The Battle
for
Baptist Integrity

John F. Baugh

To Order Additional Copies of
The Battle for Baptist Integrity
Please use the Order Form
on page 245

The
Order Form
may be freely reproduced
to meet additional needs.

Published by
Battle for Baptist Integrity, Inc.
Austin, Texas
Copyright © by John F. Baugh
P.O. Box 160244
Austin, Texas 78716

Library of Congress Catalog Card Number: 96-86809
International Standard Book Number: 1-889872-00-8

Acknowledgments

Numerous men and women have made significant contributions to the research and development of this publication. I am most grateful for their advice and valuable assistance.

The constant encouragement, patience and wisdom of my loving wife, Eula Mae—who has enriched my life for more than sixty years—and her understanding of the need to restore integrity in our beloved denomination greatly facilitated the research and preparation of this book.

It has been most rewarding to experience the depth of several friends' love for the Savior and commitments to His ways. Their lives are governed, day by day, by choosing to do that which is right in the sight of God. Thus, my deepest appreciation is expressed to Karen Carlson, Anna McLean, Roger A. Pendery, William J. Reddell and Drs. Herbert H. Reynolds and Daniel G. Vestal for their counsel, advice, guidance and selfless contribution of their time and energies to the writing of this book.

Dr. Eugene W. Baker has been invaluable in the creative process and has been tireless in shaping the content and in the production of this book. I am greatly indebted to him.

I am grateful that God granted this opportunity to share with fellow Baptists these certain concerns related to the cause of Christ.

Finally, I express my gratitude to the many friends who encouraged me to undertake this endeavor.

Table of Contents

Preface

It is my prayer that the content of this book can be of encouragement to *mainstream* Baptists as they seek to determine the best of ways by which they, as individuals and members of congregations, can honor Christ in their lives as they serve His causes.

It is *not* intended for the author to profit financially from this publication. Therefore, all financial aspects of this endeavor are being monitored by one of the nation's most respected public accounting firms, Arthur Andersen & Co., which can provide audited statements of all financial transactions related to the development and distribution of this book.

To the extent that proceeds from book sales exceed costs of its preparation, printing and distribution, such income will be expended to support ministries and mission enterprises of *mainstream* Baptist churches in this manner: Should the members of a Denominational Relations Committee or another group of *mainstream* Baptist laypeople purchase 100 or more copies in a single shipment, their church will receive a check in the amount of $300 or more ($3.00 per copy) which can be invested in the church's ministries and missions enterprises.

Purchases of 50 to 99 copies or 25 to 49 copies in single shipments will be similarly reimbursed at the rate of $2.75 and $2.50 per book respectively.

All remaining net proceeds from book sales, if any, will be forwarded, first to the churches whose members have purchased in single shipments 25 or more copies of the book, then to other *mainstream* Baptist mission endeavors.

From the Author

I would prefer a private discussion in which to share with each *mainstream* Baptist the tragic shattering of the hopes and dreams of the Baptist people over the last seventeen years. In such a setting, not only could I hear your meaningful comments, but I would benefit further from your facial expressions, tonal inflections and gestures that are so important to a conversation between friends.

However, since that is impossible, please allow me to present, *as if in a personal conversation*, the story about the intrusion of startling occurrences and the unfolding of incredible events that have destroyed the trust, divided the allegiance and severed the loyalty that had existed among Southern Baptists for more than 130 years.

The opinions expressed in this book reflect factual information—to which reference is made throughout its content—as well as reasonable and prudent conclusions based on individual experiences and observations.

If you are willing to consider the important information presented in this publication, you may have some questions. Let's talk about a few of them now—and others later.

"Who is John Baugh?"

I am a layman. More than sixty years ago I was baptized as a believer in Christ and accepted into the membership of a Southern Baptist congregation. Mrs. Baugh and I are members of the Tallowood Baptist Church of Houston, Texas. During our almost sixty years of marriage, we have been members of but two churches, both Southern Baptist.

Many wonderful fellow believers—men and women, laypeople and ministers—have enriched our lives. Among those who now bring special blessings to us are the pastor of our present church, Dr. Daniel G. Vestal, and other members of that sweet congregation of believers.

This book is not about me. But you have a right to know of some influences that have impacted my life.

I am one who has benefited from the lives of those whom I perceive to be heroes—men and women, Baptists and others.

Mrs. Baugh's parents were among my heroes and heroines. Both were graduates of Baylor University and Southwestern Baptist Theological Seminary. Her father was an honorable and effective Southern Baptist pastor. During his retirement years and until his death, he was a member of the Tallowood Baptist Church of Houston.

The photographs of some of my heroes are in my office—Dr. Russell H. Dilday, Mr. Earl C. Hankamer, Judge Abner V. McCall, Dr. Herbert H. Reynolds, Dr. Robert B. Sloan, Dr. Daniel G. Vestal and others. Mrs. Baugh was one of my heroines even before 1936 when we agreed to love and cherish one another " 'til death do us part."

My mother was a gracious, happy and generous woman who was devoted to the well-being and happiness of all with whom she came in contact. As a diligent member of the Woman's Missionary Union, she *was* "in contact with the world."

We were members of the Columbus Avenue Baptist Church of Waco, Texas. My father was an ordained deacon of that church. Baylor University was important to us. My father's memorial service was conducted by his close friend, Dr. J. B. Tidwell, for whom Baylor's Tidwell Bible Building is named.

My dad was kind and gentle, a man of good will. He also possessed a sense of humor that, along with patience, was required to guide his three sons. His rules were few—but memorable:

1) Never disappoint your mother,

2) Think about what you say and do. Jesus, in the Holy Spirit, is always by your side. Do not disappoint Him.

3) In many ways you are different from other people—but not better than they. Do not disappoint them.

Personal Prejudices

As you will discover, I have some personal prejudices. Therefore, it seems only appropriate to acknowledge that certain experiences heavily influence my analysis of the conflict in our denomination. Thus, the following:

Intolerance of Phonies

Most people have had some exposure to devious individuals who say one thing and mean another—commonly called "doubletalk." Among this group are those who make their living as con artists, gaining riches by embezzlement and other dishonest machinations. There also are those who boast of their array of adulterous affairs and are proud of having gotten by for so long in their promiscuous lifestyle.

I confess that I am disturbed by such phonies. I will not do business with them and I am uncomfortable around them in social settings. The most disgustingly revolting of all phonies are the "religious types" who make a mockery of God and prey on vulnerable men and women to achieve their own selfish purposes.

"Why would you write a book about the Baptist conflict?"

I am neither a theologian nor a scholar and I have never written a book. I had not intended to do so, but knowledge of Fundamentalism's evil intent and unwarranted actions *called* me to express deep concern about its impact upon the ministry and mission endeavors of *mainstream* Baptists.

"So, what can be done?"

Laypeople comprise far more than 95 percent of the Baptist family. Each of us has the responsibility to make our lives count more for Christ. A significant way for us to do this is to work cooperatively with equally trustworthy fellow Baptists. As laypeople, we must begin the process to offset the politicized wrongdoing within Baptist life. We must demand that Christlike conduct be the hallmark of those with whom we work. Let us not support or become a part of the current wrongs so widespread in the *"official"* Southern Baptist Convention; otherwise, we could inadvertently become involved in them.

"Is this just more about Baptist politics?"

No, this book does not seek to immerse you in Southern Baptist Convention politics. Indeed, it will suggest that you not attend SBC annual meetings. Mainstream Baptists have learned the futility of trying to vote the ugly controversy out of existence. The members of my family and I have determined to be set free from the evil of today's SBC politics.

"To what extent will you discuss Fundamentalism?"

During the many years that Mrs. Baugh and I have participated in denominational endeavors, I have had more than ample opportunity to observe the obsessive spirit of Fundamentalism. I have seen firsthand its progressive ambitions and have experienced the arrogance of its political avarice. Therefore, the accounts of fanatical Fundamentalist evil reflect "up close and personal" perspectives.

Some Southern Baptists may disapprove of my public discussion of the despicable attitudes and inexcusable acts perpetrated under the influence of Fundamentalism. However, since June 1979, I have hoped and prayed that the Fundamentalist brethren would relate anew to Christ and restore Christian integrity in our denomination. Instead, their malicious misdeeds have accelerated.

"Why discuss Mainstream Baptists' future?"

Fellow Americans' perceptions of the Southern Baptist Convention are increasingly negative. Our denomination has been stripped of much of its moral soundness that we have cherished as *mainstream* Baptists. Still, we can be confident that our future can become brighter than ever before, subject to:
- our being obedient to Christ alone;
- praying for and listening to God's guidance;
- making God-honoring decisions about clear-cut choices;
- working diligently while adhering to Christian principles;
- being redemptive in spirit; and
- exercising vigilance against the loss of religious freedom and other time-honored Baptist distinctives.

"Why should Baptists consider this information?"

This information must be shared. You have a right to know, and I believe all Baptists need to consider, some of the attitudes and deeds that have fomented irreconcilable strife among us.

Some Southern Baptist men and women whose lives are impacted by the spirit of Fundamentalism are confronted daily by certain questions such as: "How may I work more effectively in God's Kingdom?" Or, "Will my life be more closely drawn to Jesus Christ today or will it be captivated by ungodly influences?" Inevitably, sincere Christians must live out the answers to those questions of conscience.

Risks are Involved

What chance do we have for the future, if we are not willing to consider the past? My writing this book—and your reading it—subjects us to certain risks. But other sincere Christians who are Baptists are subject to even greater risks. When a believer understands what Jesus expects, but deliberately fails to respond, the resulting spiritual void can prevent that man or woman from continuing to experience the joy of salvation and to respond to the Master's expectations.

Sincere Christians Cannot Remain Unconcerned

As you read this book, I trust that you will recognize the challenges before us. I pray you also will realize that correcting the situation will require your *personal* involvement. The *first step* of that involvement will be identified throughout these chapters.

The Christlike Solution

In every church of which Christ is the head, the restoration of Christian integrity can begin in ways that can be rapidly expanded throughout the denomination.

Reestablishing Christian integrity in Baptist life is up to the people, for God has granted to them both the responsibilities and democratic means to govern their churches, to choose to work with like-minded Christians and to share the Gospel so that hearers throughout the world might gain the faith-saving grace for which Christ paid the price on the cross.

Prologue

Thank you for considering this book. In fairness to you, I believe a review of the following brief comments—which will require only a few minutes of your time—will indicate the possible value of your reviewing the book's entire content.

About This Book

What is this book about? There are several matters to be pondered:

> • Why has an oligarchy been established to rule over the Southern Baptist Convention (SBC)?
> • Why is the oligarchy, comprised of approximately eighty close-knit and well-organized radical Fundamentalists, so fanatically committed to the absolute control of the SBC?
> • Why have the Southern Baptist people allowed Christian integrity to be systematically diminished, then overrun, and finally, corrupted in their convention?

We can understand the motivations underlying the takeover strategy that was developed in the 1970s, the means employed to establish the oligarchy in 1978—then comprised of fewer than thirty men—and the resulting attacks against the SBC beginning in 1979.

We can understand why the oligarchy's inner circle has been increased year-by-year since 1979.

We can see the oligarchy's power in the nation's political processes.

We can envision the oligarchy's ultimate goal.

We can understand the confusion caused by the whirlwind rapidity of the 1978 and 1979 events and the paralyzing shock created by the blitzkrieg attacks against the SBC.

But why the Southern Baptist people have allowed Fundamentalist evil to completely overtake their denomination is beyond understanding.

The Baptist People's Dilemma

Will the paralyzing shock experienced in 1979 permanently immobilize the good Baptist people? Possibly a letter I recently received from a Baptist friend indicates a reason for the ascendance of Fundamentalist dishonesty as a way of Baptist life.

The letter says in part, "As you and I know, Fundamentalism is deeply entrenched within the Southern Baptist Convention. It is here to stay. There is nothing any of us can do to correct the direction of our denomination . . . ."

My friend is in error. *Mainstream* Baptists can begin restoring Christian integrity in Baptist life at any time of their choosing—without even leaving the inside of their churches, and without attending an associational, state convention or SBC meeting. I believe *mainstream Baptists* will agree that the suggestions in Chapter 14 are simple, honest and straightforward and that they can and should be achieved without delay.

The Southern Baptist Family

The Southern Baptist family is not the same organization as the Southern Baptist Convention. However, the men and women who comprised the Southern Baptist family from 1845 to 1979 *were* the Southern Baptist Convention, and they were the heart and soul of the Southern Baptist denomination.

In 1979, control of the SBC was seized by a rancorous Fundamentalist minority. That minority, identified as the *official* Southern Baptist Convention in this book, could be accurately called the Fundamentalist Baptist Convention.

In 1979 the SBC was comprised of approximately 10 percent Fundamentalists. The remaining 90 percent were mainstream Southern Baptists who loved, worked in and supported all their denomination's enterprises. *Mainstream Southern Baptist men and women remain the heart and soul of the denomination, even though they have no say in its affairs.*

Identifying Characteristics
of the Hybrid Fundamentalist Religion

The characteristics of *old world Fundamentalism* as well as the *hybrid Fundamentalist religion* are clearly defined in Chapter Eight.

Democracy and Fundamentalism Cannot Coexist

Fundamentalism's long-term goals and democratic principles are incompatible. Fundamentalist ideology mandates a self-perpetuating body of hierarchical rulers and, therefore, cannot coexist with a true democracy which is characterized by principles of equality and in which the supreme power of governance is retained by the people.

Fundamentalists never allow themselves to be distracted or deterred from seeking to capture a targeted objective. As "patient revolutionaries" they wait for openings to advance their ideology—step-by-step. Whether related to a religious or a governmental entity, Fundamentalism's restless stirrings are intensified until control of the designated object is seized, whether it be church or state.

The spirit of Fundamentalism reasons, "inasmuch as we represent only a minority of the people, we must use untruths, slander, hate and dirty tricks to achieve a 'level playing field.'"

Therefore, as presented in Chapter 9, possibly the above explains the Fundamentalist pronouncement, "if it takes dirty tricks to take over the Baptist General Convention of Texas, we will use dirty tricks to do so." Always, Christian integrity is the victim that falls to Fundamentalism's "spiritual warfare" charade.

Fundamentalists openly state "the fight over the Bible will never be over." Therefore, seemingly, the battle to restore Christian integrity in Baptist life also must remain a never-ending struggle. Vigilance is the price to be paid for religious freedom.

Greed for Money and Lust for Worldly Power

The ultimate cost of Fundamentalism's greed for ever more money and its lust for ever greater worldly power are impossible to determine. It is sickening to contemplate the ongoing damage that has been done to the Southern Baptist sector of God's Kingdom because of Fundamentalism's domination over the SBC for the past seventeen years. No doubt Fundamentalism will seek to continue—even intensify— its adverse impact on *mainstream* Baptists who are serving the cause of Christ.

Insulting behavior to Mainstream Baptists.

The ongoing spawning of Fundamentalist power plays, augmented by shrewd public relations ploys, is insulting to the Southern Baptists whose only desire is to spread the Gospel of Christ so that those who hear might experience a saving faith in Jesus.

The transformation of the SBC into a base for the expansion of Fundamentalist worldly powers is insulting to our Baptist heritage.

Attempts to whitewash the evil that has been unleashed in the denomination in the past seventeen years is insulting to the memories of the honest Baptist leadership that served the denomination for so many years.

Handing the control of SBC seminaries over to hardline Fundamentalist ideologies is insulting to *mainstream* Baptists' investment in denominational institutions and their commitments to God.

The disbursing of portions of tithes and offerings, the use of other assets and the expending of the convention's influences in the nation's dirt-cluttered political realm is insulting to all who are committed to ethical conduct. The spending of the people's millions of dollars in monetary gifts to whitewash Fundamentalist wrongdoing and the specific efforts to seize control of the associations and state conventions by means similar to those employed to gain control over the SBC—each of these is, and all of them are—insulting to authentic Baptists' intelligence.

Fundamentalism's Irreversible Nature

As is indicated throughout the book, it is impossible for Fundamentalism to tolerate human behavior not under its control.

- It cannot accept any creed or doctrine not created by itself.
- Fundamentalism cannot abide any institution, church or governmental entity that was not created by itself or that is not under the control of its spirit.
- In order to achieve its purposes, its call is for never-ending warfare, even though our Lord and Savior called us to peace.
- Fundamentalism's principal trademark is hate, even though Jesus practiced and admonished His followers to extend love to one another.
- Fundamentalism enforces its coercive demands by the exercise of punitive retribution that includes the diminishing or

destruction of the reputations, Christian careers and personal lives of "opponents." Yet, Jesus practiced and admonished His followers to enrich the lives of one another.

The central purpose of this book, from the beginning of Chapter One to the end of its final page, is to entreat fellow *mainstream* Baptists to heed the Holy Spirit's leading in the restoration of Christlike integrity in Baptist life.

Men and women who now understand the spirit of Fundamentalism and continue to support its evil practices, in effect, are certifying to their approval of untruth, hate, slander and persecution in the church of which Jesus Christ is the head.

1

Mainstream Baptists' Legacy
Current Identity and Future

❋❋❋❋❋❋❋

In all things, be of good report—

> "Every follower of Christ knows the Christian highway is paved with love. It is on that road that we would entreat all Baptists—who are able to thrust aside the spirit of Fundamentalism—to again walk arm-in-arm with a transformed Southern Baptist family that is committed solely to Christ."

Mainstream Baptists' Legacy
Current Identity and Future

The most important matter discussed in this book relates to the restoration of Christian integrity in Baptist life. Other concerns that significantly impact the lives, ministries and missions work of the Southern Baptist family also are presented.

Particular attention is given to the expanding credibility gap that has been created by the attitudes and actions of the *"official"* Southern Baptist Convention (SBC). The devious devices that have led to the loss of trustworthiness within our denomination must be stopped, then remedied. The dastardly practice of *segregating for "special treatment"* certain persons, institutions and groups is particularly repulsive and potentially devastating to the denomination. It, too, must cease.

The Southern Baptist Family

As indicated in the Prologue, the Southern Baptist family is not the same as the Southern Baptist Convention, the corporate organization. Rather, it is the good and godly men, women and children:

- who, under the leadership and guidance of honest pastors, faithfully seek to emulate the servanthood spirit of Christ;
- who are the heart of ministering to the needy and witnessing to the lost;
- who, by their tithes and offerings, provide a very sizeable majority of the support for Baptist evangelism and mission efforts around the world; and
- who seek to shape their personal conduct to reflect Christian integrity and honoring of Christ in the communities in which they reside.

These "Mainstream Baptists" who comprise approximately 90 percent of the denomination, have loved, respected, trusted and witnessed with one another for many decades.

Mainstream Baptists
An Historical Perspective

It is said that in 1845 when the Baptists met in Augusta, Georgia, to form the Southern Baptist Convention, they were united by their love for a lost world and their submission to God's Word as the inviolate standard for Christians' conduct.

In the late 1970s, the respected and trusted Southern Baptist Convention was the largest non-Catholic body of organized Christians in the United States. It also was the most rapidly growing Christian denomination in the world.

The great majority of the men and women who comprised the Southern Baptist Convention at that time were "Mainstream Baptists." They were not perfect, but they were committed to the witness and work of their churches. They were striving to model their personal lives upon the teachings of Christ.

Mainstream Baptists treasured the Bible. It was their guide; it was God's Word! Its holy pages clearly defined Christ's standards for human conduct. The straightforward faith of mainstream Baptists was the source of their joy as they eagerly sought to serve the Master in ways consistent with the straightforward Bible.

Wherever there were needs—whether nearby or in a distant land—*mainstream* Baptists responded in Christian love! Evangelism was uppermost on their minds and the imperatives of the Great Commission were embraced in their hearts. Success in winning the lost was unprecedented, and countless numbers of people across America were seeking Jesus. The nation seemed to be on the verge of a great revival.

Fundamentalism's Presence Recognized

In addition to *mainstream* Baptists in the late 1970s, there was a relatively small number of fanatical Fundamentalists within the SBC—men who believed that they alone were competent to interpret God's Word. Among this group were some who were willing to go "as far as is necessary" to force others to submit to their dictatorial Fundamentalist control.

Although *mainstream* Baptists were aware of Fundamentalism and knew a little about its aggressive nature and rigid demands, they had no apprehensions about working with that small minority in the SBC. This was because *mainstream* Baptists were unaware of the Fundamentalists' intention to take control of the Convention. That scheme was a closely guarded secret.

J. Frank Norris

The blight of Fundamentalism, of course, is not a recent phenomenon in Baptist life. In the 1930s—and persisting for several years thereafter—Dr. J. Frank Norris, pastor of the First Baptist Church of Fort Worth, Texas, did everything he could to seize control of the SBC. He shot and killed a man who opposed him—and it happened in the church office! In addition, a Grand Jury indicted him for arson—setting fires in buildings that housed the First Baptist Church.

Norris was an absolute dictator over his congregation, and he did things his way. He did not brook criticism nor accept suggestions; he did not bother with the civilities and niceties of life. And, in typical Fundamentalist style, he claimed he did everything "for the glory of God."

I consider Norris to have been a Fundamentalist beast in Baptist clothing. Possibly, he was even worse, since he paraded his Fundamentalist evil in the justifying cloth of the clergy. However, in order for Norris to have been able to display his immoral conduct proudly, as a peacock preens its plumage, there had to be a sizable number of gullible Baptist laypeople willing to support him. This was evidenced by the several thousand followers who attended his burial, many of whom wept openly. Some even said, "To me, J. Frank Norris was God."

Possibly my prejudice against J. Frank Norris and *his* worshippers is too harshly expressed. But he invoked Fundamentalism's *segregation for special treatment* on one of Baptists' greatest heroes, Dr. George W. Truett. Norris singled out the good and godly Dr. Truett for *incessant persecution*.

His stated intent was to destroy the venerable, trusted and otherwise respected pastor of the First Baptist Church of Dallas. Fortunately, Norris' evil intent to diminish Dr. Truett was unsuccessful and subsequently, Norris was kicked out of the SBC.

4

Mainstream Baptists
in 1979

In June of 1979, immediately preceding the Southern Baptist Convention's annual meeting in Houston, fifty thousand *mainstream* Baptists gathered in the Astrodome for a Bold Mission Thrust Rally—the historic beginning of an all-out effort to "go and make disciples of all nations."

Dr. Presnall Wood, editor of the *Baptist Standard*, called the rally—the largest gathering of Southern Baptists ever assembled in the United States—"impressive and inspirational." The filling of the cross-shaped flag by more than 1,200 people who responded to the mission commitment appeal was one of the highest points in Southern Baptist history. The dedication of 1,100 persons for mission service was unprecedented in American Christendom.

Those who participated in the rally wanted to tell the story of Jesus—more tenderly and more boldly than ever before. They felt compelled to tell of His life, to recount His pain and suffering, to tell *why* He died and *for whom* He died.

Unbelievable Turn of Events

But then, on the next day, as the SBC's annual meeting got underway, an incredibly harsh and unprecedented sneak attack was launched by a small band of fanatical Fundamentalists who were motivated by desires for worldly power. Their efforts resulted in the exploding of a "bombshell" that blasted apart and decimated—*in a single day*—the love, trust and mutual commitments that had existed among Baptists for more than 130 years. These Christian principles had characterized the denomination and had been the foundation for Southern Baptist ministries, witnessings and missions since 1845.

Dr. Presnall Wood wrote in the June 20, 1979, issue of the *Baptist Standard:*

> The 15,947 messengers to the Convention had a dose of politics that left some ill. A coalition led by Paige Patterson, President of the Criswell Center for Biblical Studies, and Paul Pressler, proved to be massive and ef-

fective in electing their candidate, Adrian Rogers, pastor of Bellevue Church, Memphis, president on the first ballot without a runoff.

In a reported meeting attended by more than 400 of the Patterson/Pressler coalition Monday evening prior to the convening of the Convention Tuesday, it was revealed that their campaign had spanned fourteen months with an organization of state chairmen who recruited from two to ninety assistants in each of the thirty-three states where Southern Baptists have conventions.

Further in the proceedings, a well-known Kentucky pastor, who was a former SBC president, pointed to the upper level skyboxes (privately owned booths at the top of the Summit facility) and stated that they were being used for caucuses—a procedure that was contrary to Convention bylaws.

The former SBC president also challenged the credentials of one of the persons in the boxes though he did not name the individual [Paul Pressler]. In response, Pressler immediately came to the rostrum to defend his use of the skyboxes. Pressler attempted to explain his "messenger credentials" though he did not mention that the way he obtained his "special status" was a blatant violation of the SBC constitution.

A respected pastor, who was a guest in one of the skyboxes, rejected the claim that no politicking had been done in the area when he reported in his church newsletter that, at one point during the convention proceedings, Pressler excitedly rushed into the skybox saying, "We're going to rout those liberals. We're going to run those liberals out from the Sunday School Board and everywhere else."

At the 1980 SBC annual meeting in Los Angeles, Paige Patterson confronted the pastor regarding what he had written. The pastor replied, "I was there and saw what happened, and it was a lie that they had not done any politicking." Later the pastor wrote, "Needless to say, I have not been welcome among the Fundamentalist fellows in the years since then."

In further discussing the events. Dr. Wood wrote:

Pressler, experienced in political operations and procedures, arranged for caucus rooms, staffed with hostesses and food, in the skyboxes overlooking the Summit Convention meeting facility where advantage could be made of the closed-circuit television of the convention. This was in violation of Article III of the constitution of the convention that says, 'No meetings other than the convention services shall be held in the convention hall during the sessions of the convention.'

He concluded with:

The 1979 Houston Southern Baptist Convention was marked by a combination of bold missions and bold politics never seen before in the annual session. Only time will tell which will have a greater influence on the future of the Southern Baptist Convention.

The Fate of Bold Mission Thrust

Unfortunately, time has revealed the terrible truth. The spirit of Fundamentalism cannot tolerate anything not created by itself. Those who succumb to this spirit are committed—contrary to biblical standards of conduct—to "power politics" and obsessively militant mind-control tactics in order to gain their extremist worldly goals.

This was certainly evident following the 1979 SBC meeting because Bold Mission Thrust was practically destroyed as fanatical Fundamentalists systematically swallowed the SBC boards, commissions, agencies and assets. As a result, *mainstream* Baptists were severely limited in their goal to take the Gospel of Christ to the entire world by 2000 A.D.

Mainstream Baptists
Today

Most laypeople recognize that the controversy that has raged for so long in our denomination continues to diminish Southern Baptists' reputations as Christians. Many believe the "infighting" has seriously diluted the witness for Christ in their own communities and states and could eventually inflict irreparable harm on all Southern Baptists' ministries and missions. Some are even apprehensive over the detrimental impact this prolonged iniquitous feud could have on the future of our nation— and the world.

A growing number of *mainstream* Baptists want to know and understand the causes of the controversy. They wonder why Fundamentalists make so many charges against fellow Baptists but offer no factual evidence to support the accusations. They want to know if mutual trust and genuine love for one another can ever be restored in our denomination. . . and if not, then what? Who will survive? Will it be the fanatical Fundamentalists? Or, will it be the good and godly mainstream Baptists whose only desire is to respond to the Macedonian call?

Over the past several years some *mainstream* Baptists have attempted to stem the flow of the spirit of Fundamentalism's politicized deceptions and unwarranted slander, but others have done little about them. This limited resistance to evil has allowed Fundamentalists' ongoing control machinations to impose a sense of spiritual paralysis on many mainstream Baptists. It also has significantly contributed to the enshrining of corrupt practices of secular politics throughout our denomination and has resulted in transforming the Bold Mission Thrust dream into an awesome nightmare.

In addition, the uninterrupted tension fostered by the spirit of Fundamentalism has created an intolerable level of apprehension within the denomination. As a result, Baptists' credibility in telling the Good News has been impaired.

Yet, the world still needs to be reached for Christ, and all the work envisioned for Bold Mission Thrust remains to be accomplished. Thus, it is a matter of the greatest urgency that *mainstream* Baptists vigorously testify to the verity of the Gospel of Christ. Only in this way can Baptists' integrity as sincere Christians be restored and the Gospel of Christ reach all the world.

Mainstream Baptists today have a sense of yearning and a pensive longing to find a way again to fall "head over heels" in love with Christ and His call to service. They aspire to live Christlike lives, to extend ministries of mercy to those about them and to support missions throughout the world. Can this be accomplished within the "official" Southern Baptist Convention—

now under the heel of fanatical Fundamentalism—or will the response to His call have to be expressed outside the traditional SBC structure?

Things to Remember

Certain matters that occurred during the 1979 SBC meeting where fanatical Fundamentalists launched their plan to seize the Southern Baptist Convention should never be forgotten. Among them are the following:

• Fundamentalists who comprised that ideological organization violated the constitution of the Southern Baptist Convention. The decorum, order and decency by which the SBC had been characterized were cast aside.

• It was revealed that Paul Pressler, who was then a member of the First Baptist Church of Houston, had not been elected a messenger by his own church. He claimed to be an "honorary member" of First Church, Bellaire, which had "elected" him a messenger—a violation of Article III of the constitution of the Southern Baptist Convention.

• There were "untold registration irregularities" and, as subsequently reported by Dr. Lee Porter, the Southern Baptist Convention registration secretary, widespread voting "improprieties" occurred.

Since 1979 we *mainstream* Baptists could have had our "best of times," had we not been denied opportunity to devote our capabilities to the Bold Mission Thrust enterprise. Instead, fanatical Fundamentalism has imposed the "worst of lifetime experiences" on many followers of Christ.

Dr. Wood was discerning as he wrote and inquired:

> The type of bold politics revealed in Houston results in contentions, divisions, diversions, and angry spirits. The implications are staggering. Will there be other groups organized on the scale of the Patterson/Pressler coalition? What will be the name of the group? Who will they represent? Will there be a challenge to Adrian Rogers next year at the convention? Should Southern Baptists become obsessed when applying secular politics to a spiritual organization?

The Fundamentalist struggle for power has made "losers" of

us all. It has sullied the Word of God in whose name these biblically immoral actions have been perpetrated. As a result, "Spiritual Warfare" activities—fostered for so long by fanatical Fundamentalists—continue to plague Baptist life today, and there is compelling evidence that Fundamentalists' greed for power is irreversible.

Over the last seventeen years the Southern Baptist Convention of the past has been corrupted by Fundamentalism's unprincipled acts. The unleashing of politicized hate intended to induce widespread intimidation of genteel Baptists has:

- adversely impacted the enthusiasm of some to serve our Lord and Master;
- extensively damaged the public perception of Baptist beliefs and the effectiveness of our Christian witness;
- destroyed the mutual trust in the denomination; and
- irreparably injured scores of honorable Baptists by the corrosive misdeeds perpetrated by those with "the-end-justifies-the-means" mentality.

Fundamentalists will not join *mainstream* Baptists to reestablish denominational integrity nor will they cease to interfere with the honest efforts of others to do so! Therefore, if our passion to share the Gospel is to prevail, we must reject the ideological pursuit of worldly power and separate ourselves from Fundamentalism's evils. Hesitancy to accept and fulfill our Christ-centered responsibilities could dramatically reduce the effectiveness of our witness as individuals and drastically diminish *mainstream* Baptists' work around the world.

A New and
Joyful Era

It has been said, "Those who fail to learn from history are doomed to repeat it."

The difficulties experienced in the SBC over the last seventeen years have caused some laypeople to lose the joy of their salvation. But the exhilaration of striving to become that which Christ would have us be can be regained. Indeed, a "new and joyful era" of service and hope *is available*:

10

- If we cling to our long-held Christian principles and Baptist distinctives, and
- If our churches retain their autonomy under Christ.

If mainstream Baptists are to experience renewal, we laypeople must open our hearts and minds and become a part of the new era in which God will do a new thing with us.

> Remember not the former things, nor consider the things of old. Behold I am doing a new thing. Now it springs forth, do you not perceive it? I will make a way in the wilderness and rivers in the desert. (*Isaiah 43:18-19 RSV*)

The cost of not following God's way out of the SBC wilderness of worldly powers could be the loss of one's priesthood as a believer and the loss of the competency of one's soul. The cost also could include the loss of religious freedom as well as the individual liberties that are guaranteed in this democratic nation.

As "men and women of the pews," we can remove ourselves from the ungodly political fight, and our congregations *can* grow and serve as faithful members of the Body of Christ. This can be accomplished without conferring with others and without attending an associational meeting, state convention or the SBC annual meeting. Chapter Fourteen suggests some clear-cut choices in this regard and explains how God can reign supreme in our lives.

Decisions About Baptist Morality

There may be some who do not wish to hear the truth about the awesome controversy that has decimated our Baptist family. There may also be some who are inclined to close their minds and hearts regarding how to end the politicized conflict in the Southern Baptist Convention. If you are one of these, then I say, without intended offense, "You may not wish to read further." However, if you are interested in documented truths, evident conclusions and the possibilities for Baptists' future, please read on.

Principles of Authentic Baptists

Dr. Carl E. Bates, one of God's Baptist giants who served as president of the Southern Baptist Convention in 1971-1972, is a remarkable expositor of the Word. One of his outstanding sermons addressed three questions: What makes one a Christian; what makes one a Baptist; and what makes one a Southern Baptist?

He answered the first question by simply stating that only God can make a Christian. He then enumerated the seven precious principles of authentic Baptist people.

1) The absolute authority and Lordship of Christ—we must do what Jesus commands, no matter what men may say.

2) The New Testament is the only and all sufficient rule of faith and practice—our doctrines and practices are found in God's Word and are not man-made creeds.

3) The competency of the soul in religion—no person, ordinance, or institution shall come between a soul and Christ.

4) An experience of Grace—a person must be converted to Christianity before becoming a member of a Baptist church.

5) The independence and autonomy of the local church—each church must govern itself, and all churches have equal—as well as separate—authority.

6) The separation of church and state—a free church in a free state.

7) The symbolism of the ordinances—baptism of believers by immersion, and the Lord's Supper.

Southern Baptists, he explained, are identified by their "love for a lost world and a willingness to get on with the work for the glory of God—whatever it costs."

In essence, these principles and total acceptance of God's Word as the inviolate standard of Christian conduct are the virtues of which authentic *mainstream* Southern Baptists are made.

The Haunting Question

As has been pointed out, we Baptists of today are "in a mess." Even so, Baptists cannot forego their commitments to Christ—for the world is at stake!

Baptists also cannot ignore the haunting question, "Is it possible to restore integrity in the "official" Southern Baptist Convention?" I believe the answer to that question is, "No—not as long as fanatical Fundamentalists are in control of the SBC—

12

not as long as the spirit of Fundamentalism continues to trample underfoot our Christian principles and Baptist distinctives."

But how long will Fundamentalism prevail over all of Baptist life?

That depends on the *mainstream* Baptist laypeople who comprise more than 90 percent of the Baptist family. It is up to them to discern the ways and to make the decisions necessary to get out of this "Baptist Mess."

2

The Baptist Mess
Its Moral Implications

****

In all things, be of good report—

"All active mass movements claim that 'the ultimate and absolute truth is embodied in their doctrine and that there is no truth or certitude outside.' As Henri Bergson said in his 1935 book, *the Two Sources of Morality in Religion*, 'So tenaciously should we cling to the world revealed by the gospel, that were I to see all the angels in heaven coming down to tell me something different, not only would I not be tempted to doubt a single syllable, but I would shut my eyes and stop my ears, for they would not deserve to be either seen or heard.'

"This is the source of the Fundamentalist's constancy. He is 'not frightened by danger nor disheartened by obstacles nor baffled by contradictions because he denies their existence.' Strength of faith in such personalities, as Bergson pointed out, manifests itself not in moving mountains, but in not seeing mountains to move."

The Baptist Mess
It's Moral Implications

The term, "Baptist Mess," was coined by newspaper reporters when privately discussing the denominational controversy that piqued widespread media interest following the dropping of the "bombshell" by Fundamentalists at the 1979 SBC annual meeting. To a layman who has observed Southern Baptists for more than sixty years, Fundamentalists' unprecedented belligerent posturing and ongoing pursuits of worldly power since that time have been greatly disturbing.

Today's "Baptist Mess" is the result of premeditated public violations of Christian conduct that have repeatedly occurred over the past seventeen years. Buried deep beneath the volcanic fissure from which erupted the "Baptist Mess" lie the disregarded virtues that formerly characterized the Southern Baptist Convention. The moral principles of love and trust that undergirded Baptists' harmonious cooperation in their work and witness to the Lordship of Christ from 1845 to 1979 have been torn to shreds.

One of the wisest laymen I know, a man deeply devoted to the cause of Christ, said to me, "We're in this mess. What are laypeople's options to bring it to an end?"

In order to provide an appropriate response to that very important question, I believe it is necessary to recognize:

Mainstream Baptists can begin ending the "Baptist Mess"— **even without stepping outside of their churches.** *The main question facing them is this: Will a sufficient number of good and godly men and women take the steps necessary to strengthen and build upon their Christ-centered beachhead of belief and witness? Will they stand tall and hold fast to our Baptist distinctives? If so, those men and women can restore the foundation of true Christian principles to the noble legacy of our Southern Baptist forebears, and thereby serve well the cause of Christ.*

15

It also is necessary to recognize that this can be accomplished without sacrificing fidelity and integrity.

Fidelity and Integrity

Among the virtues now largely cast aside by the calculated acts of unprincipled men is *fidelity*—one's faithfulness to a trust, steadfast loyalty to beliefs and to persons.

Another, which also has been disregarded by those with an insatiable hunger for worldly power, is *integrity*—the reliability of one's honesty, devotion to sincerity and to unbroken commitments. These are the virtues that Christ expects of His followers and that His followers expect of one another.

Fundamentalism's Master Plan

In 1979, after several years of secretive planning, a Fundamentalist attack was launched against the fifteen-million member Southern Baptist denomination. Although the assault was advanced under the guise of "spiritual warfare over the Bible," I believe the actual purpose, in addition to the immediate goal to seize control of the SBC, was to gain worldly powers sufficient to establish rule over some of the nation's important governmental and other institutions.

The Plan's Basic Method: Designated Victims

Inasmuch as the premeditated attack could not be leveled simultaneously against fifteen million persons, living within and outside the U. S. borders, a smaller group of respected and trusted denominational leaders was designated to be *segregated* and subjected to the heinous practice of *special treatment*.

This *special treatment* involved the direct persecution of those good men and women with the intent of besmirching their denominational careers and diminishing their personal lives. It was done to intimidate into silence the *mainstream* Baptists who comprise approximately 90 percent of the denomination.

This effort to achieve Fundamentalist mind control sufficient to mute significant opposition to the aggressors' wrongdoing repeatedly violated the spirit and letter of God's Commandments and admonitions.

No One Knows the Cost to Christendom

From the Christian perspective, the Fundamentalist siege could not have occurred at a more unfavorable time. It was during the period that the restoration of moral practices was sorely needed in our nation. It was at a time that spiritual revival in America seemingly was stirring, as was evidenced during the *Bold Mission Rally*.

It was when the human spirit of many Americans of all ages was yearning for the emergence of a sense of spiritual idealism, for the clarity, beauty and purity of Christianity as a faith undefiled by greed, dishonesty or personal ambition.

The nature of Fundamentalism, as defined in Chapter Three, suggests the near impossibility of its adherents returning to Christ. That haunting reality clearly portends the decimation of the Southern Baptist Convention.

However, Fundamentalism will not prevail forever. It ultimately will fall under the weight of its own evil, although this could require the passing of several generations and thus, wreak untold havoc upon the nation.

Remaining True to Christ: The Rewards

As you contemplate the plight of the Baptists who are committed to remain true to the cause of Christ, the account of their valor is stirring. They continue to honor those principles that contributed to Southern Baptists becoming the largest non-Catholic denomination in America and the fastest growing in the world.

Authentic Baptists will desire to consider the following questions and glean from the content of this book the responses to those inquiries which are of such grave consequence.

- **What caused the "Baptist Mess?"**
- **Who made the mess?**
- **How did they do it?**
- **Why did they do it?**
- **What has the "Baptist Mess" left behind it?**
- **What can be done about it?**

Certain Other Troubling Matters

There are additional topics that, I believe, sincere Christians and authentic Baptists will wish to consider. I trust that some of those who have been snared by the spirit of Fundamentalism also will ponder these matters:

- Without doubt, Fundamentalists have "made themselves felt" in the Southern Baptist Convention. The stated motive underlying the Fundamentalist takeover of the SBC—to "*Save* the Bible"—was, I believe, entirely phony.
- The premeditated unethical methods employed to seize control of the SBC, when examined under the light of biblical instruction, are viewed as having been highly erroneous, if not heretical. Therefore, seemingly, certain Fundamentalist leaders have arrogated unto themselves the unfettered use of odious worldly powers for "the glory of God."
- Pious pronouncements of absolute allegiance to the Holy Bible have the hollow ring of hypocrisy—particularly as some of the most powerful of Fundamentalist leaders attempt to disclaim responsibility for the ungodly depravity unleashed within the SBC. Yet, the complicity of the leaders is undeniable in light of the effects that their corrupting "punishment and reward" system has had on the denomination.
- When evaluated by God's Word, the politico-religious plots cannot be construed to be Christian. Since this is true, how do Fundamentalism's evils continue to be predominant in the SBC? Given the history, legacy and responsibility of the Southern Baptist denomination, what is to be the ongoing impact of Fundamentalism's politico-ideological thrust on Baptist life, on American Christendom and on the nation?
- How heavily will Fundamentalists' attitudes and actions weigh on the hearts and minds of mainstream Baptists?
- How will *mainstream* Baptists respond to Fundamentalism's ongoing persecution and oppression?
- Will *mainstream* Baptists capitulate to Fundamentalism—or will they take the steps necessary to restore integrity in Baptist life—and thus, be empowered to invest their lives in ministries of mercy and witness under the Lordship of Christ?

The straightforward answers to these questions, I believe, will demonstrate to *mainstream* Baptists the necessity to join with cooperative missions and other enterprises—not controlled by the "*official*" SBC—to serve in the nation and throughout the world.

Participants
in the "Baptist Mess"

The participants in the "Baptist Mess" include both the Fundamentalists—who caused it—and mainstream Baptists—who have been, and are continuing to be, affected by it.

The Nameless and Faceless Oligarchy of Eighty

The oligarchy that now numbers about eighty was begun by approximately thirty men who masked themselves in anonymity in 1978 and shrewdly designed the scheme to seize the SBC. Their secret plan was and is to take ever greater control of the denomination.

• These hooded masters have at their command "religious" jackals bent on persecution of others in exchange for personal rewards. Some of these acts of persecution are enumerated in Chapter Seven.

• Leaders of the oligarchy continue to wear the masks of anonymity as they select puppet after puppet to be their "front men" to serve as presidents of the SBC. Psychological factors related to leaders of politico-religious mass movements are described in Chapter Three.

• The men who compose the oligarchy created the apartheid in Baptist life which is described in Chapter Ten. Some of the acts of evil for which they are responsible are discussed in Chapter Five.

• The men of the oligarchy blatantly barter away the approximate 1200 "elected" positions in the SBC as lures in their reward/punish schemes. They consign some of the SBC's influences and assets for the gaining of worldly powers by dangerously ambitious politicians—as discussed in Chapter Eight.

• The faces of the oligarchy can be partially recognized by a study of some of the defining characteristics of Fundamentalism that are presented in Chapter Four. These are the men who brought about the poisoning of the SBC Pastors Conference which also is described in Chapter Four.

• The men of the Oligarchy manipulate the decisions made by those who govern the six SBC seminaries, Foreign Mis-

19

sion Board, Sunday School Board and other SBC agencies and boards. They will continue tightening their grip on Baptist life until the mainstream Baptist laypeople *literally* force the restoration of Christian integrity in the SBC.

• The several means to reestablish Christian integrity in Baptist life are suggested throughout the book. However, more specific means to restore integrity in the denomination are presented for your consideration in Chapters Nine, Twelve and Fourteen.

• The men of the oligarchy are responsible, at least in part, for virtuous women being called "whores of Satan." The oligarchy's desire to diminish or destroy the Woman's Missionary Union is discussed in Chapter Six.

• The men of the oligarchy are to be held responsible for shouting the epithet "liberals" at the pastors of churches who remain committed to Christ and who have resisted the spirit of Fundamentalism as discussed in Chapter Eleven.

• The oligarchy holds out rewards for those who attempt to seize additional state conventions. This is mentioned in Chapter Twelve.

• The men of the oligarchy instituted the dastardly practice of segregation of individuals, groups and institutions for persecution in 1978.

• The men of the oligarchy are responsible for the evil acts of persecution that have been committed in the past. These men are to be held responsible as the persecution of "opponents" continues—and as more "opponents" are designed for *special treatment.*

• They will be responsible for the violence most likely to occur as the spirit of Fundamentalism continues to fester.

Fundamentalists—as Described by Dr. James T. Draper, Jr.

In the 1974 Broadman Press book, *The Church Christ Approves,* Dr. Draper, president of the Southern Baptist Convention Sunday School Board—the largest religious publishing organization in the world—wrote:

Fundamentalism is more dangerous than Liberalism because everything is done in the name of the Lord. In the name of the Lord, the Fundamentalist condemns all who disagree with him . . . . He uses the Bible as a club with which to beat people over the head, rather than a means of personal strength and a revealer of God.

. . . . To the Fundamentalist, the test of fellowship is correct doctrine. If you do not agree with his doctrinal position, he writes you off and will not have fellowship with you. There is no room in his world for those who have a different position.

Another fact that Draper shared in his book is the reason *why* Fundamentalists are so mean-spirited.

A Fundamentalist feels threatened by diverse convictions and writes them off as sinister and heretical. As long as you support his position, he is with you. Cross him, and he has no use whatever for you . . . . the Fundamentalist tactic is simple: hatred, bitterness, and condemnation of all whom they despise.

When the Fundamentalist-propelled "bombshell" exploded at the 1979 SBC annual meeting, shrapnel of hatred, bitterness and condemnation were strewn across the denomination. Fatally wounded were the trust and fellowship for which Southern Baptists had become known. The joyous sounds of loving Baptists singing "Onward Christian Soldiers"—as they vocalized in unison their commitment of service to the Lord—were all but drowned out by the ferocious drum beating of the mutant *spirit of Fundamentalism.*

Sharing his candid description of the faithful followers of the Fundamentalist philosophy, Draper tells *how* fanatical Fundamentalists persecute their victims.

In the name of the Lord they will launch vehement attacks on individuals and churches. In the name of the Lord they attempt to assassinate the character of those whom they oppose. They direct their attack most often on other Christian leaders with whom they find disagreement.

Hard-line or Hard-core

"Hard-line" or "Hard-core" is synonymous with Fundamentalism and is, therefore, redundant. Nevertheless, to some, these

21

terms describe the "ambitious malcontents in Southern Baptist life who seek to control and manipulate a large mass of people to satisfy their own unhealthy personality needs."

Fundamentalists in Evangelicals' Clothing

As reported by Mark Wingfield in a January 12, 1996, *Associated Baptist Press* news release, few American Protestants want to be labeled Fundamentalists or "liberals" anymore, but "it seems almost everyone wants to be classified as an evangelical."

Dr. Leon McBeth, professor of church history at Southwestern Baptist Theological Seminary, was quoted as saying, "As an historian, I can demonstrate that the new evangelicals originated from the old fundamentalists in an effort to rehabilitate, to overcome the awful, awful public image of Fundamentalism."

Another church history professor, Dr. Timothy Weber, said that classical Fundamentalists have claimed the evangelical label in recent years because of the highly negative associations in the press between the word "fundamentalist" and bomb-throwing international terrorists.

Weber, who has ties to Fuller Theological Seminary and Denver Seminary, two self-described evangelical schools, also stated that the difference between evangelicals and fundamentalists was not so much theological as attitudinal. He said,

> Evangelicals were not content to remain marginalized. They wanted to enter mainstream American life. This desire to move into the larger world created a major rift between evangelicals and fundamentalists beginning around the 1940s. "This is what got Billy Graham in trouble," he explained. "He was preaching what they were preaching but throwing his arms wide open and allowing even liberals to support him." That didn't sit too well with true Fundamentalists, who insist on maintaining separation from those who claim to be Christian but don't act or believe exactly in the same way as Fundamentalists.

"Conservatives"

Classically, a theological conservative is one who believes in the basics of evangelical Christianity: salvation by grace and not works; inspiration and authority of scripture; perseverance of the saints; believer's baptism; bodily resurrection; a literal heaven and hell, etc.

In more recent years, while addressing the SBC conflict, the secular media has tended to identify the protagonists as "moderate-conservatives" and "fundamentalist-conservatives."

The word "conservative," as used by Fundamentalists, is perceived by some as seeking to impose a movement's politico-religious ideology on others and, in so doing, to control the minds and actions of its conscripts.

Those who dare to resist Fundamentalism's politico-religious views—and the behavior and methods associated with them— are subject to Fundamentalist leaders' efforts to diminish or destroy such persons' reputations.

"Conservative resurgence" refers to Fundamentalism's ever growing worldly power in the United States.

"Moderates"

"Moderates" did not choose to be called by that name. Nevertheless, "Moderates" are the many honorable *mainstream* Baptist men and women who are committed to the *fundamentals* of our Baptist faith—religious liberty and the concept of the Priesthood of the Believer—as well as to the tenets of evangelical Christianity.

"Moderates" are opposed to *Fundamentalists* and to the *spirit of Fundamentalism*. Fundamentalists label "Moderates" as "Rats," "Liberals," "Skunks," etc., because they refuse to capitulate to the Fundamentalist rulers who are at large in the SBC.

Although aware of their shortcomings, "Moderates" abhor the meanness of spirit by which mind control and manipulations are accomplished. They respect the rights of others to exercise their own "priesthood of the believer."

"Moderates" also consider all believers in Christ competent to interpret the Bible for themselves—and to enjoy personal freedom—in matters of belief and in the practice of faith.

Differences Between the Participants in the "Baptist Mess"

Fundamentalists employing worldly devices seek to gain power over many dimensions of American life. *Mainstream*

23

Baptists, in their work, lives and witness, strive to abide by scriptural admonitions.

Baptist Faith and Message

The 1963 Baptist Faith and Message statements that *main-stream* Baptists embrace identify the several significant factors underlying their living faith and their striving to consistently honor Baptist beliefs concerning:

- The Scriptures,
- God the Father,
- God the Son,
- God the Holy Spirit,
- Man,
- Salvation,
- The Church,
- God's Purpose of Grace,
- The Lord's Day,
- Baptism and the Lord's Supper,
- The Kingdom,
- Last Things,
- Education,
- Evangelism and Missions,
- Stewardship,
- Cooperation,
- The Christian and the Society Order, and
- Peace and War and Religious Liberty.

For many decades the Baptist Faith and Message statements provided encouragement and guidance for Southern Baptists. These statements have now largely been discarded by fanatical Fundamentalists—except when the statements are useful for public posturing purposes.

The Centerpiece of Fundamentalism's Rejection of the Baptist Faith and Message: *Fundamentslists Call It "Inerrancy"*

Dr. Grady C. Cothen, in his outstanding book entitled *What Happened to the Southern Baptist Convention, A Memoir of the Controversy*, tells of a conference on Biblical Inerrancy that was held at the Ridgecrest Conference Center in 1987. At this meeting, more than a thousand people attended the conference to which the "best known available scholars—Baptists and others—on the nature of Inerrancy and scripture were invited." Eleven major papers—covering the history, definition, and parameters of Inerrancy—were presented.

Responses from those who agreed or disagreed with the premise of each paper were also delivered. In addition, seven other presentations were made during special seminar sessions.

There was a wide variance in the positions taken at this meeting regarding Inerrancy, as well as the definitions of the term. Dr. Cothen wrote, "One or more of these definitions would include most Southern Baptists."

Regardless of the fact that Inerrancy was a little used term, and one that was highly difficult to define, Fundamentalists picked it as their first carrot and prod.

Individuals who accept what Fundamentalists *say that they* believe about "Inerrancy" can move up the political ladder. However, if an individual differs in any detail, he will be cast aside.

**Poles Apart—Dr. Billy Graham's Comments
About small "f" fundamentalists
(referring to the fundamentals of the Gospel)
and capital "F" Fundamentalists
(referring to bigoted extremists, etc.)**

Seemingly, there are no matters that have mystified Southern Baptist laypeople more than have the disparate meanings of "the fundamentals of our faith"—and "the spirit of Fundamentalism."

The following story about Billy Graham can assist every Baptist to understand the "poles apart" differences between "the fundamentals of our faith" and "the spirit of Fundamentalism."

In the 1950s—when Dr. Graham was a young evangelist and not well known in America—it was announced that he was to lead a major evangelistic crusade in New York City. A major magazine reporter asked Dr. Graham about his theological beliefs—whether he was a Fundamentalist.

Dr. Graham replied, in effect, "If by fundamentalist you mean a person who accepts the authority of the Scriptures, the virgin birth of Christ, the atoning death of Christ, His bodily resurrection, His second coming and personal salvation by faith through grace, then I am such a one."

Dr. Graham continued, "If, however, by Fundamentalist you mean 'narrow, bigoted, prejudiced, extremist, emotional snake-handler without social conscience'—then I am definitely not a Fundamentalist."

Almost half a century has passed since that time. Dr. Graham has never spoken or acted as Fundamentalists do. He is recognized throughout the world as a beloved Christian leader, a man known to be entirely trustworthy and, therefore, one who is universally respected.

Conversely, men who are imbued with the spirit of Fundamentalism, individually and corporately, are involved in the spreading of hate, in deceptions, in harmful whispering campaigns and in the shattering of love and trust in the Southern Baptist Convention.

The personal life and Christian influences of Dr. Billy Graham, as compared with those of fanatical Fundamentalists, who are narrow, bigoted, prejudiced extremists without social conscience, are poles apart. The differences in moral character and commitments to Christ between Bible-believing Southern Baptists and those who obliterated the line of integrity in Baptist life is evident.

The beliefs about God's Holy Word, as espoused by each mainstream Baptist whom I know, are similar to those I have heard from the lips of Dr. Graham.

Fundamentalists' Design
for Seizing Control

God's Holy Guidance Exchanged for
Political Gurus' Shrewd Schemes

As proclaimers of God's Word, Fundamentalists exude dubious sounds, for

• As practitioners of God's Word, Fundamentalists have shaken public confidence in Baptists' commitments to stated beliefs, and

• As profaners of God's Word as related to personal conduct, Fundamentalists have segregated honest Baptists for **special treatment**, i.e., persecution, and thereby have abused, defamed and harmed these men by vilifying them as "Rats," "Liberals," "Skunks," etc.

Therefore, to some traditional mainstream Southern Baptists, Fundamentalists are perceived to be impersonators.

Euphemistically Misleading Names and Image Polishing

Fundamentalists misled honorable Baptists by the use of euphemistically dishonest names such as "Baptists speaking in Truth and Love" and "Baptist Faith and Message Fellowship."

In addition, they often use a variety of public proclamations—that I believe to be phony—to polish their images. Some of these include, "No compromise about the Bible," "Public service must conform to His will," "We are committed to faithfulness to Scriptural guidelines" and "We are for fidelity to the faith."

By proclaiming such statements as "The government has not done enough to fight religious persecution," etc., men who would restrict religious freedom for others are enabled to achieve their public posturing goals.

However, Fundamentalism's image-polishing has tended to reject the principles of love and Christian service—the very principles proclaimed by our risen Savior—and for which He was crucified.

Establishing A "Market" for Fundamentalism

An extremely simplistic definition of "marketing" is to cause potential customers to desire specific products. Whether toothpaste, food, automobiles or other products, the ongoing viability of the producer is dependent upon increased product sales.

Similarly, "markets" must be established for concepts as well as products. Within the Southern Baptist Convention, the Fundamentalists' marketing plan was created to cause Southern Baptists to "buy in" on an addictive product—hate, for hate "sells" better than love.

Fundamentalists have been quite successful in this endeavor as can be attested by the sizable and growing market for political hate in America.

Did God Make Mistakes?

It seems that some Fundamentalists believe that a mistake was made by God when He sent to dwell among men a Messiah who declined to serve as an earthly ruler of nations. Did Fundamentalists seek to correct God's error by declaring themselves rulers of churches? If so, possibly, one can be designated the ruler of the Southern Baptist Convention, then of the nation.

Another Error?

Fundamentalists apparently believe that God also was in error to send a Messiah who loved sinners, was compassionate and told us to love our neighbors. Fundamentalists cash in on the fact that hate "sells better" than love and that hate can rally masses of men to persecute others. Those so recruited anticipate being rewarded for their efforts in making possible the rulers' growing and increasingly feared worldly power.

Thus again, Fundamentalists determined the way to "correct" Jesus's error of preaching and admonishing His followers to practice love.

In summary, Fundamentalists have learned how to reject those portions of Jesus's spoken word with which they disagree. The very heart of the Lord's ministry, His manifestations of patient love and the spirit of forgiveness are disavowed by Fundamentalists' actions.

Supplanting the Holy Spirit

Is it inherent in those who comprise the Oligarchy of Eighty to displace the power of the Holy Spirit and to take upon themselves the right to exercise its authority over followers of Christ?

Some illustrations of the wrongful assumption of the powers of the Holy Spirit are included in Chapter Ten. Usurpation of the Holy Spirit's power lies at the feet of those who instituted and continue to prosecute the phony "spiritual warfare" *games*. The Oligarchy of Eighty's dictating who are to serve as president and as other officers of the SBC also rejects the Holy Spirit's leadership of God's people.

Pretense About Interpreting God's Word

By persecuting those who resist demands that all Baptists blindly accept their interpretations of the Bible—Fundamentalists seek to forcefully impose those demands.

It's In The Bible

Authentic Baptists know that under the guidance and inspiration of the Holy Spirit, every sincere believer in Christ can gain an ongoing understanding of God's messages.

Followers of Christ who hear sermons, participate in Sunday school and study the Bible in private are fully competent to understand God's responses to major questions that His followers ask:

Who is God? It's in the Bible.

What is God like? God's Son is like the Father. Read about what Jesus said and did. It's in the Bible.

What does God expect of His followers? The Ten Commandments along with many other Old Testament scriptures, including God's clear and beautiful word in Micah 6:6-8—and the accounts of Jesus' life and ministries and other admonitions contained in the New Testament.

All of these provide answers about what God expects of His followers.

What do fellow believers in Christ expect of one another? Should not they expect one another to be true to *God's expectations?* It's in the Bible.

What Does the Bible Say and Mean?

The Bible means what it says and says what it means. The imprint of God's moral laws on one's conscience provides common sense understanding of biblical truths. A straightforward believer in Christ recognizes that even though the Bible is filled with the mysteries of prophecy and poetry, one can understand God's straightforward Word

Yes, Baptist laypeople are fully competent to understand God's Word. They are equally capable of discerning whether the conduct of Fundamentalists is consistent with God's Word. If not, can any *mainstream* Baptist give reason to be yoked with those imbued with the spirit of Fundamentalism?

Fundamentalists' Devices
To Gain Control

Segregation for "Special Treatment," i.e., Persecution

The *segregating* of individuals, groups and institutions for **special treatment** is a primary Fundamentalist control practice.

Political persecution and mind control practices—whether in America or elsewhere—have evolved throughout history. Even before the birth of Christ, totalitarian nations engaged in **special treatment** practices that isolated political prisoners for subsequent torture or death.

Segregating certain people for intended harm or diminishment is one of the most despicable practices evident in today's *official* SBC. More than two hundred years ago Baptists played a major role in winning for all Americans the right to enjoy religious freedom.

Today—ironically and shamefully—Fundamentalist Baptists are unleashing inexorable pressures and purposeful punishment on other Baptists who exercise their rights of religious freedom and who seek to practice the tenets of their Christian faith without outside interference.

In Nazi Germany more than fifty years ago, Jews were *segregated* for *special treatment.* In 1996, Jews have once again been *segregated* for *special treatment*—this time by the *official* Southern Baptist Convention. Of course, whereas the Nazi intent was to take the lives of millions of Jews, the SBC plan is stated to be for the saving of Jewish souls.

However, to many Jewish leaders, as pointed out by Rabbi A. James Rudin, national inter-religious affairs director of the American Jewish Committee, the Southern Baptist Convention's appointment of a special missionary for "Jewish evangelism" appears to leave the impression that Southern Baptists are targeting Jews as if they are some sort of trophy to be won.

Rabbi Rudin was quoted by the Religion News Service as saying:

> Oddly, these biblical literalists [Fundamentalists] seem to give no credence to the covenant that was established, through Abraham, between God and the Jewish people. Though Southern Baptists may believe otherwise, for Jews, it is a covenant that still stands. And the Southern Baptist leaders' attempt to tamper with the integrity of that covenant is offensive and infuriating to Jews. To us, Southern Baptists are putting yet another spin on a tragic historical pattern—singling out Jews for special treatment.

Some Baptists who have been persecuted have cause to wonder if the SBC resolution to segregate our Jewish friends for special treatment was inevitable rather than inadvertent.

Accept Fundamentalist Control or Be Relegated to the Trash Heap of Baptist Life

In order for Fundamentalists to achieve their goals of domination and control of the Southern Baptist Convention, they had to impose certain "corrections" on all aspects of Baptist life.

• Since Fundamentalism did not create or control the SBC, that condition was intolerable and it had to be "corrected," regardless of the possible damage resulting to the denomination.

• Since Fundamentalism did not create or control the six SBC seminaries, that situation had to be "corrected." To do so, Fundamentalists seized the seminaries.

• Since Fundamentalism did not create or control the Mission Boards, the Sunday School Board and other SBC agencies, Fundamentalists considered that to be intolerable. All had to be "corrected" to their satisfaction.

• Since Fundamentalism did not create or control the SBC Annuity Board, that situation also "had to be changed."

• Since Fundamentalism did not create or control the writing of the Baptist Faith and Message statements in 1963, Fundamentalists had to "correct that situation."

Now that the "necessary corrections" have been completed, the Oligarchy of Eighty "owns" all of the approximate $10 billion in SBC assets which the Baptist people, reflecting their loving support, felt that God had entrusted to their stewardship.

Fundamentalists' devices are amplified throughout the book, buit specifically in Chapter Five.

Some Things Fundamentalists Say and Do To Camouflage, Justify and Cover Up Some of their Misdeeds

---

One of my heroes, the late Judge Abner V. McCall, advised me never to get into a quarrel with a newspaper editor whose resources include the ability to buy paper by the roll and ink by the barrel. He also cautioned about the unfairness of denominational debate with Fundamentalists whose resources include the ability to spend millions of dollars of the people's tithes and offerings for the one-sided slanting of "public relations." Those tithes and offerings also can buy the services of the best of "spin masters" for the "justifying" of wrongful acts.

Unfortunately, I am unable to follow all of Judge McCall's sage advice. The evils of Fundamentalism, so prevalent in Baptist life since 1979, compel me to speak out, to call attention to some of the things that Fundamentalists have done to seize control of the SBC. Their shrewd practices continue unabated—even while attempting to "justify" their inexcusable and dishonorable use of some Southern Baptist assets—in the quest for ever greater worldly power.

• Fundamentalists will not even bother to defend any misuse of tithes and offerings. Their control of the SBC is absolute.

• They will rationalize the reorganization of the SBC, never suggesting that it is a major step toward transforming it to become a monolithic "Consolidated Southern Baptist Church of America."

• Fundamentalists will say that they are the ones being persecuted for the sake of righteousness. They will deny that those who have embraced Fundamentalist evil are accessories to the sin that effectively places the gods of worldly powers above the Almighty God.

• They will attempt to perpetuate the charade that biblically immoral worldly powers are Christian in character—and that promiscuous tactics of gutter politics are Baptist in principle.

• Fundamentalists will say it is a difference in belief about the Bible that causes themselves and *mainstream* Baptists to be poles apart. However, if Fundamentalists believed the Bible, they would not violate God's commandments; they would not engage in hateful acts that would negate the testimony of Jesus's life and ministry; and they would admit their differences with other Baptists are not about the Bible.

• Fundamentalists will continue to talk about their "theological recovery"—putting a pious spin on "Inerrancy" that has little to do with honoring the Scriptures, but much to do with rationalizing the use of ungodly hate to gain worldly powers over fellow Baptists.

• They will talk about the "conservative resurgence" in order to obscure the power-seeking evil that has been imposed upon the Southern Baptist Convention.

• Fundamentalists will rationalize the trampling of Baptist polity by waging the phony "spiritual warfare" strategy of worldly politics.

• They will pontificate about Matthew 7:3 (RSV)—"Why do you see the speck that is in your brother's eye, but do not notice the log that is in your own eye?"

• Fundamentalists will deny that their reward/punishment system of granting or withholding positions of power and prestige is a means of mind control.

• Fundamentalists will say the fight over the Bible was settled by the Peace Committee. They will not admit that their seizing control of the Peace Committee was a shrewd ploy to extend Fundamentalist powers and to throttle the possibility of peace in the SBC.

• Fundamentalists will falsely claim allegiance to the Baptist Faith and Message statements but promote Inerrancy as the exclusive justification for the continuing "spiritual warfare."

• Even though Bold Missions Thrust has been relegated to obscurity for seventeen years, it will be brought out of the political closet—as a deceptive "public relations" ploy.

• Fundamentalists will continue to "justify" use of any means—deception, slander, character assassination and other dishonesties of choice—to maintain control of the Southern Baptist Convention.

• Fundamentalists will continue to shrink from openly discussing and publicly debating the placing of some Baptist tithes and offerings on the altar of worldly-powered politics.

• Fundamentalists will put a pious spin on their demand to remove members of the Southwestern Baptist Theological Seminary's faculty who, though admittedly "theologically conservative," needed to be replaced to provide "political balance" in the institution.

• Fundamentalists will continue to lie about and *segregate for special treatment* men such as Winfred Moore, Richard Jackson, Daniel Vestal, Russell Dilday, Lloyd Elder, Keith Parks and others to be vilified and persecuted as "liberals" who "don't believe the Bible."

• Fundamentalists will say that mainstream Baptists are

33

a group of "religious-left" activists and/or that they suffer from a Messianic complex.

• Fundamentalists will continue to rely on human nature to place a far higher value on the preaching of hate rather than proclaiming the love of Jesus.

• Fundamentalists will continue their pious prattling about "the decline in Christian values."

• Fundamentalist leaders call for "Southern Baptists" to work with "other Christian groups" in order to witness to every person in America.

• Yet, honorable Baptists who choose to serve Christ by associating with like-minded believers in the Cooperative Baptist Fellowship, or in other Baptist groups, are segregated for *special treatment* by the fanatical spirit of Fundamentalism.

One wonders if the central purpose of the Fundamentalist rhetoric about "other Christian groups" is nothing more than an effort to develop a worldly-powered alliance designed to control America?

Some Things Fundamentalists Will Not Say or Do

• Fundamentalists will not admit that some of their more wild-eyed radical young colleagues have been granted permanent participation in the Oligarchy of Eighty—and places of high authority in the SBC. Those younger extremists will be able to perpetuate the Fundamentalist stranglehold of SBC institutions and assets at least until they reach retirement age—thirty to forty years hence.

• Fundamentalists will not confess that some tithes and offerings have been spent to place a twisted political spin on adverse events that have occurred in the SBC in recent years; or that the purpose of such "public relations" ploys is to persuade Southern Baptists to accept the worldly evils of the past; or that efforts must be made to obscure some of those recurring evils.

• Fundamentalists will not hold that individual Baptists can be blessed to serve as extensions of the life and ministries of Christ even if not under the control of the SBC rulers' ecclesiastical authority.

• Fundamentalists will not discontinue parroting that preachers are rulers of churches and will not say that congregations will continue to be manipulated in pursuit of their rulers' personal and worldly ambitions.

• Fundamentalists will not affirm the freedom, worth and dignity of every Baptist; instead they will continue to rationalize that the true value of each person is measured in one's service to the politico-religious movement's ideological pursuits.

• Fundamentalists will not recognize that the inviolability of the human conscience is a gift of God; that freedom and exercise of conscience is an inalienable right of every person; that conscience demands freedom from tyranny over one's mind, heart and soul. Instead, Fundamentalist leaders of the mass movement will continue to demand that every Baptist be submissive to Fundamentalist rule.

Justifiable Dishonesties?

The spirit of Fundamentalism fashioned and fostered the massive politico-religious movement that has overwhelmed the Southern Baptist Convention. This same spirit is propelling its ideological concepts beyond the borders of Baptist life into every village, hamlet, town and city of the United States. As the "Baptist Mess" spreads, the credibility of sincere Christians recedes.

Is it possible that one can follow the spirit of Fundamentalism and simultaneously be faithful to the precepts of Christ? Is it possible that a pastor, who has been called by God to servanthood leadership, has also been "justified" by God to become a ruler among rulers who initiate practices that are based on untruths and slander and who join in other dishonest seekings of unprecedented worldly powers over the denomination?

Perhaps, understanding the psychological profile of Fundamentalism—as presented in Chapter Three—will provide insight into possible answers to those questions.

3

The Spirit
of Fundamentalism
A Psychological Profile

✳✳✳✳✳✳✳

In all things, be of good report—

> "Once the organizers of a mass movement are committed to changing their world, they must identify with an issue and a worthy adversary—since they cannot effectively modify their own personality characteristics and shortcomings—in order to rally the masses to their cause."

The Spirit of Fundamentalism
A Psychological Profile

Have love and trust—previously so evident in our denomination—been torn asunder over the past seventeen years? Have men who call others derogatory names refused to have fellowship with anyone who does not join in Fundamentalism's militant lockstep?

Have good and honest Baptist men and women been thrown out of their denominational roles because of differences in opinions with proponents of Fundamentalism?

Have loving and God-fearing *mainstream* Baptists, who told the truth about the behind-the-scene antics of the Fundamentalist leaders, been shunned and removed from their denominational responsibilities? The answer to each is a resounding "Yes."

Even though the ongoing misdeeds of SBC leaders are evident, some laypeople have not recognized such wrongful acts to be unchristian. Other patient and godly laypeople have not yet realized that their Southern Baptist Convention has been seized by fanatical Fundamentalists.

Most laypeople are aware that evil has befallen their denomination and that something is terribly wrong, but many do not understand what specifically has gone wrong or how or why it went wrong. Perhaps this is because the malignant spirit of Fundamentalism in Southern Baptist life is highly complex and difficult to comprehend.

Secular newspapers and periodicals have often reported on the spirit of Fundamentalism, and a significant amount of space has been devoted to the accounts of Fundamentalist wrongdoing in various Baptist state papers.

However, in spite of this information, many Southern Baptist men and women still do not have a clear understanding of Fundamentalism and the spirit that it exudes.

Defining
Fundamentalism

Numerous studies of Fundamentalism have been made over the years. One of the best is "The Fundamentalism Project" of the American Academy of Arts and Sciences which is edited by Martin E. Marty and R. S. Appleby. Another, as mentioned in the previous chapter, is James Draper's book, *The Church Christ Approves*.

Draper wrote that book while he was pastor of the First Baptist Church in Euless, Texas. It seems paradoxical that he could pen such words and, then, knowingly—and with both eyes open—join the ranks of the Fundamentalists. However, after openly embracing the Fundamentalist camp, he reaped the rewards of the presidency of the Southern Baptist Convention and then the presidency of the SBC Sunday School Board.

Characteristics of Fundamentalism

The spirit of Fundamentalism, in all of its present expressions, arises out of a militant mentality that is the same whether among Moslems, ultra-orthodox Jews, Christians or others.

- It has an insatiable appetite for worldly power.
- It imposes its mind-control views on others.
- Its secret actions disclose its distrust of all persons.
- It covets all that comes into its sight that may advance its cause.
- Its ultimate objective is to control all that can be brought under its purview.

The spirit of Fundamentalism desires to dictate, and it demands that others become exactly like itself. *It enforces mind-control tactics by threats of persecution.*

Goals of Fundamentalism

The obsessive goals of the spirit of Fundamentalism vary greatly from the Christian principles that *mainstream* Baptists have believed in and practiced for so long. The spirit of Fundamentalism seeks:

1) To achieve mind-control over all persons within the Fundamentalist orbit and to make them available for both denominational and worldly assignments;

2) To obtain power sufficient to control vast sums of money. Always, ever more money is sought;

3) To control every organization and every asset that can be utilized to achieve Fundamentalism's insatiable appetite for worldly powers; and

4) To capture territory after territory en route to its ultimate quests, even worldwide Fundamentalism.

Psychological Profile of Fundamentalism

Most *mainstream* Baptists want to know the reasons for the controversy. They also want to know why it has raged on for so long and has affected the lives of so many people across the nation. To comprehend these things it is necessary to understand the psychological makeup of the "spirit of Fundamentalism."

In 1990, Baylor University President Dr. Herbert H. Reynolds, a widely experienced and eminent psychologist, made a special presentation ". . . to portray the characteristics of yet another mass movement in history in which there is significant socio-pathology."

Through this means Reynolds, who is currently serving as Baylor University chancellor, shared some perceptions regarding the *spirit of Fundamentalism*. Never before had *mainstream* Baptists had such an opportunity to obtain a straightforward understanding of Fundamentalism. (I have provided the subtitles to facilitate your reading.)

Lay Definition

A good lay definition of the word Fundamentalist is "one who knows what he is doing is wrong but does not care."

Underlying Deficiencies and Insecurities

"A mass movement appeals basically to those who crave to be rid of an unwanted self. They seek a new life, a rebirth or a chance to acquire new elements of self-esteem, confidence, hope and a sense of worth by identification with a holy cause.

"As with most mass movements throughout history, this one was begun by ambitious malcontents who would never have achieved personal visibility had it not been for their vision of creating a milieu and structure that would allow them to control and manipulate a large mass of people to satisfy their own unhealthy personality needs.

39

Desire to Submerge Themselves in Something Spectacular

"The renowned longshoreman philosopher Eric Hoffer stated that such persons 'see their lives and striving beyond remedy and . . . they crave to dissolve their spoiled, meaningless selves in some soul-stirring spectacular communal undertaking.'

Need to Create an "Issue"

"Once the organizers of a mass movement are committed to changing their world, they must identify with an issue and a worthy adversary—since they cannot effectively modify their own personality characteristics and shortcomings—in order to rally the masses to their cause.

Need to "Create" an "Enemy"

"As Adolf Hitler said in the early days of the organization of the Third Reich, 'The masses do not want freedom of choice. They want a simple doctrine and an enemy, preferably just one enemy. Truth is irrelevant: emotional appeals are better than intellectual arguments' . . . and with his propaganda chief, Joseph Goebbels, Hitler made it clear that if the Jew had not existed, they would have had to invent him. And they also understood all too well that 'any lie, frequently repeated, will gradually gain acceptance.' You see the Hitlers and Goebbels of all eras know that 'the big lie' will work because most people are innately trusting and, therefore, have a limited capacity to fathom the deception on a grand scale.

Unification by Hatred

"A requirement of mass movement strategy is that individuals must be identified and victimized from time to time to keep the hatred and fires burning in the bellies of mass movement members. In other words, they have to see live evidence of the demeaning punishment and even destruction, physical or psychological, of the worthy adversary. As Eric Hoffer has discerned, 'Hatred is the most accessible and comprehensive of all unifying agents.' And Heinrich Heine has suggested that 'What Christian love cannot do is effected by a common hatred.' Finally, it has been said that 'Mass movements can rise and spread without a belief in a god . . . but never without a belief in a devil.' The strength of a mass movement is proportionate to the vividness and tangibility of its devil.

Abnormal Cravings

"The leaders of Fundamentalist movements possess classical mass movement personality characteristics in that they have demonstrated time and again that they have an unfulfilled craving for work, power, recognition and goals that cannot be found in their ordinary pursuits; they required separation from self and something they view as more creative and fulfilling than that of a servant role in a lost world filled with travail. They are motivated by a blemished self which manifests itself in bibliolatry in hot pursuit of the worthy adversary. Their personality structure involves the proclivities and behavior indigenous to a frustrated mind.

Claims of Truth

"All active mass movements claim that 'the ultimate and absolute truth is embodied in their doctrine and that there is no truth or certitude outside.' As Henri Bergson said in his 1935 book, *The Two Sources of Morality in Religion*, 'So tenaciously should we cling to the world revealed by the gospel, that were I to see all the angels in heaven coming down to tell me something different, not only would I not be tempted to doubt a single syllable, but I would shut my eyes and stop my ears, for they would not deserve to be either seen or heard.' This is the source of the Fundamentalist's constancy. He is 'not frightened by danger nor disheartened by obstacles nor baffled by contradictions because he denies their existence.' Strength of faith in such personalities, as Bergson pointed out, manifests itself not in moving mountains, but in not seeing mountains to move.

Unchanging Behavior

"Since it is doubtful that the involved mass movement extremist who deserts his holy cause, or is suddenly left without one, can adjust himself once again to an autonomous individual existence without incurring much self-hatred, then it is also doubtful that the leaders and many followers of the movement will change their behavior. It would be like the loss of life itself to those who are most psychologically afflicted.

Power and Persuasion

"In view of the preceding statements, what will be seen in a mass movement's future if not thwarted? First, fanatical orthodoxy will continue as long as the movement is in possession of power and can impose its doctrine by force as well as by coercive persuasion. Persistent coercion is of nonpareil effectiveness, not only with those who lead a less complex existence, but also with those who consider themselves leaders and intellectuals.

Attacks on Innocent People

"At some point, even those who consider themselves to be strong and resilient . . . but not a part of a mass movement . . . may rationalize their cowardice and finally capitulate to Fundamentalism if they are not constantly alert and totally unyielding to such ungodly tactics.

"Therefore, it must be accepted as fact that innocent people will continue to be deliberately accused of misdeeds and sacrificed in order to keep suspicion and hatred alive.

Discrediting Tactics

"There is always a continuation of doctrinal purification, use of slogans and an interpretation of 'historic new days' to try to reinvigorate those involved in the Fundamentalist movement and to attract new adherents. There will also be increasing attempts to discredit prevailing beliefs and institutions and to remove them from the love and allegiance of those not involved in the mass movement.

Eventual Downfall

"Some leaders of the mass movement will live long enough to observe the downfall of the movement. A mass movement with a concrete objective, e. g., to take over and control an organization, is likely to have a shorter life than a movement with a nebulous, indefinite objective nurtured by chronic extremism. Oliver Cromwell was quoted by J. A. Cramb in his *Origins and Destiny of Imperial Britain* as having said, 'A man never goes so far as when he does not know whither he is going.'

Ultimate Result

"Furthermore, it is a fact of history that when a mass movement begins to attract and reward people who are primarily ambitious in their personal careers, it is past its most viable stages and is committed to deserving the power of the present. Hoffer has said that, 'It ceases to be a movement and becomes an enterprise'. . . . The more posts and offices a movement has to hand out, the more inferior stuff it will attract, and in the end these political hangers-on overwhelm a successful movement in such numbers that the honest fight of former days no longer recognized the old movement . . . when this happens, the mission of such a movement is done for."

The Madness of Fundamentalism

The *spirit of Fundamentalism* within the Southern Baptist denomination has defined itself—by its muscle, by its meanness, by its marauding nature and by its manipulative methods that have misled millions of Southern Baptist people.

The malignancy of Fundamentalism is choking the true spiritual breath out of Baptist life. Its politico-religious ideology has cast a pall over the Southern Baptist Convention. Month-by-month and year-by-year Fundamentalism's tentacles throttle the basic freedoms enjoyed by Southern Baptists. Simultaneously, Fundamentalism is using the Convention's influences and assets to expand its worldly powers.

Fundamentalists cannot escape the fact that they are responsible for the carnage that has scattered the debris of malevolence over our denomination. Fundamentalists must eventually reckon with the realities that have twisted their lives and brought havoc to the careers of so many others.

I believe, as do other *mainstream* Baptists, that "surrender to Christ" is the only antidote to quell the spreading of the spirit of Fundamentalism. Down deep in my heart I am troubled about the anguish to be suffered by those who have succumbed to Fundamentalism's evils.

Every follower of Christ knows the Christian highway is paved with love. It is on that road that we would entreat all Baptists—including those who are able to thrust aside the spirit of Fundamentalism—to again walk arm-in-arm with a transformed Southern Baptist family that is committed solely to Christ.

4

Footprints Of
Fundamentalism
Trail of the Baptist Travail

In all things, be of good report—

> "A mass movement appeals basically to those who crave to be rid of an unwanted self. They seek a new life, a rebirth or a chance to acquire new elements of self-esteem, confidence, hope and a sense of worth by identification with a holy cause."

Footprints of Fundamentalism
Trail of the Baptist Travail

Throughout history, Fundamentalism has caused people to suffer from its malignancy of estrangement. Beginning well before the birth of Christ—then, from Constantine to Calvin—from the Spanish Inquisition to the Crusades—from the hanging of Christian "witches" in Salem to J. Frank Norris and now beyond, the ravages of Fundamentalism have resulted in broken-hearted families and troubled churches and institutions. In all cases, the Fundamentalist claim was to serve a "Holy Cause."

It is difficult to comprehend the complexities of Fundamentalism. It is puzzling to understand how some Fundamentalist preachers can exhibit religious characteristics behind a pulpit and, yet, seemingly are driven by the forces of evil at other times. Review of the J. Frank Norris material in Chapter One may be appropriate at this point.

It also is bewildering to attempt to fathom the reasons why certain laypeople whose lives had been enriched by the idealism of Christianity could transfer their allegiance from Christ to Fundamentalism and its flagrant wrongdoing.

How Can Laypeople
Identify a "True Believer" Fundamentalist?

Does the spirit of Fundamentalism gradually acquire the power to overrule its clients' (or victims') vows to God—or is it men's prideful ambition that leads to a flirtatious affair with Fundamentalism—that will ultimately control their hearts and minds?

In either case, the affliction seemingly is both irresistible and incurable, and it often leads men to flagrantly foster personal sins of the soul even as, from pulpits, they piously condemn sins of the flesh.

Usually, it also leaves men's hearts and minds pathetically and irreparably twisted.

The Spirit of Fundamentalism
and Its Lucrative Marketplace

Fundamentalism's successful marketing of itself evokes envy in a tradesman's heart. Fundamentalism's principal product—the promise of worldly power over men and nations—is inordinately seductive *and* potentially profitable, for the manufacturing cost of this "product" is negligible.

Fundamentalism's clergy conscripts attempt to explain and justify their use of worldly power with such proclamations as "to restore the honor of the nation," "for the glory of God" or "to right the wrongs within the realm." These false claims magnetically draw foot soldiers to support the "cause." These enthusiastic followers seek the privilege—and some even pay money—to serve in the army of such a massive ideological movement.

The Personal Power of Each Fundamentalist Ruler Reinforces the Oligarchy's Invincibility

The Fundamentalist ruler's public demeanor is benign, even winsome. His facial expressions, gestures and words communicated from the pulpit are, first and foremost, designed to cement his control over the church—his power base and guaranteed stream of money.

> "I report to no man. I am responsible to no governmental entity. I am accountable only to God."

Who can question the Fundamentalist as he stands behind the pulpit and tells the people about the special words that God spoke to him—and to him only. He pauses—as much as thirty seconds—for the people to contemplate that they are listening to God's Special Messenger. After such a scene, who would question the ruler's imperial wisdom? Who would dare to challenge this proclamation of absolute authority?

Such rulers of churches, along with other Baptist potentates, created the controversy in Baptist life in order to obtain ironfisted worldly powers. They reinstituted persecution similar to that which J. Frank Norris employed so effectively. They brought about fragmentation. They ended civil discourse. They abandoned love. They destroyed trust. They made a mockery of Christian values, bartering them away for worldly powers.

It is obvious that some men believe gaining worldly powers for current aggrandizements is worth the ultimate eternal costs.

Spiritual Schizophrenia

The spirit of Fundamentalism distorts preachers' abilities to chose logically between right and wrong. This limitation—called "spiritual schizophrenia"—is evidenced by these characteristics:

- On Sundays, the face that the preacher turns to the congregation is one of engaging persuasion. He seeks the warm approval and hearty applause of the church's members
- The Fundamentalist's face in associational meetings, state conventions and in media presentations is to "carefully pick and choose the right scriptures for support of his public posturing." In dealing with sensitive matters such as his opposition to women serving as deacons, the preacher will say, "I cannot be committed to God's authentic Word and go against what God said." He always attempts to justify his Fundamentalism-induced position, even while knowing of other scriptures that affirm women serving as deacons and in other church offices. Nevertheless, the preacher puts a "spin" on his occasion-selected scripture-of-the-moment.
- But the Fundamentalist's real face—the real person—is evidenced in secret Fundamentalist meetings. It is important that he be perceived as the most macho among men. Each ambitious preacher would like to be known among those who participate in the secret meetings as being the one who will go farthest in the persecution of victims targeted for *special treatment.*

Fundamentalism's
Consuming Passions

Obviously, seeds of the spirit of Fundamentalism can be propagated only by men who are captivated by and committed to its consuming passions which are:

1) an obsession to control the minds and actions of all persons whose submission could contribute to the gaining of Fundamentalism's politico-ideological ambitions,

2) an unquenchable thirst to obtain and control increasing streams of money with which to acquire ever greater politico-religious power, and

3) an insatiable desire for personal aggrandizement, as necessary, to be proclaimed "The Greatest."

The Numbers Game

Numbers are vitally important to Fundamentalist preachers. They are meaningful internally in order to consolidate and retain control of the church's members. They are significant externally in order to demonstrate who is the greatest among Fundamentalists. In essence, numbers determine who is to be granted the most powerful denominational and political plums of power and position.

Christian Love Dispensed at 11:00 A.M. on Sundays

On Sundays, it is exceedingly difficult to distinguish between current-day Fundamentalist preachers and good and godly pastors who are Southern Baptists' servantlike spiritual leaders.

On Sundays, except on those occasions preceding secular political elections, Fundamentalist preachers read and quote the scriptures. They exhort hearers to have faith in Jesus. They preach and conduct worship services typical of those held in other Southern Baptist churches.

Making Important Statements

Some Fundamentalist preachers are strongly inclined to "make statements." Some of these "statements" that are so fashionable in Fundamentalist circles include:

- Hiring full-time bodyguards;
- Driving an "important" automobile with darkened windows;
- Having opulent personal offices reserved exclusively for entertaining public personages and important visiting Fundamentalists; and
- Leading the church, if located in a major city, to join in one dimension of the "who is the greatest" contest—by vying in the acquisition of ever-larger tracts of land.

"These Are the Specific Words God Told Me To Say"

"God gave me a strong word." Strong words come directly from the Bible—but those who violate God's Word have no hesitancy to superimpose their own will over God's will.

Unquestionably, God speaks to His followers. He has provided the Bible as the source of guidance for each of us. In addition, God grants special gifts of capabilities, discernment and wisdom upon which to draw. He allows experiences from which expertise is gained. He speaks to us through the dynamic wonders of nature and by other means.

Many have heard Fundamentalist preachers say things such as, "God spoke directly to me this morning and told me to stand on this very spot to say to you . . ." One Fundamentalist phoned me to say that God called him that morning and told him to tell me what I was supposed to do—for him—not for God.

A prominent Fundamentalist preacher stood before the congregation and said, in effect, "God talked directly to me and told me what to tell you—that you are to 'bug off.' " And, of course, many other such self-serving proclamations are based on similar claims that "God told me to do it."

Mind Control is a Theocratic Necessity —Not a Prideful Plaything

When a "true believer" Fundamentalist—one who insists that his interpretations and conclusions are the *only* ones that are acceptable—finds what is desirable to him, his mind never wanders and his eyes never waver from the objective. The target is zeroed in, as if locked into the guidance system of a Cruise missile. The quest is not ended until the prized objective has been seized.

Then, when such a Fundamentalist preacher is called to be the pastor of a church, his first goal is to become the church's ruler. Whether preaching "hellfire and brimstone" sermons or being ingratiatingly charming and entertaining, the Fundamentalist preacher's need is to quickly gain hearty approval and hear flattering applause from his listeners.

Successful Fundamentalist preacher-rulers are serious students of psychology. Prior to their taking over a church, current staff members must be terminated. After the Fundamentalist preacher arrives, other changes—such as the church's physical facility, location of the pulpit or changing the lights—are deemed necessary to highlight the predecessors' deficiencies.

However, possibly the greatest change is reflected in the church's Finance Committee. The new Fundamentalist preacher will gain control of the church's money or he will leave. *The Finance Committee is the preacher's private turf.*

Many thousands of sincere Christian Baptists are members of Fundamentalist-ruled churches. They are tolerated as long as they pose no difficulties to the ruler.

Each member of the congregation is expected to submit to the Fundamentalist preacher's will. Whether for window dressing, image polishing or other reasons, some of the most influential members may serve on church committees if they are appropriately submissive.

However, staff members serve as chairpersons of the committees; and members of the staff remember who controls their paychecks.

The Laypeople's Spiritual Torment

Few, if any, laypeople, after careful reflection, would choose to be a part of that which is wrong and then say to themselves, "I really don't care."

Yet, many members of Fundamentalist-controlled churches are confronted by a disturbing dilemma.

Some church members are unwittingly mobilized as reluctant mercenaries in the struggle for worldly power. Others who would resist Fundamentalism, as a matter of conscience, in order to honor Christ's expectations that believers obey His word, are surreptitiously labeled as *"opponents* of the preacher."

Loyal foot soldiers in the "spiritual warfare" are expected to join in the persecution of "opponents" by whisper campaigns and other forms of denigration.

"Opponents" are dangerous to the Fundamentalist "cause," for they would oppose a Fundamentalist takeover of governmental institutions and other entities by the means used to seize control of the Southern Baptist Convention.

Most of the laypeople in such circumstances recognize that the preacher's three obsessive goals are to control their minds, build an ever-growing base upon which to amass greater worldly power and to expand the sources of increasing sums of money.

Seemingly, the laypeople have but three choices:

1) Strive to reestablish democratic processes in the church's governance,

2) Move their membership to a congregation that practices unfettered democratic participation by all of its members in the church's affairs, or

3) Continue their submission to further Fundamentalist mind control.

Rank and File Members of a Fundamentalist Church

If some members of the congregation are not enthralled by the Fundamentalist preacher—and are aware of his diminished integrity that coincides with his increased power—they can remain members of the church as long as they continue to be discreetly silent. They also can attend services and place money in the offering plate if they do not ask questions about the church's operations or its finances. Thus, those who are willing to accept the status quo can avoid being consigned to the *special treatment* category.

About Deacons Who Should Not Ask Questions

Ordaining a sizable number of new deacons is necessary to achieve control of the church quickly. In some Fundamentalist churches, the number of deacons expands into the hundreds. When enough of "his loyal men" have been elected, older deacons can be segregated as "road blocks to the church's progress."

It is not unusual for the new deacons to be told, "Don't ask any questions. Consider yourselves to be the 'spiritual leaders' of the church."

As spiritual leaders, their primary responsibility is to bring in ever more people to join in the "spiritual warfare" to save the Bible! Always, ever more recruits are to be mobilized for the benefit of Fundamentalism.

However, if a deacon becomes a persistent questioner, the preacher or a staff member is likely to tell the inquirer, "The governance of this church is not democratic. It is theocratic. Perhaps you should not come to another meeting."

In some Fundamentalist churches, following biblical guidelines as related to ordaining men to serve as deacons and selecting women to serve in church-elected positions is a farce. Many of the deacons are not biblically qualified to serve in the position due to divorce, use of strong drink and for other reasons. But they can attest to the churches' rulers being "the greatest."

On the other hand, even though biblically qualified, women are prohibited from responding to God's call to service. Nevertheless, the fact remains that *the ruler is the ruler*!

However, rejecting those scriptures in the Holy Bible that would tend to restrict the purposes of *Rulers' Personal Aggrandizement Society* is a standard Fundamentalist practice.

Sundays Provide Special Opportunities.

What are some popular methods used to draw some of the people ever closer to the preacher?

- Bring in big name entertainers;
- Bring in big name politicians; and
- Bring in big name visiting Fundamentalist preachers.

Younger couples are impressed by "prosperity" sermons, but they may be unaware that such sermons are not biblical.

Feeding the Poor

Image polishing, public relations, window dressing or for whatever reason, on rare occasions the needy are fed—but always while being televised with the preacher.

The preacher gets the publicity, but, then the poor have been fed—even if it is just once a year!

Pull of the Ladder

Never in any experience of life—corporate, community, professional, societal or other organizations—have I observed "ladder climbing" obsessions to be greater than those of Fundamentalist preachers.

Indeed, the compulsion to establish a Fundamentalist's superior self-worth seemingly is the driving force of his life.

Incredible Arrogance

There is an incredible arrogance evidenced in men who say, "The United States must turn from its wicked ways, humble itself and pray for God's deliverance"—yet continue to wage "spiritual warfare" games against true followers of Christ!

Apparently, these men consider it better not to discuss publicly the sins that were committed in seizing churches and the Southern Baptist Convention.

Fundamentalists
Not All Alike

While I was a teenager in Waco, Texas, the spirit of Fundamentalism was made manifest on two separate, but startling, occasions. One of these emanated from a radio broadcast; the other occurred in a personal confrontation that I witnessed. In later years, I would conclude both identified with the "true believer" sect of Fundamentalism.

As I listened to the radio, I was astonished to hear a Fundamentalist preacher, who was berating an elected McLennan County official, say, "God, I ask you to take that man's life. Lord, it would be the greatest blessing of my ministry if you were to strike him dead even while I am calling on you to do so. Praise God!"

The other incident occurred when I was a high school senior. While at Baylor University to obtain enrollment information, I walked across the street from the campus to the Baylor Drugstore. There were numerous students inside visiting, shopping and eating.

Suddenly a young man stood on his chair, stepped to the top of a table, pointed to two students at another table and shouted, "God will take your sinful lives for drinking those Coca-Colas!" I felt the students were in far greater danger of Fundamentalist hate than from a God of love.

The Driving Force:
Who Is The Greatest?

Every Fundamentalist whom I have observed making a public presentation—or with whom I have conversed privately—has seemed to have as his major concern the relative attractiveness of his public image. His unspoken central theme appears to be, "I am superior. I am the greatest. I am in control. I am the ruler. I shall brook no question or challenge to my authority." Only after the underlying factors related to his dictatorial power have been reiterated, can he proceed with his conversation or sermon.

Seemingly embedded at the epicenter of the Southern Baptist Convention controversy is the Christian world's tallest imaginary billboard. The identical imaginary messages emblazoned on each side of the fictitious giant sign convey the query, "Who is the greatest?"

Approximately two thousand years ago, Jesus provided a clear-cut answer to the question "Who is the greatest?" Apparently, those mesmerized by the spirit of Fundamentalism's search for *"Who is the greatest?"* deem the Lord's response to be unsatisfactory.

"I am to be the greatest!"

A member of a church, pastored by one of today's most powerful Fundamentalist leaders, shared this incident that occurred in the early years of that preacher's career. During an after-church Sunday evening young people's fellowship that was being held in the member's home, the Fundamentalist preacher abruptly stood on a coffee table in the living room and announced to the group, "I am going to become the greatest preacher that Christendom has ever known."

The addiction to power usually proves itself to be as destructive as an addiction to alcohol and other drugs. Practically all Baptists who have been blessed with longevity of life have seen pitiable results of self-proclaimed greatness such as the interruption of potentially successful careers, destruction of business organizations, wife and child abuse and the wrecking of homes, among other things.

One can only wonder about the outcome of the life of that young Fundamentalist preacher had he succumbed to the leadership of the Lord rather than the desire to be designated as "the greatest in Christendom."

Fundamentalist Ownership Practices

Many Fundamentalist preachers have obtained absolute control over congregations. Some own the church buildings—literally—and even the land on which the church facilities have been constructed.

The "committees" of the church are allowed no latitude whatsoever regarding decision making. The preacher directs all operations and functions of the church. He is the ultimate ruler!

Private Enterprises

Fundamentalist preachers of some Southern Baptist churches have established themselves—individually or through corporations they control—as owners of certain aspects of the churches' functions. Such Fundamentalist rulers often control the cassette, television, personal appearance and other such "ministries of the church." In many instances, the church pays all of the costs, but the Fundamentalist preacher receives the monetary proceeds from those "ministries."

Pride and Politics

Most Baptists try to be courteous to each other. They want to become more Christlike. Yet, some selectively ignore the teachings of Jesus—except from pulpits on Sundays! At other times, whether by dyspeptic nature or by intent, they either cannot or will not engage in civil discourse. Far more damage is done to Baptists' Christian witness by what is said *about* people than by what is said *to* people.

Seeds of Hate

I am not ambivalent about the spirit of Fundamentalism and, as is apparent, I cannot be submissive to it or supportive of its pursuits. Still, I have sympathy for those whose lives have been caught up in the "righteousness" of the evil that rigidly interposes itself against the Christian principles that have warmed the hearts of believers since Jesus taught the tenets of faith and love to His disciples.

Yes, the plight of those committed to Fundamentalism is regrettable. But one wonders about the dichotomy of a sincere belief in inerrant scripture and apparent unwillingness to accept our Lord's designation of love as the centerpiece of Christian conduct.

In my presence, a preacher, deeply imbued with the spirit of Fundamentalism, prefaced his remarks about what he would do to another man with the words, "Were I God . . . ." Fortunately, for persons such as I, he isn't! My God is a God of love—not hate.

The Great Commandment: Matthew 22:36-40

In Matthew 22:36-40, the lawyer asked Jesus, "Teacher, which is the greatest commandment in the law?" Jesus replied,

"Love the Lord your God with all your heart and with all your soul and with all your mind. This is the first and greatest commandment."

Then Jesus astonished the man by saying, "And the second is like it. Love your neighbor as yourself." How could an ordinary hearer of the Word understand that *anything* could be the equivalent of that first and great commandment—to love God completely. Yet there it was—in the words of Jesus—and there it still is! What does it mean if one deliberately chooses to violate one of those commandments?

World Congress Identifies Fakes

Can you imagine anyone calling W. A. Criswell a fake? Dr. Robert Terry, then editor of the Missouri Baptist paper, *Word & Way*, wrote an article that was carried in the December 1, 1994, issue of the Georgia Baptist paper, *The Christian Index*. In it Dr. Terry wrote:

> The name George Sweeting may not be known to the majority of *Word & Way* readers, but most will recognize the names of W. A. Criswell, pastor of First Church of Dallas, Texas, and Jerry Falwell, pastor of Thomas Road Baptist Church in Lynchburg, Virginia. All three have identified themselves as Fundamentalist Christians in various ways. But according to the World Congress of Fundamentalism, all three are fakes.
>
> Sweeting was president of Moody Bible Institute in Chicago . . . . W. A. Criswell is currently celebrating his fiftieth anniversary as pastor of First Church, Dallas. He is a former president of the Southern Baptist Convention and continues to travel widely and speak regularly. . .
>
> Jerry Falwell. Who needs to say more? Falwell has become one of America's most widely known personalities . . .
>
> Few would argue the credentials of any one of the three to their identity as Fundamentalist Christians. But to the World Congress of Fundamentalists (WCF), their credentials are not good enough.
>
> In 1985, the Congress (WCF), under the leadership of Bob Jones, Jr., president of Bob Jones University, and Ian Paisley, a militant Protestant leader in Northern

Ireland, passed a resolution condemning all three men. The resolution read: 'We believe that it is not enough just to proclaim biblical principles of separation but that it is further necessary in scripture to identify men, institutions and movements that are involved in apostasy or compromise with it. To this end the World Congress of Fundamentalists warns Bible believers against . . . such men as W. A. Criswell, Jerry Falwell, George Sweeting and Jack Van Impe.' (Van Impe is a Fundamentalist evangelist.)

In his book, *Heart Disease in Christ's Body*, Van Impe recalls, 'I always felt that my best preaching took place when I was stirred by 'righteous indignation' and I often ended up tearing people to shreds in ungracious tones with unkind words. When I blasted alleged compromisers by name publicly, those steeped in Fundamentalism responded with enthusiasm because it was negative and inflammatory.'

'Preaching on the crucifixion, the precious blood of Christ, assurance of salvation or other edifying topics produced just a few rare 'Amens.' Conversely, preaching against rock music, dancing, hair length or pantsuits created deafening applause. . . .'

Inevitable Questions

Seemingly, consciously or otherwise, preachers have two choices. They must decide,

1) whether ". . . to tear people to shreds in ungracious tones and with unkind words" to obtain the applause of men—men whose base nature causes them to gravitate to the negative and inflammatory, or

2) whether to preach " . . . the crucifixion, the precious blood of Christ, assurance of Salvation . . ." and thereby subject themselves to the ignominy of receiving only a few "Amens."

How difficult should that choice be for men called of God? It is either to seek Fundamentalist ego-massaging and deafening applause or the simple reward of seeing people quietly and thoughtfully respond to the love of Christ. Unfortunately, there are some who claim to believe Jesus's words to "love your neighbor" but by their actions demonstrate a conviction that Jesus was wrong to define love as the imperative practice of those genuinely committed to His call.

Indisputable Answers

Michael Clingenpeel, editor of the *Virginia Religious Herald*, wrote

> A few Baptists in our Southern Baptist and Virginia Baptist fellowships are dyspeptic by nature. They define themselves more by what or whom they oppose rather than what they favor. When they define an enemy and territory to conquer, it is difficult not to respond to their agenda. Fortunately, these contentious believers are in a minority, and most Virginia Baptists prefer to be motivated by a more positive, Kingdom-advancing agenda.

Even though reference could be made to the current Fundamentalist SBC leaders as no more offensive than being "dyspeptic by nature," the Fundamentalists waging of "spiritual warfare" against *mainstream* Baptists, rather than following the ways of Christ, is evidence of their intention to harm.

Characteristics That Differentiate Categories of Fundamentalists

---

Some followers of the Patterson/Pressler political machine were fully aware of its commitment to seize all that it could—with its resulting goal being the amassing of ever-greater worldly power. Yet, I believe thousands of others did not know what they were getting into when invited to support Fundamentalism's hate.

"True Believers"—in Fundamentalism

Deep within the heart of the Fundamentalist revolutionary—the "True believer"—lies the lust for personal power to seize control of a church, an institution or a nation. Absolute control of others is necessary:

1) to "legitimize" mind control,
2) to discredit or to destroy opposition and
3) to seize specified targets.

The following may be said of Fundamentalism's "True Believer."

• The "True Believer" possesses strong "theological motivation" to enforce acceptance of his particular "interpreta-

58

tion" of God's Word.

• The "True Believer" insists that each facet of his interpretation of the Bible is inviolate.

• The "True Believer" is confident that all practices of the Fundamentalist religion are right and all others are wrong.

• The "True Believer" has no doubt that those who hold a different view or interpretation of the Bible are dangerous to God and to the "True believer."

• The "True Believer" almost always must be involved in "spiritual warfare"; otherwise, he/she no longer will be acceptable to other "True Believers."

According to the "True Believer's" creed, anyone who refuses to accept the "True Believer's" interpretation of the Bible must be ridiculed as a fool and branded a liberal. His Christian testimony also must be damaged and his personal integrity diminished or destroyed.

In the event a layperson resists a Fundamentalist preacher's rulership, that individual's conversion is questioned. When a layperson resists a Fundamentalist preacher's control, the recalcitrant is subject to a whisper campaign designed to discredit him. In some instances, the "offender" is laid open to "religious blackmail" based on confidences previously shared with the preacher.

The "True Believer" Fundamentalist is not merely mean-spirited or "dyspeptic by nature." He is a mirror reflection of Fundamentalism's ***tyrannical mindset***.

Counterfeit Citizenship?

Even though desiring to protect his public posturing—if pinned down about even the most blatant of evil acts—every "True Believer" Fundamentalist will tell you, as I have been told by more than one, and as mentioned previously:

> "I report to no man. I am responsible to no governmental entity. I am accountable only to God."

Inasmuch as the God known by *mainstream* Baptists incorporated His rules of life in the Ten Commandments, seemingly, men who intentionally violate them would seek the approval of another god, one invented for that purpose.

59

With further regard to "True Believer" Fundamentalists' allegiance to religious freedom and individual liberties of the nation's citizens, possibly Chapter Ten will be of special interest to authentic Baptists.

"Go Along to Get Along"

The "go along to get along" Fundamentalists want to be close to the power base where their future can be more assured. They are the foot soldiers who do the dirty work of the Fundamentalist movement, and they are rewarded accordingly.

I have great sympathy for the sizable number of Southern Baptist pastors who—perhaps unwittingly—have given support to the Fundamentalist movement. It is possible many of them did not understand the nature of revolutionary Fundamentalism.

Unfortunately, naiveté concerning their leaders' commitment to the seizure of power, regardless of methods employed, is now subjecting many pastors—those who are caught in the middle—to significant disquietude.

A logical question would be, "Upon finally understanding the nature and political goals of Fundamentalism in the SBC, why would any pastor, who is honest with God and honest with fellow Baptists, not be willing to stand on the high ground and publicly oppose Fundamentalism?"

A parallel question, especially for laypeople, could be, "Are those who have been misled for a few years by Fundamentalists willing to consign the remainder of their lives to that ideological movement—especially when realizing that Fundamentalism intentionally rejects Christ's command to love one another?" The answers to these questions lie in each layperson's heart.

Believers Choice

I continue to wonder, "Why do laypeople, knowing full well that something is terribly wrong in the SBC, continue to allow their tithes and offerings to be sent to Nashville—where the SBC Executive Committee, in determining the portion that each SBC board, agency, commission and institution will receive—has the power to allocate significant amounts of money to be used to finance Fundamentalist enterprises?"

How much of our tithes and offerings have already been devoted to harming our state conventions? I believe you will be shocked by some of the information presented in Chapter Nine.

"Well, I'm Doing My Part."

Some Southern Baptist laypeople, without giving serious thought to where Fundamentalism is taking the Convention, remain committed to certain of the irrational concepts of the spirit of Fundamentalism. A dear friend of mine is a member of a Fundamentalist-controlled congregation. He understands Fundamentalist evils and is aware of the pastor's many unchristian acts, yet he voices no opposition to those dishonesties. His defense is the statement, "Well, I'm doing my part. I go to church, hear a sermon, leave my money and get out. What they do with my offering is their problem."

If my friend is alive twenty years hence, I wonder about his inevitable regret regarding the ongoing course of Fundamentalism and its impact on his children and grandchildren and upon all of America.

Poisoning of the Pastors Conference

Approximately fifty years ago an unknown teenager perished in a Nazi death camp. But the diary she left behind revealed her identity and still touches the hearts of millions around the world. Even on wintry, wet mornings in Amsterdam, people line up outside the unremarkable four-story building at No. 263 Prinsengracht. They wait their turn to climb the steep stairway to the secret annex where Anne Frank recorded her thoughts and her daily life of seclusion and hiding.

Every reflection upon the tragedy of the SBC Pastors Conference reminds me anew of the tragedy of Anne Frank. A recent issue of the *Reader's Digest* told her poignant story and quoted from her diary in which she wrote:

> When it's dark, I often see long lines of good, innocent people walking on and on . . . I feel wicked sleeping in a warm bed and get frightened when I think of close friends now at the mercy of the cruelest monsters ever to stalk the earth. All because they are Jews!

Later she wrote, "I want to go on living even after my death." On August 4, 1944, the end came after Anne and her family had passed 761 days in hiding. Around 10:30 a.m. a car drove up to 263 Prinsengracht. The Frank family was whisked away. Later that day friends found Anne's diary that had been left behind. In it she had written, "I still believe, in spite of everything, that people are truly good at heart." She remains a candle in the dark for us all.

Christlike Pastoral Leadership

Our pastors are highly important in our lives. There is a yearning for our pastors to be Christlike—for them to shape us spiritually by the truth of God. We greatly desire to admire, respect and love them. We want our "shepherds" to challenge and lead us in ways as would Jesus were He the pastor of our church.

As we know and believe, God revealed himself through Jesus Christ. He specifically determined that Jesus was to reflect the spirit of servanthood, not the ambition, avarice and arrogance of unyielding dictatorial leadership. But something has gone wrong—terribly wrong.

Some pastors have succumbed to single-minded quests, single-minded pursuits, single-minded demands, single-minded obsessions, single-minded malice and single-minded corruption—all of which are components of the political guile of Fundamentalism.

Disquietude in congregations grows commensurably as incidents of conflict between the people and pastors of Baptist churches continue to escalate. The authentic Baptist people want their pastors free of Fundamentalism—to live clean lives in private and honest lives in public and to practice Christlike leadership from the pulpit. Unless these are the standards by which our pastors live, more and more Baptists will be impacted by influences that first diminish, then deny the importance of Christ to this lost world.

Christian Conscience Can Prevail

Conscientious pastors seek to live their seven-days-per-week lives according to God's word—the same as preached on Sundays. Some Fundamentalist preachers talk about Christ on

Sundays; but, during the rest of the week, as if in a fashion show, dictatorial power is paraded as a political statement.

Please hear the words of an honorable and highly respected pastor whose lifetime commitments and work have undergirded the cause of Christ and whose ministries of mercy and mission commitments are performed in the servanthood manner of the Master. He wrote:

The Stated Plan for Control
Several months before the 1979 annual meeting of the Southern Baptist Convention, which convened in Houston, Texas, I was visited by Judge Paul Pressler and enlisted as one of his many workers. The object of his campaign was stated as being a victory over the liberals in the SBC. He identified the liberals as members in our midst who did not believe in the inerrant, fully inspired word of God. He was very disturbed over what he perceived to be a strong liberal drift in our six SBC seminaries. His stated plan was to capture the presidency of the SBC and then, through the appointive powers of the presidency, all convention boards and agencies could be completely controlled by the true Bible believing members of the SBC.

Judge Pressler then revealed to me a map of the United States and proceeded to show how the various states were broken down into units over which various individuals were being assigned. The assignment had to do with informing the people, enlisting the people, organizing the people and getting out the vote. A line of communication was being established whereby Judge Pressler and his co-laborer, Dr. Paige Patterson, could be in close contact with each leader in every assigned field throughout the nation.

Responsibilities Accepted
I agreed to be responsible for a rather large area of my state [Texas] and to report directly to Judge Pressler. Once locked into the campaign I received regular phone calls and a constant flow of information and instructions from Judge Pressler. As convention time grew nearer, Judge Pressler pressed for quotas of voters from my area

and made many offers relative to meeting needs of messengers such as transportation and rooms in Houston.

When the convention time actually arrived and immediately prior to the election of the president, Judge Pressler and Dr. Patterson arranged a luncheon for well over four hundred of the enlisted workers from across the convention. The luncheon was at the Colonnade Cafeteria near the convention site. The purpose of this meeting was to finalize plans and to have every worker informed, or perhaps the better word would be programmed. Judge Pressler and Dr. Patterson obviously orchestrated every movement of that meeting. The workers were simply told what to do and none were given an opportunity to make any kind of contribution.

A Growing Uneasiness

Two things, in particular, occurred during this meeting that caused me to decide that the uneasiness which had been growing in my heart and mind was justified. I knew for certain when these two things happened that I was in the wrong camp.

Shortly after we were seated at our tables in the cafeteria, a messenger was sent to each table to instruct us to be watching a certain entrance. We were informed that at any moment a very important man was going to appear at that entrance and that we must jump to our feet and give him a rousing welcome. Just then the evangelist James Robinson appeared. He stood there in the doorway as some proud prince and all of the people jumped to their feet and began to clap their hands with much enthusiasm. Evangelist Robinson was presented to us as one of the great champions of our faith and as a powerful enemy of all the liberals who were determined to destroy the SBC. Moreover, he was extremely agitated over the "alleged" fact that there were so many liberals teaching in our seminaries. He was sent to clean up the convention.

Preempting the Holy Spirit

The second event which occurred settled the matter for me once and for all. Again messengers were sent to each table and this time each person was given a blank piece of paper. We were then informed that there were two men who were at this time acceptable to Judge Pressler and Dr. Patterson. Either of the two would make a great president of the SBC and would start us on the road to ultimate victory.

The Revelation

The names were then revealed to be Dr. Adrian Rogers and Dr. Bailey Smith. Following this revelation, we were told to get down on our knees and to ask the Holy Spirit to enlighten us as to which of the two He wanted to become the new president of the SBC. Once we had the divine enlightenment we were to write Smith or Rogers on the blank piece of paper. Soon after this sacrilegious farce, limiting the Holy Spirit to the two men previously chosen by Judge Pressler and Dr. Patterson, the ballots were taken up and counted. Shortly thereafter, we were informed that the Holy Spirit had selected Dr. Adrian Rogers. Though I had nothing against either Dr. Rogers or Dr. Smith, I was glad that I had turned my blank piece of paper back as I had received it.

Free Refreshments for Political Conformity

Now that the Holy Spirit had supposedly settled the matter, we were sent out to line up our people so that they would be sure to vote for God's chosen man. This was simply too much for me. Here were some men doing some very raw politicking and attempting to make everything appear up and above board by attributing the results to the work of the Holy Spirit. We left with the reminder that there would be plenty of free refreshments provided for us during the convention and that we would be informed as to the progress relative to the meeting of our common goal.

I resigned that day from the so-called holy crusade and I believe I'm a better man and Southern Baptist for it.

(This good man was willing for his name to be shown, but I withheld it to shield him from Fundamentalist hate. He is available to confirm his experiences in person with any *mainstream* Baptist.)

Poisoning Procedures

Throughout our conversation, I have provided a significant amount of documented information. But, inasmuch as the following statements reflect my personal opinion, the point should be made clear. I was there; I saw it take place; I heard it all!

Over the years I have "sat in on" pastors conferences that preceded SBC annual meetings. At the 1986 meeting of pastors held before the SBC annual meeting in Atlanta, I was practically mesmerized by what occurred. While it was happening I thought about fellow *mainstream* Baptist laypeople and was grateful that they were not hearing what was being "preached." I thought about fellow Americans who would not have believed it possible that something of this nature could transpire before an overflow crowd of Baptist "men of the cloth."

Bailey Smith was standing before that crowd of Fundamentalist preachers, whipping their emotions into a frenzied state. He repeatedly waved the Bible over his head and vehemently shouted staccato sentences such as, "It isn't what they think. It's what God says." And the Fundamentalist preachers responded as if puppets on a string—guttural sounds emanating from their throats.

I sat there, as if paralyzed in the midst of the Babylonians who cheered for the lions thousands of years ago. As Bailey Smith continued to speak, I thought about Dr. Draper's book, *The Church Christ Approves*, in which he wrote

> Fundamentalism is more dangerous than liberalism because everything is done in the name of the Lord. In the name of the Lord, the Fundamentalist condemns all who disagree with him . . . he used the Bible as a club with which to beat people over the head, rather than a means of personal strength and a revealer of God.

I remembered the Fundamentalists' anger that followed their inability to seize control of the SBC at the 1972 annual meeting in Philadelphia. It was during that era when Fundamentalists established the Luther Rice Seminary (1968), Criswell College (1970) and Mid-America Seminary (1971). Many graduates of those Fundamentalist institutions—as well as some alumni of the six SBC seminaries who had been converted to Fundamentalism—were at the 1986 SBC Pastors Conference that I attended. I then thought back to the Conference of Southern Baptist Evangelists that had been held in Dallas the previous year. At that meeting, one evangelist said it was time for a "bloodletting." It was reported that another evangelist, Sam Cathey, said, " . . . for years I've been saying we've got to take off the kid gloves. People who don't believe the Bible can be mean as hell . . . we've got compromise; we've got liberals. They've come out of the woods. We know who they are. Let's go get 'em."

I recalled that Charles Stanley, the SBC president, had addressed that group of evangelists in 1985. Instead of exhorting Baptists to relate to one another in a spirit of love and forgiveness, his comments on that occasion did nothing to quell the highly inflammatory mood of the bloodthirsty "evangelists" who were ready to dash out into the streets to "Go Get 'Em!"

I found myself wondering, "What if the Lord were to make an appearance in this room? What if Bailey Smith had invited Jesus to speak to this restive crowd? Would these angry, belligerent Fundamentalists heed him? Or would they continue seeking Southern Baptists 'liberals' to revile, slander and diminish?"

It was at that moment I felt the poisoning of the Pastors Conference had been completed. It was at that moment I wondered if those particular Southern Baptist pastors would ever understand the change that had come over them, would ever regain their senses or would ever return to Christ.

Here it is 1996. The Southern Baptist Convention, having been seized in 1979 by underhanded means, is now under the thumb of the Oligarchy of Eighty. Only the most naïve could assume that the SBC leaders would turn away from their worldly power ambitions in order to serve the Savior. Only the most gullible could justify acquiescence to Fundamentalist evil by "not wanting to be involved."

Had Anne Frank attended the Pastors' Conferences over the past seventeen years, one wonders if she would continue to say, "I still believe, in spite of everything, that people are truly good at heart."

One also is caused to wonder to whom Jesus will say, "I never knew you."

5

Vignettes Of Evil
The Great Divide: Intention of the Master Plan

✳✳✳✳✳✳✳

In all things, be of good report—

"The leaders of Fundamentalist movements possess classical mass movement personality characteristics in that they have demonstrated time and again that they have an unfulfilled craving for work, power, recognition and goals that cannot be found in their ordinary pursuits; they require separation from self and something they view as more creative and fulfilling than that of a servant role in a lost world filled with travail. They are motivated by a blemished self which manifests itself in bibliolatry in hot pursuit of the worthy adversary. Their personality structure involves the proclivities and behavior indigenous to a frustrated mind."

Vignettes of Evil
The Great Divide: Intention of the Master Plan

The spirit of Fundamentalism's contagious malignancy has invaded many Southern Baptist churches. It has brought turmoil and has divided congregations.

Fundamentalists now control the six SBC seminaries to which—in some cases for over a hundred years—they provided little, if any, support for development, facilities and operations. In addition to the six SBC seminaries that they have seized, the Fundamentalists also have the three institutions *they* established in the late 1960s and early 1970s—Luther Rice Seminary, Criswell College and Mid-America Seminary.

Evidence indicates the origin of the Patterson/Pressler strategy, designed to *divide and conquer*, occurred in the mid-1970s. Over the past twenty or more years, graduates of the Fundamentalist institutions have become rulers of numerous Southern Baptist churches. During this time a significant number of members of those Fundamentalist-ruled congregations have stormed Southern Baptist Convention annual meetings to vote as desired by the radical oligarchy.

In 1979 the power of God was deliberately and shrewdly defied by Fundamentalists in order to seize control over the Southern Baptist Convention. As a result, the SBC has been completely transformed by Fundamentalism. Today, it is creedalistic. Its Oligarchy of Eighty is totalitarian.

Segregation for Special Treatment

Early on, state conventions, associations and churches were individually targeted to be conquered. According to the September 24, 1980, issue of *The Virginia Religious Herald,* at the same meeting in which Pressler stated, "The conservatives [Fundamentalists] are going for the jugular in their campaign to get control of Southern Baptist institutions and the convention itself," he also suggested an organized chain of communications.

That chain to achieve further conquest was, "A layman in each church—someone in each association, etc."

Baylor University, An Early Target

Baylor University was *segregated* for **special treatment** by the current cadre of ruling Fundamentalists in the 1970s. Indeed, even in the 1960s, Fundamentalists started circulating lies about Baylor and certain members of its faculty.

Unquestionably, Baylor was a prized trophy target, for it was and remains the largest Baptist university in the world. If Baylor could be captured, all Baptist colleges and universities could fall to Fundamentalism.

In the fall of 1989, by a premeditated and secretive scheme typical of Fundamentalism's shrewdness, the attack against Baylor University was intensified. It was accelerated early in 1990 and thereafter until Texas Baptists, in their state convention's 1991 annual meeting, formally brought to an end Fundamentalism's further plots to seize control over Baylor.

It was Baylor's courageous president, Dr. Herbert H. Reynolds, who, after being subjected to ongoing extreme and excessive Fundamentalist provocation, stood tall against the intensified pressure. Dr. Reynolds led in a resolute stand against Fundamentalist evil. He placed his career and life at stake to preserve academic freedom and the autonomy of individual Baptists and religious liberty at Baylor and to honor those principles of Christian rights and justice throughout the world.

A very sizable majority of the university's trustees concurred and, as a result, Baylor's charter was amended to change the method for selecting members of its governing board.

As mentioned previously, Texas Baptists approved the charter change in 1991. Thus, Baylor was removed, as far as is possible, from Fundamentalism's grasping tentacles.

Although Baylor has been insulated from seizure, the Fundamentalists will continue to hate and will further their attempts to harm the university. Other Baptist colleges and universities, if not already under Fundamentalist's control, also remain under similar danger.

Purifying the Denomination

"Conservatives"—the image-polished name of men imbued

with the spirit of Fundamentalism—say they want to "purify" the denomination. In the process, they have corrupted others to join in their wicked Fundamentalist ways and have triumphantly pontificated the righteousness of their own wrongs. Yet, these same men who flagrantly violate scriptural conduct in their "purification" processes continue to call *mainstream* Baptists "liberals," "moderates," "rats," "skunks" and other vilifying "names-of-the-day." Fundamentalists have not said, "when we are through purifying the denomination, possibly we will turn again to the ways of Christ."

Adrian Rogers Calls for Spiritual Warfare

The 1995 convention edition of *Texas Baptists*, a publication by Fundamentalists for Fundamentalists, contains an article entitled "Adrian Rogers on Spiritual Warfare." Typically, Rogers chose a text from the Old Testament. (Completely ignored was Matthew 22:36-40 that encourages believers to love one another and thus denies justification for spiritual warfare among us.)

Rogers, whom I recognize to be a mesmerizing preacher, made the following statements in that article:

> Now I want to say to every mother's child in this building tonight, there is a battle, and if you don't get in it, you have *sinned against the Lord.* Listen to me. The Bible says in that same chapter, "And Moses said unto the children of Gad and to the children of Reuben shall your brethren go to war and shall ye sit here?" [Numbers 32:6, KJV]

> Now I hear a lot of people say, "Well, you know I just don't want to get involved." No man has a right to be at peace when his brothers are at war. We've got a job to do, and it is a big job. We've been in a battle against unbelief, against liberalism, against modernism. And it's a battle. Now we have a young generation who say, "Well, it's time to stop fighting." The fight will never be over until Jesus comes.

> There is a mandate for victory. We're at war, and we will always be at war. You read every one of Paul's epistles, he's fighting someone or something. Don't get the idea now that it's going to be all honey and no bees. The mandate is for victory.

71

The Stream That Flows Away from God

The corporate and personal conduct of men who occupy the Southern Baptist Convention's highest offices has created the "Great Divide" in Baptist life. In the Rocky Mountains, the Continental Divide determines the direction of the runoff of melting snow—whether to flow toward the Pacific Ocean or to the East.

Similarly, in Baptist life, deceptive and wrongful acts have fed the cascading river of Fundamentalism which has divided our denomination. Fundamentalism's resolute course has supplanted Christian principles and attempted to intimidate authentic *mainstream* Baptists.

The spirit of Fundamentalism seeks the applause of men whose base nature stands guard against yielding to Christian love. It enlists others to join in inflammatory actions and to rejoice in evil. Because of this, the "people of the pews" are being further separated from the denomination that they have cherished, in which they have worked and to which they have given their tithes and offerings.

To be true to their heritage, *mainstream* Baptist laypeople must cope with the ravages of that out-of-banks river of wrongdoing. If not, Christian love and honorable conduct will continue to be torn asunder by Fundamentalism's "spiritual warfare," born of the desire for ever greater worldly power.

But, can Fundamentalists be deterred from stirring further hatred in the Southern Baptist Convention? If so, it might be possible for hate ultimately to be dispelled and for the renewal of love among some Baptists to begin. Then, in the *"official"* SBC, God could be restored as the One to be glorified—rather than revering the gain of ever more worldly power. However, these things cannot happen if Fundamentalists continue to prefer to " . . . tear people to shreds in ungracious tones and with unkind words."

Fundamentalism's
Prized War Trophies

Tributaries of dishonesty feed the swollen stream of Fundamentalist deceptions by which Baptist life is plagued. The next section of this chapter presents only a small percentage of the thousands of evil acts perpetrated by the spirit of Fundamentalism. Should anyone wish to obtain documented evidence of additional wrongful acts, please see the last paragraph of this chapter.

Conduct and Relationships

It is the violation of God's laws and the compromises of traditional standards of Christian conduct that have divided our denomination. Knowledge of that fact is of increasing importance to many Baptists.

The Ten Commandments were codified to enunciate the morally acceptable conduct expected in relationships between God and humankind. The life of Jesus Christ—His words and His ministries—demonstrates the depth of love, kindness, patience and helpfulness. He expected these qualities to be visible in the lives of His followers.

The apostle Paul, inspired by the Holy Spirit, wrote:

> Let us then cast off the works of darkness and put on the armor of light; let us conduct ourselves becomingly as in the day, not in reveling in drunkenness, not in debauchery and licentiousness, not in quarreling and jealousy. (Romans 13:12-13, NIV)

Jesus said:

> You shall love the Lord your God with all your heart, and with all your soul, and with all your mind. This the great and first commandment. And the second is like it, you shall love your neighbor as yourself. On these two commandments depend all the law and all the prophets. (Matthew 22:37-40)

The Point of No Return?

You and I are at a critical juncture. We are possibly approaching a crisis point, but please hear me out. What I say in the next several paragraphs could cause us to be uncomfortable with one another. I realize that my telling this segment of the controversy story subjects my credibility to risk. Yet I—as do you—face a far greater risk. Both of us are held accountable by God for the way we seek to do that which is right in His sight.

73

It is important to hear again the words of some of the men who are accountable for the "great divide" that is growing deeper and deeper in our denomination. James Draper wrote in his book, *The Church Christ Approves*:

> Fundamentalism is more dangerous than liberalism because everything is done in the name of the Lord. In the name of the Lord, the Fundamentalist condemns all who disagree with him. . . he uses the Bible as a club with which to beat people over the head, rather than means of personal strength and a revealer of God. . . . In the name of the Lord they will launch vehement attacks on individuals and churches. In the name of the Lord they attempt to assassinate the character of those whom they oppose. They direct their attack most often on other Christian leaders with whom they find disagreement.

Paige Patterson, president of Southeastern Baptist Theological Seminary, presented a paper dated November 17, 1994, entitled *Anatomy of Reformation—The Southern Baptist Convention 1978-1994*. I perceive it to have been an attempt to justify some of the evils of worldly power used to seize the SBC.

In this presentation Patterson said he met Paul Pressler for the first time in 1967. On that occasion, they reviewed several matters, including the failure of prior Fundamentalist efforts to take control of the Southern Baptist Convention.

Patterson stated:

> . . . while many such efforts have been attempted, they have uniformly failed because they had been attempted either by little-known leaders or else by isolated individuals who knew little of the value of organization or political process.

In the years that followed, Patterson and Pressler studied the SBC constitution. Then they developed the scheme to seize control of the convention by political machinations. Their plan breached Christian conduct and directly violated the SBC constitution that they had "studied."

The 1978 Secret Meeting

Patterson also said, ". . . In the fall of 1978 a group of pastors

74

and laymen from many states convened in the Airport Ramada Inn in Atlanta for a meeting that would launch 'the controversy' as it is now called." Several agreements developed out of this clandestine Atlanta meeting. The "conservatives" [Fundamentalists] would seek to "rescue the denomination." It was agreed that the pastors who attended that secret meeting would have their identities protected as long as possible.

A Fateful Decision

In the presentation, Patterson additionally commented:

> Furthermore, conservatives generally suffered from a paucity of political acumen and sophistication which made it almost impossible for them to outflag the experienced operatives of the denomination.

Nevertheless, history has attested to the fact that Fundamentalist leaders garnered "political acumen" sufficient to recognize that "any lie, frequently repeated, will gradually gain acceptance."

It also has been demonstrated that "The big lie works because most people are innately trusting and, therefore, have a limited capacity to fathom the deception on a grand scale."

It seems apparent also that the pastors who met in that secret meeting were seduced to seek the benefits and seize unto themselves the power that could be obtained by plunder politics.

Seemingly, it was at that moment those pastors—possibly having unwittingly let down their guards—forsook God's guidance for that of political gurus.

Gary North, Reconstructionist Leader

In a radio interview with Reconstructionist leader Gary North, Pressler indicated that in 1977 and 1978 he began "with prayerful reflection and study to see how the system could be retaken . . . ." Pressler further indicated in the interview that over the next several months (after the secret 1978 meeting) he made weekend trips to various locations in Texas (where the 1979 SBC meeting was to be held) and to other states where he spread the Fundamentalist story that would entice many others to succumb to the wiles of worldly power.

Rampant Rumor

In 1985, at a time when it was thought the Fundamentalist rulers could be unseated, a rumor related to Billy Graham ran rampant during the SBC annual meeting. The rumor claimed that Dr. Graham personally favored a Fundamentalist leader in the election for the SBC presidency. There was no truth to this information. Dr. Graham was out of the country, and he had not endorsed either candidate. But that did not stop Fundamentalists from spreading the false rumor which played a significant role in their candidate's narrow victory.

The Heresy File—Intent to Divide?

In 1987, just a week before ending two years as president of the Baptist General Convention of Texas, Dr. Paul W. Powell, then pastor of the Green Acres Baptist Church in Tyler, was interviewed by the then associate editor of the *Baptist Standard*, Toby Druin. After presenting information about the demanding schedule he had to follow during 1985-1987 because of his BGCT leadership position, as well as his pastoral responsibilities, Dr. Powell discussed the vision that many within Texas had for furthering the Kingdom of God.

He stated that Texas Baptists ". . . have a vision of reaching this state for Christ, they have a plan for it and are motivating and inspiring us to get on with it." It was the desire to serve the Master and the setting of "greater programs" that led Dr. Powell to indicate

> the secret of Texas avoiding controversy that has plagued the Southern Baptist Convention the last nine years. . . . If we do that [serve the Master] we don't have time to fuss and fight with each other. The horse that is pulling the plow doesn't have time to kick against the traces . . . .

Dr. Powell then stated that during the first year of his BGCT presidency, he met with one of the leaders of the Fundamentalist movement who had stated that he had "evidences" of liberalism in the Southern Baptist Convention. Dr. Powell asked for and finally was given a packet of material purported to be the "evidence." He examined the material that for many years had become commonly known as Paige Patterson's "Heresy File" and discovered that it contained fifteen names—only fifteen names—

from among more than *fifteen million* Southern Baptists! As reported in the *Baptist Standard*, Powell stated:

> Three were pastors over which the SBC exercises no control. Four were college professors over which the SBC has no control [colleges are owned by state conventions or have agreements of cooperation with state organizations]. Of the remaining eight, three were retired.
> "That leaves five persons," Powell said. "I am not saying there are five liberals; I am saying there are five on his list."

Dr. Powell concluded with the statement, "They have spent 10 years getting information, and I am assuming he gave me his best. You could put all the liberals they can document in a Volkswagen." He summarized the actions of the Fundamentalists by saying, "The Southern Baptist Convention has been hoodwinked" and the Fundamentalists have been putting up a "smoke screen" to avoid showing their real motives.

Don't Want to Fight—Just Want to Get on with the Work

Perhaps Dr. Powell's concluding comments, as reported in the *Baptist Standard*, give us an insight into the hearts and minds of most Baptist men and women in the pews. Powell said that Baptists are a "big-hearted people who love God and love His work and don't want to fight. They just want to get on with the work." How true!

The Peace Committee Charade

To help you understand the Peace Committee charade, permit me to provide some background comments:

Having not controlled its writing, Fundamentalists were dissatisfied with the 1925 Baptist Faith and Message statement regarding the Scriptures. For the same reason, they were equally displeased with the 1963 Baptist Faith and Message statement.

Nevertheless, prior to 1979, the Southern Baptist Convention's work was cohesive because it encompassed evangelism, worldwide missions and mercy in Christ's name. When belligerent Fundamentalists were organized into a massive force that dropped the political bombshell at the 1979 SBC meeting, Adrian Rogers was elected president of the convention. *That election turned the Southern Baptist Convention far to the po-*

litical right—to the fanatical right of Fundamentalism that thrives on slander and dirty politics. In due course, the SBC was delivered to the obsessive Religious Right that, by its very nature, must control, diminish or destroy its opponents.

By 1985 the controversy had greatly escalated. Approximately 45,000 people attended the SBC meeting at Dallas. The Fundamentalists and "Moderates" were not talking; they were brawling. There was great concern—but it was too late—the Fundamentalists were in power. They would retain that power over everything. They would never allow fairness in anything.

Baptist people largely looked in the other direction. Their attitudes were, "We don't want to be involved" or "We don't want the controversy to become a problem in our church." Amazing! *It was the "uninvolved" tithes and offerings of such congregations that undergirded the Fundamentalist misdeeds that destroyed peace in the denomination.* Thus, how can a Baptist congregation remain unaffected by the spirit of Fundamentalism?

At the 1985 SBC annual meeting, attorney Charles Pickering, president of the Mississippi Baptist Convention, called for the formation of a group balanced in nature. This group was to talk through and resolve disagreements. Hopefully, the group would be able to find common ground so the SBC could put the controversy aside and get on with its traditional ministries and missions.

The SBC messengers agreed and a "peace" committee was formed. The body, composed of twenty men and two women, was largely chosen by Fundamentalists and, unquestionably, manipulated by Fundamentalist political muscle.

The first meeting was held in August 1985. Members were forbidden to discuss anything that transpired during the sessions. Only the chair, Charles Fuller, was allowed to discuss publicly the work of the committee.

Fundamentalist Plan

The Fundamentalists offered a plan whereby people in the SBC who were unhappy with specific institutions or individuals could direct their complaints to the Peace Committee. The committee would request an accounting/explanation from the individual or the head of the specific agency or institution.

If the Peace Committee determined the agency or individual was performing according to the Baptist Faith and Message statement, then the accused would be deemed "innocent." If not, the Peace Committee would take the charge to the SBC in session. The elected messengers at the annual meeting would render judgment according to the Baptist Faith and Message statements.

Please keep this is mind. This is the planned procedure to which all members of the Peace Committee were committed— except, as would be demonstrated—for a few fanatical Fundamentalists.

Now here comes one of the several Fundamentalist twists. Nineteen complaints were received from Baptists who were unhappy with the stewardship of Southern Baptist Theological Seminary in Louisville, Kentucky. The complaints were sent to the seminary president, Dr. Roy Honeycutt, and he was given adequate time to prepare answers to each complaint.

In January 1986, the Peace Committee members assigned to consider these complaints—Drs. William Crews, Winfred Moore, Adrian Rogers and Cecil Sherman—met with Dr. Honeycutt at Southern Seminary. With President Honeycutt were the seminary attorney and the chair and vice chair of that institution's board of trustees. One of the participants indicates that the session was serious but not mean-spirited.

The meeting was recessed for dinner after which the discussion continued. By nine that evening, Dr. Honeycutt had addressed all nineteen charges. According to the procedures established by the Peace Committee, the complaints had been properly reviewed. Thus Drs. Crews, Moore and Sherman thought their work was finished as did Dr. Honeycutt.

Peace Committee Plan Not Honored by Rogers

Then, to everyone's surprise, Adrian Rogers removed from his briefcase a stack of papers—illustrations of the "heresy and infidelity to the scriptures" that he had privately gathered but failed to disclose against Southern Seminary and its faculty.

He probed, punched and pounded on President Honeycutt who tried to respond in good humor. Typical of the questions with which the president was badgered was, "When did teachers at this school begin to teach that the first eleven chapters of

Genesis were not literally true and that the world was not made in six twenty-four-hour days?" As he did with all the accusations, President Honeycutt responded patiently and respectfully.

The inquisition went on until eleven that evening when the committee requested an adjournment until the next morning with the expectation to conclude all matters prior to noon. The next day's meeting began the way it had ended the previous night—Rogers questioning Honeycutt. He did so until early afternoon with no break for lunch. Obviously Rogers was advancing the thought that Southern Seminary was guilty of teaching heresy, at least according to his interpretation of what the Baptist Faith and Message required. Ultimately, Dr. Honeycutt was replaced by a Fundamentalist zealot.

Peace Committee Tapes

The Southern Baptist people paid all of the expenses of the Peace Committee. At that time, the SBC still was the people's denomination.

It was expected that all Peace Committee meetings would be recorded. It has been stated that this did occur. Nevertheless,

- as far as is known, no editor of any state convention paper has heard even one of the tapes;
- as far as is known, not even one Southern Baptist (other than certain SBC leaders) has heard any portion of the tapes.

Is there a legitimate reason for this withholding of such vital information?

Death Threats in SBC Struggle for Worldly Power

A few months later, at the 1988 SBC annual meeting in San Antonio, Dr. George Harris, pastor of Castle Hills First Baptist Church, San Antonio, nominated Dr. Richard Jackson, pastor of the North Phoenix Baptist Church, for the office of convention president. *San Antonio Express-News* reporter, J. Michael Parker, wrote that Dr. Harris did so because he felt the nomination would help "bring healing to the Convention."

Parker reported,

> Though theologically conservative, Jackson is not aligned with either faction. Moderates quickly supported him as their best hope against the powerful forces. . . .

80

Harris' nomination of Jackson brought death threats and criticism from Fundamentalists . . . .

Parker's article also indicated Dr. Harris

had offered to nominate the Reverend Jerry Vines, a Fundamentalist pastor from Jacksonsville, Florida, who eventually won the 1988 election, but Vines insisted he would not run . . . . The Reverend Ed Young of Houston, another Fundamentalist, also refused to run, so Harris approached Jackson.

The *San Antonio Express-News* reporter also stated that many people who favored Dr. Jackson were Moderates, but that many others were "conservatives who were not happy with the Fundamentalist takeover." It was one of the closest elections in SBC history as Dr. Jackson failed to win by less than three hundred votes.

Parker further declared that Dr. Harris said,

Fundamentalists labeled Jackson a moderate and a liberal and circulated many lies about the candidate. Jackson was his own man and did not stand for either faction. That's probably why he lost.

Exploitation of the Bible as Related to Inerrancy

The Bible is the centerpiece of plunder politics strategy. As Draper wrote:

In the name of the Lord, the Fundamentalist condemns all who disagree with him . . . he uses the Bible as a club with which to beat people over the head . . . .

It is valid to inquire about Patterson's and Pressler's seeming fidelity to the Bible. But if we are going to do that, let me express my belief that the Bible I study, carry to church and read to others is precisely as defined by the Baptist Faith and Message statement regarding the scriptures:

The Holy Bible was written by men divinely inspired and is the record of God's revelation of Himself to man. It is a perfect treasure of divine instruction. It has God for its author, salvation for its end, and truth, without any mixture of error, for its matter. It reveals the principles by which God judges us; and, therefore, is, and will remain until the end of the world, the true center of Christian union, and the supreme standard by which all human conduct, creeds and religious opinion should be tried. The criterion by which the Bible is to be interpreted is Jesus Christ.

Further, I believe that the Bible that I hold in my hand is precisely that which God has entrusted to me as the central guide for life. That is what the laypeople whom I know also believe about the Bible.

The "Inerrancy" Issue: Keystone of Political Strategy

Pressler said in his interview with Gary North, "Everybody knows there are not 5 percent liberals in the Southern Baptist Convention." Then I must inquire, "Is there as many as 1 percent?" And what percentage of Fundamentalists preach the Bible on Sundays and, as Fundamentalists, refuse to live by it Mondays through Saturdays?

I have never seen the original autographs of the Bible—but neither has Pressler nor Patterson, even though the statement was made that Patterson's views of the Bible were related to the original autographs. No Fundamentalist has seen the original autographs of the Bible. But I do not need to wait until the original autographs are found. I believe the Bible is precisely that which God intended it to be.

However, since the centerpiece of the political foray was "Inerrancy," let us discuss it. Fundamentalists cannot deny that "Inerrancy" has been used as a political weapon. In the June 26, 1986, issue of the Oklahoma *Baptist Messenger*,

Patterson said his group expects to tie the hiring of denominational employees to their positions on abortion, euthanasia, school prayer and federal budget reduction. . . . We want an open, pro-life position in all of our institutions and agencies, dealing with both abortion and euthanasia.

Patterson also was quoted as having explained that "the social agenda has not been a major focus for the fundamental-conservatives in the past . . . [but] I think it'll go over nearly as well as the Inerrancy thing."

82

Statements on Inerrancy

Statements on "Innerrancy" are far from inerrant. But that does not bother Fundamentalists for "Inerrancy" is one of their most powerful political weapons.

It seems appropriate to pause and say it is not my intent to suggest what you should think. My request is that you consider the impact that failed integrity has had and will continue to have on the members of your family, on your church and on the control and use of your tithes and offerings, and even on individual freedoms and other democratic principles of this nation.

The Criswell Study Bible

Paige Patterson, the "champion of Inerrancy," was in charge of preparing the *Criswell Study Bible* (incredibly, the King James version!) which contained study notes that astonished many theologians—even those who claimed to be "conservative." Here are examples of the *Criswell Study Bible* notes that have puzzled Bible-believing theologians and laypeople:

> And when Abram heard that his brother was taken captive, he armed his trained servants in his own house, three hundred and eighteen and pursued them unto Dan. (Genesis 14:14, *Criswell Study Bible* p. 24.)

The explanatory note from the *Criswell Study Bible* states, ". . . However, scribes may have updated intermittently the names of communities, special sites and cities which would explain this as a scribal efficiency and not error." This is amazing! Here Patterson and those who worked with him used the very method that they so widely deplore. This is exactly the same thing for which Fundamentalists condemn others, labeling them as "liberals."

Here is another.

> And Moses and Aaron did so, as the Lord commanded . . . and all the waters that were in the river were turned to blood. (Exodus 7:20, *Criswell Study Bible*, p. 82)

The *Criswell Study Bible* notes state, ". . . which suggests that the 'blood' was filtered out by the sandy soil. This is not possible with literal blood. Thus, the word may suggest merely a change in color." This statement made by an inerrantist is most interesting.

Seemingly the *Criswell Study Bible* editors have humanized a miracle. They suggest the water merely changed color rather than that God actually turned it into blood. Truthfully, who are the liberals?

Criswell liberalism continues.

. . . Therefore, Saul took a sword and fell upon it. And when his armor-bearer saw that Saul was dead, he fell likewise upon his sword and died with him. . . . He (Saul) said unto me . . . slay me: For anguish is come upon me, because my life is yet whole in me. So I stood . . . and slew him. (II Samuel 1:9, 10a), *Criswell Study Bible*, p. 370, 372)

The *Criswell Study Bible* explains it thusly, "Those verses accurately describe the death of Saul. The addition to the story in II Samuel 1:2-10 is apparently manufactured by the Amalekite soldier in an attempt to ingratiate himself to David."

Is it possible? Are those who walk in lockstep as Fundamentalists the same men who hang on every comma, every word, every line? Are they saying, "Don't believe II Samuel?" Are they saying, "It is incorrect?" Are they really saying, "The scripture is apparently manufactured?"

Then,

. . . For they trembled and were amazed: Neither said they anything to any man: for they were afraid. (Mark 16:8, Criswell Study Bible, p. 1184)

The explanation of this verse by the *Criswell Study Bible* is that, "The ending of Mark's Gospel has been in dispute among scholars. . . The presence of the abrupt termination convincingly argues that the original ending has been lost." Seemingly this explanation reflects the "higher critical" method of study that, when followed by others, elicits Fundamentalists' strong condemnation.

When questioned on September 12, 1986, about the apparent liberalism in the *Criswell Study Bible* notes over which he presided, Patterson denied that there was any element of liberalism there. As reported in the September 17, 1986, issue of the *Baptist Standard,* he applied the "soft spin" technique to the liberalism evident in the *Criswell Study Bible* by saying, "the notes certainly could have been clearer and could have been written . . . with greater care." That is spinmastery at its best—or worst!

Patterson declined to admit that the author of those notes should have been included in the politically persuasive heresy file!

The Bible and SBC Leaders

Baptist men and women in the pews not only believe the Bible is true, they expect their leaders to be true to the Bible. SBC leaders should not use the bible to gain political supremacy. They should not say something is inerrant merely to condemn others. And certainly SBC leaders should not refuse to follow the Bible as the guide for daily living.

Fundamentalists have loudly championed their belief in the Bible, but they have made up their own rules of conduct. Fundamentalists claim to have a high regard for the Scriptures, but they demonstrate a high *disregard* for its teachings. One is caused to wonder if Fundamentalists' stated belief in the Inerrancy of the Bible is more than for political propagandizing.

What Does Paige Patterson Believe About the Bible?

I have not discussed with Patterson what he believes about the Bible, but I have read some of the comments that he has made about God's Word. It was reported by the *Virginia Religious Herald* on September 24, 1980, that at a meeting held on September 12-13, 1980, at the Old Forest Baptist Church in Lynchburg, Virginia, of which Rev. Arthur B. Ballard was pastor,

> Patterson deprecated the King James version of the Bible as the 1611 translation "by a bunch of Anglicans, most of whom were lost," and cited "tragic translations" in the King James version.

That is the Bible that you and I study to understand God's instructions. One has cause to wonder if Paige Patterson interviewed the translators of the King James Bible in the year 1611, and whether their names were included in his infamous "heresy files."

Baptists' Special Concerns Explored

In the April 23, 1980, issue of the *Baptist Standard*, editor Presnall Wood expressed several "concerns" about the charges that were being made by Paige Patterson that "persons in high denominational posts are no longer true to historic Baptist beliefs." Dr. Wood was also interested in knowing about the "organizing efforts of Patterson and others to elect presidents and control the selection of convention trustees over the next several years."

In the May 14, 1980, issue of the *Baptist Standard* Patterson responded. For easy comparison, Presnall Wood's concerns and Paige Patterson's replies are presented in a two-column format. *Did Patterson speak truthfully?*

Concerns of Dr. Wood	Answers by Dr. Patterson
1) The group has the makings of a political party that smacks of an attempt to take over the convention.	1) No political party will emerge among the various groups of concerned Baptists. No "take over" is planned, desired, or possible. Baptists who believe in the full trustworthiness of the Bible are exchanging information and encouraging participation in associational and convention life. This is the full extent of what is transpiring.
2) Their charges imply all past and current boards and commissions of the SBC have not been vigilant in keeping the agencies committed to historic Baptists beliefs.	2) We have tried to warn that some serious negligence has occurred. If not reversed, there is no reason historically to believe that Southern Baptists could not be ravaged by the same dis-

belief which has led to decline in other major denominations.

3) Saying a "large group of denominational posts" no longer holds the Bible to be totally and completely true and failing to hold to historic beliefs without naming their names sows unwarranted seeds of suspicion.

3) We have no desire to sow unwarranted seeds of suspicion. Evidence cited is sufficient to suggest the potentially devastating nature of the problem.

4) The Patterson group implies they are the only concerned group and the only ones qualified to keep Baptists doctrinally correct.

4) We certainly do not believe that we are the only ones qualified to keep Southern Baptists doctrinally correct. We do believe that it is the responsibility of every Baptist to exercise vigilance in his priesthood, seeing that the convention and its agencies remain true to the doctrines for which our convention has always stood.

5) The permanency of the Patterson group could lead to other groups and political parties within the convention.

5) No agenda for permanency exists in the plans of anyone.

6) The Patterson group could drive a wedge between pastors and laymen through the suggestion that pastors lack courage to deal with denominational problems.

6) No wedge between pastors and laymen will develop. Both groups are extensively represented among concerned groups of Baptists, and lack of courage is sometimes a problem in both areas.

87

Fundamentalists have difficulty tolerating anything they do not create nor which they cannot subjugate. Since 1979, Fundamentalists have systematically seized control of SBC institutions and assets that were originally developed and paid for by *all* Southern Baptists, though the Fundamentalists made only minuscule contributions.

Ironically, it is the *mainstream* Baptist laypeople's tithes and offerings that continue to provide most of the money that keeps the Fundamentalist worldly-powered machine on its course of conquest.

Are Baptists Expected to Practice Ethical Conduct?

Ethics relate to the standard of conduct or code of morals expected to be practiced by individuals or organizations. There are numerous passages in God's Holy Word that establish proper standards for our conduct as Christians and Baptists. Among the most instructive scriptures regarding ethical conduct are those in Micah, Galatians, I John and other books in which the Gospel of Christ is recorded.

Through these inspired words we are told that the Lord requires us "to do justly, and to love mercy, and to walk humbly." (Micah 6:8, KJV) We also are informed that "the fruit of the Spirit is love, joy, peace, longsuffering, gentleness, goodness, faith, meekness, temperance." (Galatians 5:22-23, KJV). And "as we walk in the light, as He is in the light, we have fellowship one with another." (I John 1:7 KJV)

As standards for the way we are supposed to live, these selected verses from the Word of God are clear. There is no equivocation. There is no alternative.

Christian Conduct Defiled

Unfortunately, some Fundamentalists have radically departed from these standards. Their actions seem to be saying that, for them, God's standards for conduct no longer have any ethical place in their lives. This appears especially true when you consider the Fundamentalists' political sacking of the Southern Baptist Convention and their ongoing mistreatment of fellow believers.

Jesus said "love"—not theological rhetoric nor political correctness—should be how we measure our daily living. Fundamentalists are radically recasting the norms of Christianity as well as the standards of conduct which God established for mankind's guidance and the bestowal of blessings upon His followers.

To Fundamentalists, creedal beliefs and unquestioning obedience are the measures of a person's value. If you do not "believe" as Fundamentalists demand, and act according to their dictates, you are unworthy. They leave no room for the Holy Spirit's guidance of one's interpretation of God's word or for an individual's spiritual discernment.

The Apostle Paul provides us with insight concerning God's inspiration. In 1 Corinthians 12:4-6 (KJV) he wrote, "Now there are diversities of gifts, but the same Spirit; and there are diversities of service, but the same Lord; and there are diversities of working, but it is the same God who inspires them all in every one."

I ask the questions:

• If Fundamentalists believe the Bible, how is it that, rather than seeking God's purpose of peace and unity within our denomination, they advocate exclusion and divisiveness?

• If Fundamentalists accept biblical instructions—God's instructions—why do they set themselves up as dispensers of judgment when there is only one Judge—our Lord—among us?

• If Fundamentalists want to see the Great Commission fulfilled, how is it that they consider the Southern Baptist Convention and the Cooperative Baptist Fellowship to be "competitors?" This is ridiculously tragic! There is more than enough for *all* Baptists to do in resisting Satan and the evil that he fosters in our world.

In his 1995 address to North Carolina Baptists, Dr. Alfred T. Ayscue stated:

Diversity is as dead as a dodo bird in some quarters in Baptist life. Lockstep theology and unquestioning conformity have become the centerpiece for some Baptists. Where are the likes of a Roger Williams or a John Leland or an Isaac Backus or a George W. Truett, a Thomas Meredith or a Samuel Wait, who will raise voices of dissent before this denial of all that is Baptistic?

Although these great men have passed to their glory, their

89

examples remain with us. Their contributions to our Baptist faith can be emulated over and over again if laypeople will recognize the problem, decide to take a stand and resolve to make a difference.

Results of Defilement

Ignoring God's standards of Christian conduct creates dissension, discord and division. It turns brother against brother, sister against sister, program against program. It makes a mockery of Christ's suffering for us, and in reality, it denies His death and resurrection. It causes something to be wrong with all that we do.

Again, quoting from Dr. Ayscue's address. His statements about some of the things that are wrong in the SBC, which is being led exclusively by Fundamentalists, are most revealing. He says,

- *Something is wrong* when the Southern Baptist Convention can embrace evangelical groups outside convention structures, sign contracts of cooperation with them and allocate funding, and at the same time exclude other Southern Baptists because they insist on exercising freedom in diversity.

- *Something is wrong* when Southern Baptists can apologize and repent for our ancestors' involvement in the cruel practice of slavery yet sense no remorse for imposing denominational chains of restriction upon women who hear and desire to follow God's call to kingdom service.

- *Something is wrong* when convention-directed correctness takes precedence over the Christ-directed command to wear the badge of love as His disciples.

- *Something is wrong* when Baptists become more concerned about a particular human view of the Bible than they are about Baptists who live by the whole truth of the Bible.

- *Something is wrong* when elected leaders and seminary presidents and pastors assume a spiritual authority that negates the priesthood of the believer.

Something *is* wrong! And you and I have opportunities—and an obligation—to assist in correcting these wrongs.

Opportunities for Change

In biblical times, the Israelites drifted away from God on several occasions and the results were drastic—always! Unfortunately, they never seemed to connect their problems with their failure to follow God's commands. As Baptists we must realize—individually and as a denomination—following God's standards of conduct is not optional! We must also recognize the stark reality that our accommodation of Fundamentalism over the past seventeen years has allowed the diminishing of Christian principles and the negating of Baptist distinctives. During this time, the SBC has been largely transformed into a power-hungry Fundamentalist politico-religious apparatus.

If we as Baptists are to be faithful to the Great Commission, then personal and corporate Christian integrity must be restored in Baptist life. This will not be an easy task. Fundamentalists will fight the effort every step of the way. They will use political guile, clever tricks and the exploitation of hostility, hate and harm against all those who call for restoration of integrity in the denomination. Fundamentalists will also reward—by the granting of "political plums"—those who join lockstep in the ongoing dissemination of half-truths and outright untruths.

As if these measures were not bad enough, Fundamentalists will also continue harvesting souls, twisting the minds of individuals and intimidating them to embrace the perpetuation of Fundamentalism's control over Baptist life.

Which Will It Be: Christian Integrity or Fundamentalist Tyranny?

Among the first steps to take, in demanding the restoration of Christian integrity in our denomination, is *to stop accommodating Fundamentalism.* To stop accommodating Fundamentalism, we must state clearly that moral conduct is a requirement for cooperative relationships.

Some Baptists seemingly feel that avoiding confrontation is the best way to resolve the ethical problems that abound in our denomination. They believe that by merely sticking one's head in the sand, the troubles will somehow disappear and it will not

91

be necessary to respond openly to wrongdoing. However, by sticking our heads in the sand, opportunities to live by honoring our heartfelt beliefs may be forfeited in America, possibly forever.

**Baptists Who Served in World War II
Suffered because of the Compromise of Integrity**

Baptists who would possibly surrender their Christian integrity as the price to be paid for a short-lived "peace" with Fundamentalists should set this book aside to read a history of World War II.

Consider how many millions of lives were lost and the massive destruction suffered as a result of British prime minister Neville Chamberlain's surrendering of his integrity for a brief "peace" with Hitler.

Consider also the years required for the United States and its allies, under the inspiration and integrity of Winston Churchill, to lead the people of England and Europe to regain their freedom.

Once we look Fundamentalism squarely in the face and observe the results of its despicable actions, then we will understand why we must gird our loins with the truth and *boldly take action.*

This gives rise to the basic question: What can we as the people of the pews do about these matters?

Participation and partnership with like-minded Baptists are among the first substantive steps to be taken. Closely related to them is the designation of our tithes and offerings.

Who do you believe should have control over God's money for which you are a steward—

- those whose practices defy the standards of Christian conduct or those who are striving like you to be faithful to God's proclamations;
- those who would enforce their own politico-religious agenda or those whose only objective is to obey our Lord and fulfill the Great Commission?

The current SBC leaders have neither made a move to wash their hands of the worldly power-grabbing process nor attempted to restore integrity in denominational affairs. Therefore, should our financial support—our tithes and offerings—be blindly placed in their grasp? God's guidance is available to those who seek His will in that important decision. (Please see Matthew 6:19-21.)

Trust
Between Baptists

Crown Jewels of all Relationships: Trust and Love

Trust is defined as an assured reliance on another's integrity, veracity and justice.

Trust provides an unwavering expectation that two or more persons committed to mutual trust will equally and readily fulfill all expectations of one another.

Consider the potential for chaos in the marketplace should a merchant abruptly change standards of measurement. Would consumers tolerate seven inches to the foot, nine ounces to the pound or two and a half quarts to the gallon? Would you continue to do business with a banker who had fraudulently removed much of the money that had been deposited in your savings account? The answer is obvious.

Mutual Trust: The Foundation of Christian Fellowship

Mutual trust among friends brings joy to relationships and contributes to the enrichment of life. I am greatly blessed—as are you—to have trustworthy friends in various walks of life as well as trusting fellow members of the Baptist church in which I am privileged to serve. To them, I would unhesitatingly entrust the well-being of my life.

It was mutual trust that created the foundation upon which the Southern Baptist Convention was founded in 1845. Until 1979 it was that same abiding trust that served as the basis for the development of Southern Baptists' missionary, educational and benevolent ministries for the extension of Christ's Kingdom.

The Baptist Faith and Message states, "Christian unity in the New Testament sense is spiritual harmony and voluntary cooperation for common ends by various groups of Christ's people when such mutual trust and cooperation involves no violation of conscience or compromising of loyalty to Christ." It further states:

The new birth of man's spirit by God's Holy Spirit means the birth of love for others. Missionary effort on the part of all rests thus upon a spiritual necessity of the regenerate life, as expressly and repeatedly commanded in the teachings of Christ. Mutual trust undergirds the duty of every child of God to seek constantly to win the lost to Christ by personal effort and by all other methods in harmony with the gospel of Christ.

Trust Intentionally Broken

The politico-religious movement's hostility and intentional harm have been enshrined as the spirit of Fundamentalism's hallmarks of mindcontrol, coercion and persecution of opponents. Chaos in relationships between Baptists has filled the yawning chasm created by violations of trust. Without appropriate remedy, the deep gorge of distrust will continue to expand.

Fundamentalist leaders deliberately chose to rely on the power of plunder politics rather than on the power of God to achieve their purposes. Their ultimate political objective, understandably, has never been discussed openly and it is unlikely that Fundamentalists will ever publicly identify that goal of all goals. But information about the overarching Fundamentalist goal is presented in Chapter Ten, *Is Religious Freedom at Risk?*

Today, Baptists are divided by broken trust. The schism in Baptist life was caused by men who cannot tolerate freedom of speech or thought. From a human perspective, as long as Fundamentalism "rules," mutual trust cannot be restored in the Southern Baptist Convention.

R. G. Puckett wrote in the March 23, 1996, issue of the *Biblical Recorder*:

> Truth and trust are inseparably related. If truth is trampled, then trust collapses. Most of us find it hard to trust anyone who has lied to us or about us. Differences of opinion may exist and never be reconciled between persons of good will, but when truth is ignored then trust evaporates.

The immortal messages of Christ have been sullied by the immoral acts of men. Therefore, I inquire, is it reasonable to

94

expect Baptist men and women of the pews to continue forwarding their tithes and offerings to Nashville—to be controlled by men who have publicly reviled, viciously slandered and ruthlessly attacked fellow Baptist believers? The answer to this question is also obvious.

Men who have yielded their souls and linked their fortunes to the spirit of Fundamentalism have rejected the teachings of Christ. It is terribly tragic that the shooting Star of Fundamentalism, with its clever contrail of mind control, has blinded such men to the shining Star of Bethlehem that guides humankind to Christ.

Voting Fraud

Dr. Grady Cothen, in his book, *What Happened to the Southern Baptist Convention? A Memoir of the Controversy,* presents pertinent information regarding voting fraud. He wrote:

> Some churches had more than the legal limit—ten—messengers. Some messengers registered twice, and some pastors registered for all their messengers—a practice since disallowed. One pastor registered for himself, his wife, and four children. Under questioning by another pastor, he admitted that the children were out at the KOA campground and not at the convention. Another pastor told of watching a man mark eleven ballots in the presidential election and turn in all of them.

Had They Been Placed on Trial

In 1979 it was reported to the SBC Executive Committee that those who had committed voting "irregularities" were caught "with blood on their hands."

I feel that those who perpetrated the voting scheme and the Fundamentalist leaders who knowingly violated the SBC constitution should have been placed on trial before the 1980 annual meeting of the SBC.

The SBC Executive Committee, I believe, should have presented the charges to the messengers at that 1980 session. A verdict should have been rendered by the messengers according to the SBC constitution and the Baptist Faith and Message statements.

Instead, members of the SBC Executive Committee chose to be "peaceful" rather than to subject the Fundamentalists to the penalties justified by their political immorality evidenced by dishonest voting.

Perhaps that is the reason Fundamentalists call non-Fundamentalists "moderates." The "moderate" leaders of the SBC in 1980 were gentle, peace-loving and generous people. They wanted to provide Fundamentalists with opportunities to come to their senses—to get right again with God and with their fellow Baptists. I respect the leaders who served the SBC in 1980, but seemingly they did not understand the spirit of Fundamentalism.

Untruths, slander, intended harm and other manifestations of mean-spirited men—as well as the ongoing intentional stirring of hatred against fellow believers—remain as the hallmarks of the spirit of Fundamentalism.

Propaganda of Their Personal Virtues

In efforts to justify wrongdoing, Fundamentalist preachers seldom quote Jesus or refer to Paul or other writers of the New Testament as the basis of their "spiritual warfare" strategy. Rather, while defending and trying to justify their conduct, Fundamentalists usually preach about the faith of Abraham, fortitude of Nehemiah and fearlessness of Daniel—implying that their own political excesses are clothed in the virtues of Old Testament heroes.

Power Propaganda: Macho Young Fundamentalist Rulers in Training

On May 25, 1989, seventy "young conservatives" between thirty-five and forty-five years of age participated in a pre-SBC rally in the First Baptist Church of Euless, Texas. Organized by Rick Scarborough, then pastor of the Retta Baptist Church near Fort Worth, the rally's stated purpose was to encourage people to attend the Southern Baptist Convention in Las Vegas. Interestingly, the opening remarks claimed the meeting was "not to stir up controversy" and suggested that "conservatives" *promote peace and healing*.

However, one participant called "liberals" in the denomination "rats" and "skunks." He was later asked if "conservatives" would actively purge "liberals" from the convention. His response was, "The rats and skunks are still inside the walls [of the SBC]. Are we just going to leave them there?"

A television evangelist also answered, "As long as they smell, one day we're going to get them out." *Fundamentalists, of course, claim their false denigrating of fellow believers is solely for God's glory!*

"What's Sauce for the Goose . . ."

A member of the SBC executive committee, proclaimed:

> women should not be pastors and deacons in Southern Baptist churches because it contradicts Bible teaching. People who believe every word of the Bible would not ordain women.

We respectfully suggest that Fundamentalists' who speak untruths that generate slander and hate toward "people who believe every word of the Bible" should not serve as SBC leaders—because their conduct contradicts Bible teachings!

Rewards of Worldly Power

Another said, "Folks, I submit to you that we have knocked the giant down, but we are a long way from cutting off its head." This same man also commented, "Jerry Falwell is so much bigger than the SBC."

As far as is known, the macho young Fundamentalists who attended that May 25, 1989, meeting, still have not identified any "rat" or "skunk" within the walls of the SBC. However, the worldly-powered careers of those who were at that meeting have certainly flourished. Seemingly the Oligarchy of Eighty perceived the seventy "young conservatives" to be powerfully committed to the persecution of Fundamentalism's mythical enemies and rewarded them accordingly.

"Broadening the Tent" Containment

Early in the 1990s, Morris Chapman, then president of the SBC, issued statements indicating that "conservatives" were in absolute control of every facet of the SBC, and now a "broadening of the tent" would be started. The more gullible Baptists felt the section of the Peace Committee report that mandated fairness in appointments would be implemented. They anticipated SBC leadership would initiate the process of reconciliation. No doubt, Fundamentalists looked upon it as a clever ploy to insure the ongoing flow of money to Nashville. In due course, laypeople, saddened by such duplicity, reflect upon "broadening the tent" to have been no more than a cynical, cruel charade.

(Please note, hundreds of statements made by Fundamentalist leaders have been reported by the *Baptist Press, Associated Baptist Press*, state convention and secular papers, copies of which are on file. I have presented only a few for your consideration.)

Time to
Draw a Line

The political bombshell that exploded at the 1979 SBC annual meeting buried the dreams of the more than 50,000 men and women who made commitments to Bold Mission Thrust. Since that time, Fundamentalist leaders' continuing exploitations of the men and women of the pews have placed at great risk the heritage of our denomination and the very foundation of our God-granted vision for spreading the Good News.

Some of the past acts and directions of SBC leadership are financially insupportable because they are morally unacceptable. It has been demonstrated over and over that God's laws do not protect the Baptist people from hostility, hate, harm or the incredible heartbreak of a denomination gone wrong. *Still*, they are God's laws—but not necessarily acceptable to Fundamentalism!

Fundamentalism's movement has cleverly obscured the trampling of traditional Baptist distinctives and the Christian principles upon which Baptists have stood. How long will this charade be allowed to continue?

It is the Baptist people—the men and women of the pews—who are the only ones who can reverse the pattern of deceit, deception and destruction of revered Baptist tenets. The time has come to draw a line—

- a line that prohibits further manipulations by Fundamentalists to gain laypeople's passive support;
- a line that redirects our tithes and offerings from financing Fundamentalists' Nashville-headquartered political machine;
- a line that publicly disavows those who attack fellow Baptists and those who design ploys to divide the people of the pews;

- a line that points to deceptive "whitewashing" coverup of the ongoing rancorous turmoil within the SBC.

The Exercise of Discernment
Concerning Those With Whom One Can Work
in God's Kingdom

I ask laypeople to pause and think about this reality. Leaders who are allowed to remain in office reflect the integrity of those who are being led. Good people who follow God's guidance must make decisions about their leaders—whether the leaders' attitudes and actions reflect righteousness or the spirit and substance of Fundamentalism.

One could enumerate thousands of incidents considered to be grievous Fundamentalists misdeeds. Yet, I believe it not beneficial to Baptist life to unleash a litany of all charges against Fundamentalism. On the other hand, I believe it necessary, as is evident, that some of the unconscionable acts that have so terribly disrupted Baptist life be laid before *mainstream* Baptists for their evaluation.

If the enumeration of these major matters have failed to identify the level of evil that is adversely impacting Baptist life, the listing of additional incidents would be a misuse of the reader's time. Nevertheless, if desired, documented accounts of certain unconscionable acts committed in the past seventeen years can be obtained.

Therefore, scores of documented accounts of wrongful acts have been kept intact. They may be acquired by any person for the cost of reproduction and mailing by forwarding a written request to: Acquisitions Librarian, Technical Services Department, Baylor University, P. O. Box 97151, Waco, Texas 76798-7151.

6

God's Messengers
Our Foreign Missionaries and the Woman's Missionary Union

In all things, be of good report—

> "In the name of the Lord they will launch vehement attacks on individuals and churches. In the name of the Lord they attempt to assassinate the character of those whom they oppose. They direct their attack most often on other Christian leaders with whom they find disagreement."

God's Messengers
Our Foreign Missionaries
And
The Woman's Missionary Union

The Southern Baptist Convention has changed drastically in the past seventeen years. It has been transformed into Fundamentalism's largest politico-religious ideological battleground in the world. The *only* SBC agency that has not yet been radically restructured is the Foreign Mission Board (FMB). However, the FMB has been altered in substantive ways, and there is no doubt that its leadership—at home and abroad—is totally supportive of Fundamentalism's quest for worldly power.

Dr. R. Keith Parks—
Devoted Servant and Remarkable Leader

Dr. and Mrs. Keith Parks' service as missionaries since 1954 and their lifelong devotion to world missions and the well-being of missionaries has set them apart as gentle Christians and gracious Baptist leaders. Dr. Parks served from 1980 to 1992 as president of the SBC Foreign Mission Board (FMB).

Fundamentalists did not elect Dr. Parks to serve in that position. Thus, he was unacceptable to leaders of the oligarchy. The situation had to be "corrected!" To do so, Fundamentalists segregated Dr. Parks for persecution and attempted to trash his reputation as a missions leader and a lifelong worker in God's Kingdom. His service as president of the SBC Foreign Mission Board was terminated in 1992.

The following February, Dr. Parks accepted the primary leadership role of the Cooperative Baptist Fellowship's Global Missions enterprise. His many years of faithful missionary service and his leadership of the FMB had made him highly respected and trusted by leaders of several nations and by missionaries who reside in many countries around the world.

Since 1993 Dr. Parks's experience, reputation and remarkable skills have made it possible for missionaries to be sent even into some of the lands where the Gospel of Christ had never been heard.

During this time the number of missionaries sent and supported by the Global Missions Enterprise has increased sevenfold.

Mission volunteers are committing their lives to the work. *Mainstream* Baptists are committing themselves to provide financial, prayer and other support to these missionaries.

There are many Southern Baptist missionaries appointed by the Foreign Mission Board who are being pressured to perform according to the dictates of the spirit of Fundamentalism.

Therefore, without question, foreign missionaries whose commitments are solely to serve Christ will receive the encouragement, prayer and monetary support of *mainstream* Baptists who work and witness in cooperation with other sincere Christians and authentic Baptists.

No doubt Dr. Parks and his fellow workers will be enabled to commission and send thousands of missionaries to all fields as they remain white unto Christ's harvest.

Missionaries "Held Hostage" By Fundamentalist Gag Order

Some of our foreign missionaries have been placed under a gag order. They have been informed they may neither question nor criticize anything said or done by any SBC leader as they are "employees" of the SBC and not members of a voting organization.

Some missionaries also have been told to "get the big numbers quickly." It has even been suggested that foreign missionaries no longer read state convention papers, thus denying them opportunities to maintain contact with the Baptist work in their home states.

Exploiting the lives of foreign missionaries, treating them as purchased chattel and holding them as hostages in attempts to prohibit discussion of Fundamentalism's evil nature and wrongful acts, even though predictable, has placed the spirit of Fundamentalism far outside the line of Christian propriety.

One estimate is that as many as half of all foreign missionaries now serving under the auspices of the Foreign Mission Board would like to remain where they are, but would prefer to do so under the sponsorship of an organization other than the Fundamentalist-controlled FMB.

Missionaries' Statement: Painful Disillusions

Among the many personal contacts I have had and the letters that I have received, the following, from a beloved missionary couple, is one of the most revealing of such communications. Subheads have been provided for the convenience of readers.

The Foreign Mission Board

"It has been observed during the years I have been a Christian—and a Baptist—that few institutions, boards or agencies have the honor of being held in as high esteem as the Foreign Mission Board of the Southern Baptist Convention. When one referred to FMB, whether in a national or state convention setting, an association meeting or in a local church, it was always in the sense of respect and dignity.

FMB Leadership

"The leadership of the Foreign Mission Board has always been of highest quality and character. These have been men and women of God whose minds and hearts were focused on missions and winning the world to Christ in the very best possible way.

"Integrity and trust are the two main ingredients that through the years have been at the foundation of the FMB and have contributed to its effectiveness. This has characterized the organization since its beginning. Not until recent years has it been questioned by those who are Southern Baptists.

Missionaries Were Used

"In the last several years since the takeover of the SBC, I feel that missionaries have been used. Prevailing forces use the mission cause and missionaries' well-being to prove their side of an issue. Appeals were made to Southern Baptists to remain loyal to the Cooperative Program and the Lottie Moon Christmas offering on the basis of keeping our 'beloved missionaries' in the field. The donors were faced with the option of wanting to give to support the missionaries and not wanting to support the Fundamentalist-dominated Southern Baptist Convention.

"This led to designating giving which, in the past, was thought of as anathema to unified cooperative giving. It is appalling that some of those in the places of top leadership pastor churches that give very little to the Cooperative Program.

Respect For Missionaries

"There is no group of people that has my respect more than the FMB. I continue to regard the missionaries with great love and respect. Many of them are close and personal friends. I thank them for their continued good work and sacrifice around the globe.

"This is all said in the framework that in the years before and those that followed our becoming Southern Baptist Missionaries we have held the FMB in high esteem. Never would I have dreamed that we would find ourselves saying that we can no longer be a part of that once loved and respected Convention and Board.

Changes Were Almost Unbelievable

"As early as 1979 we began to see things happen with a planned escalated pace. We read of the activities of key players in this drama and read with disbelief of yet another activity leading to the present state of the Southern Baptist Convention. When we lived in Africa, we read our stateside Baptist periodicals. We saw that one by one people who had been respected and loved were being fired, encouraged to retire early or quit by the hand of Fundamentalists. Does one think that such controversy does not affect mission work? News of the ugliness is not confined to geographical borders of the U. S. but spills over and reaches far and carries with it questions in the minds of nationals with whom missionaries work and witness. These are questions not easily answered. Trust is often left to question.

SBC Annual Meetings Disappointing

"As we approach furlough we always anticipated attending the SBC annual meeting, the highlight of the time spent in the U. S. A. We went and represented our adopted country gladly, carrying the flag of that African nation and speaking on behalf of missions. To our amazement, shock and sorrow, we saw activities, heard conversations and watched what happened on the convention floor. We saw preschool children with ballots, voting right before our eyes in Atlanta, Georgia, at the convention in 1986. People around us stood and cheered, clapped and yelled. This reminded us of a junior high sports event. There were issues that caused people to rise. There were standing ovations in which we could not participate. People stared at us repeatedly and we knew that, indeed, we were out of place. This was not the convention we had known nor is it what Baptists have traditionally been.

"Where Has Our Beloved Convention Gone?"

"We asked, 'Where has our beloved convention gone? Where are the people of dignity, kindness and that reflect Christlikeness?' After attending the SBC annual meeting once again in Atlanta in 1991, we vowed we would not do this again. . . . We observed a shift from foundation and building trust among people that had never known the name Jesus, to a strong position on numbers. 'We should do whatever it takes' to get quick and immediate results.

Spinmasters At Work In The FMB

"Reports of activities sent to publications were surprising to some of us that lived there. We were unaware that the work was reported to be so large. Obviously, stories and numbers grew as they were reported. We wrote at one point and said that we were amazed how large the work in that foreign land was reported to be. We heard and read statements that caused us to ask, 'Is this the nation in which we work?'

Missionary Work Is Difficult

"Being a missionary has never been easy. No one promised that it would be. In many places in the world missionaries live in very difficult situations and encounter hardships that will never be told. Many live self-sacrificing lives in service that you will never read about. Some live in dangerous places and under conditions that most people would never undertake. With all that is burdening our missionary forces, why then should there be the added burden of hostile takeover and to live under the heavy hand of the authoritative board of trustees?

The Missionaries' View

"How do missionaries view the controversy? In a number of ways. Some missionaries said they hoped it would go away, therefore they ignored the existence of any such intrusion. Some do not want to know and don't want to talk about it.

"Others have stated that surely most of what is being said and read is rumor. How can anything so bizarre take place? You can keep quiet and keep your concerns to yourself. You can say nothing, read nothing and simply work. You also must not ask questions. Trustees and current administrators would want the missionaries not to 'know too much' or 'ask too many questions.'

The Ultimate Conclusions

"Departure is the method many have taken. If you are interested, and care for the future of missions and what can and is happening in this hostile takeover, you either choose silence, bury your head in the sand or depart. Many have anxiously awaited retirement, wanting to no longer be under the Fundamentalist banner. We understand these feelings, yet there is a place for taking your own personal stand for what is right, for what is true. Even if the future is uncertain, faith in the One who calls and the One who leads is the One whose hand we take.

"Our resignation comes from the observance of events within the Southern Baptist Convention over the past several years that have caused us great pain. The dismissals, early retirements, resignations under protests and takeovers have stunned us. Among the final straws was the firing of Dr. Dilday. We are friends of the Dildays."

The missionary couple continued:

God Calls Foreign Missionaries

"Foreign missionaries are people called by God to serve in lands other than their own. The emphasis here is upon the fact that it is God who calls, none other. The missionary normally is sent by an organization or a church or a group of churches. Sometimes that missionary goes out under different means. It is not the sending body that calls. Those called by God often seek out those agencies that help one to fulfill that calling by being the financial provider.

"Oftentimes we confuse the will of an organization with the Will of the One who calls. When God calls one to serve He will also enable as well as provide the means whereby the missionary may not only go but be sustained financially. It is God to whom the missionary is ultimately responsible. We shall all stand before a living God and give

106

an account of our faithfulness to that which we have been called.

"Laypeople have the right to designate their missions money—in order to support the missions endeavor—and the missionaries—whom the Holy Spirit has called to the attention of their fellow Baptists."

Traditional Baptist Work and Witness

The rank and file of Southern Baptist people love their missionaries. Obviously, the fanatical Fundamentalists know that; but, at this time, they seek to avoid intensifying the laypeople's anger—the normal reaction against Fundamentalist wrongs. SBC leaders want more and more "missionary" money to be sent to Nashville. Some refer to "missionary money" as being "our easiest big money."

Mainstream Baptists' Unlimited Support of Missionaries

Several alternatives that can be blessed by God exist to alleviate the predicaments now faced by many of our missionaries. Options can be made available to those missionaries who desire to continue serving Christ apart from a politico-religious ideological movement.

Arrangements can be made by which state conventions can become the sending and supporting agencies of all foreign missionaries rather than allowing them to be subjected to any type of abuse by the SBC Foreign Mission Board. *Mainstream* Baptists are capable of and singularly committed to continuing traditional Baptist ministries of mercy, evangelism, theological education and missions enterprises.

Any three or more of several state conventions have combined incomes—much of which is being sent to the SBC Executive Committee—that, combined with the Lottie Moon and other missions offerings, would be sufficient to pay the salaries and expenses of *all* SBC missionaries.

Mainstream Baptists' tithes and offerings could be channeled through trustworthy cooperative enterprises whereby they would be devoted exclusively to Christ-honoring causes. If so invested, they would make a *spiritual* difference throughout the entire world.

Those tithes and offerings, available to send missionaries,

to support theological education and to undergird ministries of mercy, could cause our cooperative enterprises to flourish as never before.

We shall love and support our missionaries for the future of the world; we are committed to love and to provide alternative support as they follow God's call to serve Him.

Systematic Persecution of the Woman's Missionary Union

Fundamentalists have a right to speak and act according to their preferences. They have a right to become the persons whom they choose to be. But Fundamentalists possess no right whatsoever to protection of their public expressions and actions from examination, evaluation and full disclosure of findings.

I, too, have a right to speak according to my convictions and conscience, particularly with regard to Fundamentalism's persecution of the Woman's Missionary Union (WMU) as well as the abuse of other noble women.

Never a Blemish on the WMU

More than any other institution or organization, the Woman's Missionary Union, since its formation more than one hundred years ago, has epitomized that which is just and pure in Baptist life. The WMU has been the backbone of missions in Baptist churches by faithfully providing information about mission needs and coordinating mission giving opportunities in almost all Southern Baptist churches.

For more than a century, the efforts of the noble women of the WMU have been greatly blessed and the consistency of their meaningful contributions has inspired mission-minded Baptists' commitments to the Great Commission. For more than a century, Baptists have rejoiced and have expressed their gratitude for the work, virtue and witness of the Woman's Missionary Union. Unfortunately, today many Fundamentalist churches no longer have WMU activities or recognize the work of the WMU to be important to God's Kingdom.

The Life of Lottie Moon

Lottie Moon was appointed a missionary to China in 1873. However, she became deeply offended by the control tactics the

Foreign Mission Board (FMB) sought to impose regarding representation of women's societies in the SBC, and two years later she resigned. Fortunately, her resignation was not accepted. Therefore, to this day her love for the lost and her servantlike work and witness in the cause of Christ symbolize the commitment of Baptists to undergird His Kingdom's work.

The life of Lottie Moon epitomizes the labors of love of countless thousands—yea, millions—of capable and gracious women who are members of the WMU throughout our denomination. The hearts of these women overflow with love for Christ and their lives are dedicated to His Kingdom. (The thrilling history of the WMU as described in Catherine B. Allen's book, *A Century to Celebrate: History of Woman's Missionary Union*, merits one's time and reflective consideration.)

"Getting on" with Baptist Missions

A formalized all-inclusive demand on Southern Baptist women was expressed in the 1984 annual meeting of the SBC held at Kansas City. Over the objections of men who heed Christ's admonitions, the *Edenic Fall Resolution* was adopted because of the number of Fundamentalists who attended that meeting. Its obvious intent was to establish an official basis for the segregation of women for *special treatment.*

> **Fundamentalist conveniently overlooked the fact that Adam could have said "No!" when offered the forbidden fruit.**

If radical SBC Fundamentalist leaders dared to be open, straightforward and honest in their public statements, they would say to women, "We might as well tell it like it is. To us, this is a basic belief: it is because you are women that you cannot be allowed to follow your call to do God's work in the Southern Baptist Convention."

Instead, being politically shrewd—always extending the politicized "justifying" process—intimidating tactics aimed at women are but a part of Fundamentalism's mind control strategy.

Paige Patterson, as reported by the *Baptist Press* in 1985, proposed that "the Southern Baptist Woman's Missionary Union should be given agency status with a board of trustees elected by the Southern Baptist Convention." Officers of the WMU did not accept the proposal. According to the same report, Home Mission Board president Larry Lewis also proposed, "that the agencies work in such close partnership that their relationships would be like a marriage."

Please let us examine such a marriage's potential for mutual love, respect and support and for the "cherishing of one another 'til death do us part."

"Whores of Satan"

At the 1990 SBC annual meeting at New Orleans, I was seated in an upper section of the Superdome. During one of the voting periods, I noticed a disturbance nearby. About a dozen men were gesturing and directing loud remarks toward a group of women seated together.

As I watched, it became apparent the men felt the women were "voting wrong" when they held their ballots up to signify a "No" vote regarding certain motions and resolutions apparently favored by the Fundamentalists.

I was dismayed by the attitudes exhibited by the men, but I was even more shocked when some of them stood, seemingly in complete agreement, as one man shouted to the women: "You whores of Satan. God will punish you for this."

It seems apparent that some Fundamentalists take great pleasure in hurling coarse, vulgar and obscene invectives against innocent women, especially when such men are shielded by anonymity. As is apparent, Fundamentalist leaders are unable to control that which the spirit of Fundamentalism has injected into the hearts and minds of some of its foot soldiers. Even though I had participated in the denomination's meetings for many years, since that incident in 1990, I have not attended an annual meeting of the SBC.

"Spiritual Warfare" Continues

By 1992, Fundamentalism's politicized "spiritual warfare" had raged for thirteen years. Would it end? If so, when? In 1996, it remains an integral aspect of Fundamentalism's politico-religious movement's strategy.

In 1992 the Executive Board of the WMU sought to expand its operations by providing information about missions enterprises and needs to churches affiliated with the Cooperative Baptist Fellowship. This was *in addition to* the normal channels of distribution by which they continue to serve other Southern Baptist churches.

The purpose of the change was to strengthen Baptists' efforts to fulfill the Great Commission. What many believed to be a giant step in Baptists' mission work was characterized as "adultery" by a newspaper's report on comments expressed by John Jackson, then chairman of the Board of Trustees of the SBC's Foreign Mission Board.

Public Condemnation

The *Chattanooga News-Free Press* reported on January 16, 1995, that Jackson, in an interview following his preaching at the morning worship service of the First Baptist Church of Soddy-Daisy, "likened the action to adultery."

Directing his remarks toward the decision the executive board of the WMU had taken to enlarge its base of operations, Jackson indicated the WMU action was equivalent to adultery for it was as if the WMU were saying " . . . I have another man that I want to be married to as well. I know that we have had such a good working relationship, but I know that you won't mind if I bring him into our bed."

Those comments, according to the Chattanooga paper, were made by this "man of God" standing in "God's house." One might wonder if God was pleased by these apparent violations of that which Jesus expressed as being the greatest commandments— to love God and to love your neighbor.

Jackson's unconscionable public condemnation of the WMU is but another example of the despotic nature of Fundamentalism. Jackson's rude and raucous denunciations represented Fundamentalism's typical malicious manipulations—purposeful attempts to harm others—to seize and impose dictatorial control over all not created by itself.

Would you want such a man to have an influence on the development of your children's minds or on their moral character? The answer is obvious, yet many Baptists who sent their tithes and offerings through the Cooperative Program unwittingly provided for the travel expenses of such men during the

111

years he was chairman of the Foreign Mission Board's trustees. At the April 18-20, 1996, meeting of the Foreign Mission Board, Bill Blanchard, pastor of the First Baptist Church of Soddy-Daisy was elected chairman of the Board of Trustees.

Further Suppression of Women

As reported in the April 30, 1996, issue of the *Associated Baptist Press*, Mark Coppenger delivered still another proclamation against women from the platform of his newest political plum—the presidency of the Midwestern Baptist Theological Seminary.

Carefully selecting scriptural passages to "support" his suppression of women while blithely ignoring other verses, Coppenger read a passage that he said requires women to "learn in quietness and full submission." He observed that Eve led Adam into original sin and said further that righteous women "will be saved through childbearing."

Coppenger is neither ignorant nor stupid. Seemingly, he simply enjoys the public flexing of his political muscle. Apparently, to some, it must be great fun to segregate women and to cover up the exultation of limitless worldly power while unilaterally unleashing Fundamentalist degradation of women.

Who Is The Greatest?

In hope of ending Fundamentalists' pious public pronouncements, one is tempted to suggest a nationwide proclamation to the effect that Fundamentalist men—only Fundamentalist men—are the greatest among all who populate the earth. However, Jesus indicated that those who would claim to be the greatest might be disappointed at the judgment.

One is caused to wonder concerning Coppenger's gleeful exultation over his male superiority. Is it not more an insult to a lost world than merely an affront to all women who are called to Christian ministry? Let us recall the God-appointed female prophetesses, apostles and teachers in the times both preceding and following the life, crucifixion and resurrection of the Master, as follows:

Correcting Coppenger's Omissions

One would expect that Baptists who are firmly committed to the whole truth of Scripture would consider all of God's Word as the basis of public remarks. In I Timothy 1:11-15 Paul urges women to remain silent and to demonstrate their godliness through modesty, good works and childbearing. Whether at a different time or in a different setting, Paul also instructs both men and women to prophesy and pray when the congregation meets for worship (I Corinthians 11:2-16).

Romans 16 records the names of several women who worked with Paul in his ministry. Among them were Phoebe, the deacon (16:1); Priscilla, a church leader (16:3-5) and Junia, an apostle who was doubtless accorded a teaching or preaching role.

In the twenty-first chapter of Acts and the second chapter of Luke, several prophetesses are mentioned including Anna, who proclaimed Jesus as Messiah.

The Old Testament names Debora, the judge, prophetess and military leader, as well as Huldah, Noadiah, Miriam and others who were prophets.

Fundamentalists' Fear Of Righteous Women

If Fundamentalists' overall political objectives are to be achieved, seemingly women must be segregated and be subjected to that segment of Fundamentalism's "spiritual warfare" strategy that calls for women, among other things, to do as they are told.

"My Women Do What I Tell Them To Do"

A fellow Southern Baptist layman whom I have admired, respected and trusted for many years wrote,

> Several years ago, when I was leading the fight against the state lottery in Florida, my son and I were at a prominent pastor's office discussing the strategy to defeat the lottery. After educating him on the issue and gaining his attention, finally he asked, "What do you want me to do?" I explained to him how our church strategy relied on the Woman's Missionary Union, who, through their missions action imperative, were asked to participate in a statewide telephone campaign to get people out to vote 'No' on the lottery.
>
> He listened politely, then leaned back in his swivel chair and put his hands behind his head and said, 'Well, we don't have WMU around here. But, my women do what I tell them to do.' At first I thought he was joking, but he clearly was not.

113

My friend wrote further,

> ... the attitudes of pastors, denominational and missions leaders—who seek to 'control their women'—is morally bankrupt.

Fundamentalists' psychological sirens sound a "Red Alert" emergency regarding significant matters they do not tightly control. The Fundamentalists did not create the WMU and they have not been able to control the decisions reached by its officers. These conditions are intolerable to Fundamentalists. They believe the situation must be "corrected" for the sake of Fundamentalism's future success—regardless of the methods required to do so.

Fortunately, WMU officers have not succumbed to Fundamentalist coercion. Neither have they accepted the "political plums" that have contaminated so many Baptist men's lives and besmirched their commitments to Christ.

7

Fundamentalist Wrath
Even the
Good and Godly
Cannot Escape It

✶✶✶✶✶✶✶

In all things, be of good report—

"A requirement of mass movement strategy is that individuals must be identified and victimized from time to time to keep the hatred and fires burning in the bellies of mass movement members.

"In other words, they have to see live evidence of the demeaning punishment and even destruction—physical or psychological—of the worthy adversary.

"As Eric Hoffer has discerned, 'Hatred is the most accessible and comprehensive of all unifying agents.' And Heinrich Heine has suggested that, 'What Christian love cannot do is effected by a common hatred.' "

Fundamentalist Wrath
Even the Good and Godly Cannot Escape It

The headline of an article recently carried in a state convention paper caught my eye: ***"Endangered Species Act Gets Mixed Reviews"***

Until reading a few paragraphs in the article, I was not certain that it did not apply to *Mainstream* Baptists.

Are Fundamentalists Christian?

Men and women who have discussed the SBC controversy with me frequently inquire, "Are Fundamentalists Christian in belief and character?"

My answer is that only God can make that determination.

But, do Fundamentalists act as Christians according to Jesus' admonitions?

The answer to that question must be discerned by *Mainstream* Baptists in order to determine with whom they will join to commit their time, energies, tithes and offerings to assure sincere work and genuine witness to Christ.

How Long Will It Take?

As have many other Baptists, I have participated over a long period of time in civic, business, social and other organizations.

Never in such settings have I experienced or seen as much evil as has been committed in the Southern Baptist Convention since 1979.

I believe it would be immoral for me to approve or to accept without dissent, the unconscionable wrongs that have been committed against fellow Baptists.

Memorandum

• No person or organization can be allowed to stand in the way of Fundamentalism's victory in the "spiritual warfare" game.

• Fellow Southern Baptists who reject mind control are to be designated as "liberals." After the battles have been won, we can become "nice" and call them "moderates" in order to polish our images.

• After a period of image polishing, the terminology to be used is "competitors."

• Finally, some must be *segregated* for **special treatment** and regarded as "enemies"—opponents to be diminished, removed or destroyed—as necessary to achieve our final politico-religious goals.

The above memorandum, of course, is fictitious—but its message rings true.

Over the past seventeen years, the spirit of Fundamentalism has been evidenced in the attacks against a significant number of good and godly Southern Baptists. Some of the punitive and slanderous actions were taken against honorable men and women whose "unforgivable fault" was their loyalty and obedience to the leadership of Christ—seemingly an offense to Fundamentalism.

I will not misuse your time by identifying each attack, but I will discuss some of the particularly heinous efforts to purge our denomination of honest and dedicated Christians such as Al Shackleford, Dan Martin, Wilburn T. Stancil, Keith Parks, Richard Jackson, Lolley Randall, David Montaya, Winfred Moore, Cecil Sherman, Russell Dilday, Daniel Vestal and others.

The evil practice of segregating individuals and groups for *"special treatment"* has been mentioned before.

As evidenced in the following pages, some of the most capable and devoted Christians in Baptist life have been subjected to such despicable persecution.

Broad-Based Abuse
—Baptists Subjected to Armed Guards

In 1990, the SBC Executive Committee fired trustworthy and experienced journalists Al Shackleford and Dan Martin. Some Baptists compared the proceedings to the Japanese sneak attack at Pearl Harbor which President Franklin D. Roosevelt memorialized as a "day of infamy."

Of course, nothing can now be done about the dismissals for the Oligarchy of Eighty is responsible only to itself. The oligarchy reports to no man nor to any governing entity.

Ironically, Mainstream Baptists' tithes and offerings were used to pay for the travel and other expenses of the Executive Committee members, plus all the costs for the meeting. Yet, some laypeople continue to blindly send their money to Nashville.

Cooperative Program funds also were used to hire armed guards to keep the Baptist people out of that closed-door meeting, a matter that received widespread publicity, both in the religious and secular media.

No official reason for the firings was ever provided to Baptists or even privately shared with the two men. I believe it was at that point the Baptist Press was transformed into the Oligarchy's private house organ.

Following the Executive Committee's action, an independent news service—the *Associated Baptist Press*—was established. Martin was involved with it for a few months, but then became a biovocational pastor in North Carolina. He subsequently moved to Texas to work on a small newspaper.

Shackleford had been a Baptist journalist for 35 years. He declined an offer of a two-year contract that would have allowed him to remain employed by the SBC until he was of age to receive full retirement benefits. Shackleford sought employment with other denominational institutions, but was unsuccessful and had to take work in a Nashville grocery store for $4.45 an hour while looking for a suitable position. Martin, a 17-year Baptist media veteran, did not attempt to join another SBC media organization.

The Cooperative Baptist Fellowship, which had established a "safety net" for victims of Fundamentalist outrages, agreed to provide a small monthly supplement to both men for a brief period. In response, Shackleford said, "I'm grateful my fellow Southern Baptists recognize the difficulty Dan and I are having adjusting professionally and emotionally to working outside the denomination."

At a meeting held in Atlanta about a year after the firings, Martin spoke to 200 Baptist pastors and laypeople. Although having been significantly damaged, both professionally and financially, Martin told the group, "I am proud I had the opportunity to work for Southern Baptists for 17 years. I would do it all over again, even if I knew the outcome."

He then shared his personal testimony that was highlighted by this comment, "You, gathered here, know more about who I am as a spiritual being than the SBC Executive Committee. They never asked."

Inerrancy Used as a Fundamentalist Weapon

Dr. Wilburn T. Stancil was segregated for Fundamentalism's *"special treatment."* The matter was reported in November 1993 by Bob Terry, editor of the Missouri Baptist Convention paper, *Word & Way.*

Dr. Terry wrote a full-page article relating to the wrongful actions of the Board of Trustees of Midwestern Baptist Theological Seminary.

The trustees had denied tenure for the popular seminary professor, Wilburn T. Stancil.

There had been much comment and concern about this matter across Missouri and the denomination, and Terry wanted to set the record straight.

He entitled his article, "Inerrancy, politics and Stancil's tenure," and began it by asking, "Was Midwestern Seminary theology professor Wilburn T. Stancil the victim of a denominational political campaign . . . ?"

He answered the question with, "Yes, he was."

119

Fundamentalist Chairman is Terribly Wrong, but Politically Correct

In April 1993 Stancil had been approved for tenure by a 16-9 vote. Tenure was denied, however, when the chair of the trustee committee decided that a two-thirds vote was necessary to grant tenure. (In October trustees agreed that a simple majority would suffice—but it was too late for Stancil who had been robbed of his rights.)

At the October 18, 1993, meeting of the seminary's board of trustees, twenty-four trustees voted against tenure for Stancil while nine voted in his favor. Although Stancil's views regarding rebaptizing people who had a genuine salvation experience after being immersed at an earlier time differed from many of the trustees, this was not the reason for the campaign against him.

Real Reason for Political Punishment

Terry explained, "The major reason for the campaign against Stancil was his refusal to describe himself as a biblical inerrantist." Trustee Ronnie Rogers of Arkansas made that point when he declared, "The whole conservative resurgence is about Inerrancy and he (Stancil) fails to meet that standard."

Although Stancil's views on the Bible and its inspiration were practically the same as the inerrantist trustees on the board, some trustees were upset because he would not describe himself as an "inerrantist." He explained that the term was "politicized, misleading and inexact." (These were the same words he had earlier written in an article that, in large part, Terry said, "set a number of trustees against" him.)

Several trustees stated they did not want a "professor at Midwestern Seminary teaching that Inerrancy was a politicized term or that it was misleading and inexact."

In his article, Terry wrote, "Inerrantists used to say it was not necessary to embrace the word 'Inerrancy,' that the important thing was one's commitment to the Bible. The way the trustees treated Stancil proves that is no longer true, if it ever was."

Terry explained that at Midwestern Seminary tenure reviews are "supposed to be based on nine clearly outlined criteria and that Stancil violated none of the nine. Nor did the instructional committee, which opposed tenure for him, charge Stancil with violating any of the nine criteria."

Bleakest Time in 30 Years

The administration, faculty and students lined up behind Stancil almost unanimously, but the trustees were emphatic in their decision. Terry wrote, "Faculty members say it is the bleakest time in the last 30 years. They ask aloud if anyone can get tenure who is not an avowed inerrantist."

Even though some trustees voted against Stancil's tenure "with tears in their eyes," Terry explained, "that does not change the situation of the whole issue being initiated by some of their fellow trustees as a political campaign around the central issue of Biblical Inerrancy. When all the rest is scraped away, that is what cost Stancil his teaching position at Midwestern Seminary. . . . No seminary can reflect the Baptist heritage of responsible theological education if the faculty is controlled by political campaigns built around favorite politico-religious issues of trustees."

After the irresponsible and ruthless persecution of Professor Stancil, the Reverend Ronnie Rogers returned to Arkansas to *"preach holiness!"*

The Most Vile
of Slanderous Attacks

This section discusses the segregation of four more of the best of Baptist men for *special treatment,* their subjection to persecution and other attempts to destroy their reputations. In Iran or other nations where Fundamentalists control the state, *special treatment* sometimes results in the victim's torture or death.

These four men—Drs. Richard A. Jackson, W. Winfred Moore, Russell H. Dilday and Daniel G. Vestal—are among the most trustworthy and honorable of God's servants. Each has been among my respected and trusted friends for many years.

In the conduct of Southern Baptist affairs, the pursuit of careers and other rights of men such as Kenneth Chafin, Grady

121

Cothen, Lloyd Elder, Keith Parks, Cecil E. Sherman and many others are protected by the laws of the land, but not by any fairness or integrity of ruthless Fundamentalist leaders.

Dr. W. Winfred Moore

The honest men and women who served as trustees of SBC institutions and held other offices prior to 1979 wanted the convention to be for *all* Baptists. Their hearts were right but they did not understand the spirit of Fundamentalism.

Dr. W. Winfred Moore's love and support of denominational work had been evident for many years, but his involvement had primarily been limited to building a mission-minded, soul-winning church that contributed *almost a million dollars to the Cooperative Program each year*. Dr. Moore attended the SBC annual meetings, but was not certain as to where the Fundamentalist "politics" that had arisen in 1979 were taking the denomination.

In 1983, things changed. Because the First Baptist Church of Amarillo, of which he had been pastor for many years, was a leading church in mission giving and layperson involvement in missions around the world, he was asked to allow himself to be nominated for office in the Baptist General Convention of Texas.

While serving as president of the Baptist General Convention of Texas, friends persuaded him to allow himself to be nominated in 1985 for the presidency of the SBC. After Charles Stanley won the position, Dr. Moore was called from the platform to meet in the press room with journalists. While Dr. Moore was being interviewed by several members of the press, he was unaware that Dr. Ray Allen was nominating him for the first vice presidency to which he was elected.

Dr. Moore felt that his election "was an effort to heal the division and let all of us have some input into convention affairs." After Henry Huff, an attorney from Louisville, Kentucky was elected second vice president, they decided "to do all we could to work with the president to bring our convention together."

Courteous Talk—But Fundamentalism Remains Mulishly Immovable

According to the SBC constitution, the president is supposed to make appointments to the various boards "in consultation with the vice presidents." These appointments must be approved by the convention in annual session.

A short while after the 1985 meeting, Winfred Moore and Henry Huff met in Atlanta with Charles Stanley. Dr. Moore said, "We gave him scores of names that had been suggested to us by state convention presidents, state executive directors, WMU presidents, directors of missions, pastors and others. He wrote them down, thanked us, provided a delicious lunch in his dining room, and then we took our leave."

When the appointments were announced, Stanley had included only one person from the large number the two vice presidents had submitted. So much for Fundamentalist observance of the "in consultation with the vice presidents" requirement specified in the SBC constitution!

"Please Sit at the Rear"

When the Convention met in Atlanta the next year, SBC President Stanley assigned Winfred Moore and Henry Huff to seats on the back row of the platform alongside the Royal Ambassadors who were serving as pages. Vice President Moore was allowed to preside over one brief session of the convention, but he had to remind President Stanley that it was convention protocol for Vice President Huff to have the same privilege. "Following this," Dr. Moore said, "Dr. Stanley did permit Mr. Huff to preside for a brief time."

During 1985-86 Dr. Moore had another unusual experience. While working on the air conditioner grill in the pastor's office, the superintendent of building and grounds at the First Baptist Church discovered a microphone and cord from a tape recorder hanging in the return air duct. "It was evident that when the recorder in the ceiling of an adjoining room was being removed, the wire and mike had caught, pulled loose, and could not be reached from that adjoining room."

After that the church brought in people from the Amarillo police department to regularly "sweep" the office area. Of course, there was never any proof that this event had any correlation to Dr. Moore's involvement in the convention struggle, but the timing of the "bugging" creates the suspicion of a direct connection.

Self-granted Exemption from Biblical Conduct?

In April 1986 a Fundamentalist political rally was held at the Park Avenue Baptist Church in Nashville. It was led by Paul Pressler, Paige Patterson, and Bill Hancock, pastor of a Kentucky church. At the rally, Lee Roberts railed against "false doctrine and destructive heresy" that he claimed were being taught by some Southern Baptist professors. He said, "False prophets and false teachers teach slop. You can't live on it." He equated the professors' teachings to spiritual "slop" that is starving students. He also said, "Many SBC pastors and professors would be tremendous United Methodists, Episcopalians, Catholics, something, but they aren't Southern Baptists."

With regard to the then forthcoming 1986 annual meeting of the SBC, Roberts said,

> Adrian Rogers, pastor of Bellevue Baptist church in Memphis, Tennessee, would be there as a candidate to support truth, sound doctrine, what Southern Baptists believe in.

He also claimed that,

> . . . All the other candidates, perhaps Winfred Moore, pastor of the First Church of Amarillo, may or may not believe in truth. [Rogers] will turn to godly men, men who believe this [the Bible] is the perfect word of God. . . . This man over here, whoever he might be, is going to have to turn to those men who don't hold this to be the true word of God . . . . So when you go to vote for a man, you're not voting for a man; you're voting for truth or untruth. That's all there is to it. (*Baptist Standard*, April 20, 1986)

Roberts' comments slandered seminary professors, "moderate" nominees for SBC offices, and others who had refused to capitulate to Fundamentalism. His public words were vulgar and crude.

One might wonder if our Methodist, Episcopalian and Catholic friends felt that they had been slandered! One could also wonder if Roberts was capable of knowing if he had "crossed the line"—or even if a line existed!

Dr. Richard A. Jackson

When it became known early in 1988 that Dr. Richard A. Jackson was to be a nominee for president of the Southern Baptist Convention, a slanderous telephone campaign cluttered switchboards across America. Purported to be providing "truth" to Southern Baptists, it was one of the dirtiest of worldly schemes designed to malign the life and reputation of the pastor of the North Phoenix Baptist Church.

Dr. Jackson, in the preceding four years, had baptized more than a thousand people annually and his church had given *more than a million dollars each year* to the Cooperative Program. Seemingly Fundamentalist elitists perceived Jackson's possible election to be a threat to their gaining added dominance over the SBC. The telephone lines were overloaded with passionate invectives and outright lies.

Relentlessly Vicious Telephone Campaign

The most prevalent theme of the telephone campaign was that "Richard Jackson is a 1) liberal, 2) a divorced man and 3) an abortionist." I have no evidence that suggests Fundamentalist leaders directed this tawdry effort.

However, it would be difficult to imagine that so great a number of Fundamentalist foot soldiers would have made so many phone calls unless instructed to do so. As a result of the spread of the premeditated lies, Dr. Jackson received numerous phone calls deriding him for being "a divorcé, a liberal and an abortionist."

How can one defend himself from the slander uttered by those who supposedly are "joint heirs" with Christ. Dr. Jackson is a rock-ribbed theological conservative. He was not, and is not, a divorcé, a liberal or an abortionist. Several of the leading Fundamentalists were well acquainted with Dr. Jackson's work and life.

During the long and trying weeks preceding the 1988 SBC annual meeting, it was expected that Adrian Rogers, Bailey Smith, James Draper, Charles Stanley or other former presidents and prominent leaders of the SBC would step forth and call an immediate halt to the "campaign of denigration" and to condemn those who were telling the lies. Those expectations were not realized.

Vengeful and
Fraudulent Procedures

The education of ministers has been highly important to Baptists since the formation of the SBC. Over the last seventy years, as more and more Baptists recognized the value of seminary training for their pastors and church staff members, the financial support given to this work through the Cooperative Program has continued to grow. During this time, many Baptists have made substantial contributions to one or more of the six SBC seminaries' special programs or operational needs.

Prior to 1979 Baptist people had faith in our seminaries and the quality of their educational programs. Most Baptists considered the spiritual preparation of pastors and staff members at the SBC seminaries to be superb.
Southwestern Seminary in Fort Worth became the largest seminary in the world. Through the years many of the greatest Baptist educators and preachers became associated with the institution either as student-scholars or teacher-mentors. The seminary had a spotless and untarnished reputation until it was determined that summarily firing seminary president Russell H. Dilday would be perceived to be politically desirable by Fundamentalists throughout the SBC.

Dr. Russell H. Dilday—
Segregated for *"Very Special Treatment"*

The complete story of the virulent attacks against Dr. Dilday and the dishonest charges made against him, and the recorded "causes" for his removal as president of Southwestern Seminary, is in hand. Permit me now, however, to provide a brief synopsis of the events that led to one of Baptists' saddest hours and created a "black eye" on the denomination.

Dr. Dilday was elected president of Southwestern in 1978. A native of Texas and a graduate of Baylor University and Southwestern Seminary, Dr. Dilday was then pastor of Second Ponce de Leon Baptist Church in Atlanta. Although a few Southwestern trustees originally favored another candidate, during his first few years as chief executive officer, Dr. Dilday enjoyed a good relationship with practically all members of the governing board.

During the first five years after the Fundamentalist bombshell exploded in Houston in 1979, the number of Fundamentalist appointees to the seminary board continued to mount, though no substantial disagreements became evident over the operation of the institution. The controversy in the denomination seemed to have little impact upon Southwestern and its mission to prepare men and women called of God to minister in His name.

Sermon on "Higher Ground"

But the controversy invaded Southwestern in 1984 following the sermon, "Higher Ground," preached by Dr. Dilday at the annual SBC meeting. In this sermon, Dr. Dilday took both Fundamentalists and non-Fundamentalists to task for being more concerned with delving into politics than with spreading the Gospel.

The next month he became more direct in his criticism of the Fundamentalists' political actions in their ongoing takeover of the SBC. His president's column in the seminary alumni publication, *Southwestern News*, left little doubt about his feelings on the matter:

> It is now clear that mainstream Southern Baptists must act to reclaim the convention from the manipulation of political machines and return it to the people. We must restore an open convention and forbid secular politicization from dominating and becoming the pattern of the future.

Hoping to encourage Mainstream Baptist preachers and laypeople to act, Dr. Dilday continued to speak out regarding the Fundamentalist movement. The public revelations he made and the calls for reform angered several seminary trustees who were "in the Fundamentalist camp." On the other hand, laypeople's voices were largely muted.

Pattern of Executive Sessions

At the October 1984 meeting of the seminary trustees, an executive session was held—the first of many over the next few years, each of which was for the purpose of removing Dr. Dilday from his leadership role at the seminary. A motion was made requiring Dr. Dilday to refrain from any public statements regarding the political situation then prevalent in the SBC. Although the motion was tabled, it was a warning sign that, regardless of how well Dr. Dilday performed his duties as president in the future, his every move would be subject to close scrutiny and punitive action could result if he did not stop criticizing the Fundamentalist movement.

Several trustees defended their actions, emphasizing that as a denominational employee, Dr. Dilday should not be critical of Fundamentalists. *Baptist Standard* editor Presnall Wood responded to this argument with: "Does drawing a salary from Southern Baptists mean buying silence of conscience? Consider applying that principle in the local church to pastors."

Major Conflagration

The following year a major conflagration occurred when Dr. Dilday recommended the dismissal of an associate professor of preaching because of unethical conduct. This recommendation was opposed by several Fundamentalist trustees led by Ralph Pulley, Bill Grubbs and Jim Bolton, all members of First Baptist Church, Dallas.

The vote for removal failed, and Dr. Dilday recalls this meeting marked an obvious shift in the board, with underlying tensions being brought out into the open. The Southwestern Dr. Dilday knew and loved was now in the midst of a change—one that in all probability would eventually have caused founder B. H. Carroll, now deceased, to no longer recognize the institution as the "school of the prophets" he established seventy-five years earlier.

Even for an Extraordinary Man—Inordinate Pressure

It is difficult to perceive the pressures upon Dr. Dilday as he led the work of the seminary over the next few years. Frequent disagreements with Fundamentalist trustees, threats of removal and constant criticism of his actions were the order of those days. It is amazing that he was able to have any success at all in the work to which God had called him.

By 1989 when the Fundamentalists had complete control of the SBC, they began to intensify the pressures on Dr. Dilday. It was widely speculated that the trustees would remove him at their October 17, 1989, meeting.

On that occasion, hundreds of people from Texas and around the denomination gathered at the seminary in an attempt to witness the proceedings. Their efforts were frustrated, however, when the board voted 22 to 11 to go into executive session.

Dr. Charles Wade, pastor of the First Baptist Church of Arlington, Texas, led many spectators in protesting the board's decision. He noted that the people there had come long distances to show their love and support for Dilday.

"The Lord Has Nothing To Do With This" Amen!

As the spectators were forced to file out, one man refused to leave, telling trustee chairman, Dr. Ken Lilly, "the Lord would have me stay." Lilly responded "the Lord doesn't have anything to do with this." It was certainly a prophetic statement, for one could feel the Lord's presence was not recognized at that inquisition.

Fundamentalism Rears Its Ugly Head—Again!

Dr. Dilday survived that meeting and relations with the trustees seemed to improve. In March 1993 the board offered Dr. Dilday $5,000 to defray expenses for a visit to a mission field of his choosing. He declined the gift, and instead suggested the money be given to the new church growth center at the seminary.

Not Enough Political Power

It was an amiable meeting with but one note of criticism as reported in the March 17, 1993, issue of the *Baptist Standard*. Damon Shook, chairman of the board, noted that while faculty members recently employed by the seminary were certainly biblically conservative, they were not sufficiently politically conservative! He called for more political balance. Ironically, Shook's statement verified what Dr. Dilday and many others had been saying for years—the controversy in the SBC was not over theology but Fundamentalist lusting after worldly power!

Rumors Abound

A year later rumors began to circulate around the seminary that the trustees would again attempt to remove Dr. Dilday from office. It was expected to occur on March 8, 1994, the date of Dr.

Dilday's annual evaluation. Although no spectators were allowed in the room, a large crowd of supporters gathered outside, singing and praying during the meeting.

Evil Scores Again

The following day the outgoing and incoming chairmen of the trustees met with Dr. Dilday and offered a retirement package that he declined. They then indicated the existence of a plan to terminate his services at the board meeting later that morning.

At that meeting Dr. Dilday was fired. A few trustees did speak on his behalf but principally only about the severance package to be offered.

Even the President's Office Was Subjected to Fundamentalism's Segregation for "Special Treatment!"

After the meeting, as Dr. Dilday was explaining to students that he was no longer president of Southwestern, the trustees were having the locks changed on his office door. In an effort to explain this Gestapo-like tactic, trustee spokesmen said they feared students would go into the president's office to seek souvenirs. One could wonder if seminary students would steal items from the president's office!

At a press conference after the firing, chairman of the board Pulley was asked why Dr. Dilday had been fired. He stated, as reported in the March 10, 1994, issue of *The Dallas Morning News,* "I don't think it's pertinent . . . . The action has been taken, there's no reason to think about the past."

Fundamentalists do not want to think about the past when Baptists loved each other and sought to do God's will and answer their call to witness on behalf of the Great Commission. Fundamentalists only think of the future as their worldly powers gain them the spoils of ever more prestigious positions.

As reported in the *Baptist Standard*—"Dr. Dilday's 'Sin of Courage did him in!' "

Dr. Daniel G. Vestal

In 1989 and 1990 Dr. Daniel Vestal allowed his name to be put forth as a nominee for the office of president of the SBC. As had occurred since 1979, the votes of the Mainstream Baptists failed to carry, and therefore, Fundamentalist control of the SBC was maintained. During both years, Dr. Vestal had been called a "liberal who didn't believe the Bible." He was viciously vilified and otherwise slandered. Dr. Vestal, as a member of the "Peace Committee," had called attention to certain members' biblically immoral actions. But, again, Fundamentalist vilification was victorious.

In a message delivered at a breakfast meeting on June 13, 1990, following the election of another Fundamentalist SBC president, Dr. Vestal emphasized that the election had not been about degrees of belief in the Word of God, but rather "about our mission for the future—whether or not we will forge a united and inclusive denomination for world missions. On June 12, 1990, that vision failed."

What We Did Was Right!

Dr. Vestal explained that he was at a loss as to why the vision failed for what they had attempted to do was right.

> I do not say that everything we did was perfect, but it was right. We spoke to the issues that are crucial to our day; openness, fairness, missions, trust, and freedom. We resisted a political movement that excludes people from decision making, assassinates people's character, questions people's integrity and commitment to the Word of God. We resisted it and we said what it is, "It's wrong, it's wrong, it's wrong!!!" We called for a return to Baptist distinctives: the priesthood of the individual believer, religious liberty, separation of church and state. We called for a return to our Southern Baptist heritage: cooperative missions, unity in diversity. . . . But we failed and now each congregation must discern and determine the will of God and the leadership of the Holy Spirit.

Fundamentalists Do Not Cooperate With or Trust Others

Dr. Vestal is now the pastor of the Tallowood Baptist Church in Houston. He is my pastor and might disapprove of my presenting these comments.

Tallowood is known as a cooperative church—both in spirit and in practice. Its people give approximately 20 percent of total receipts to the Cooperative Program and other mission enterprises.

131

Daniel Vestal is an unusual man, truly and thoroughly a Christian gentleman, with a kind and nurturing soul. There is not a more honest and honorable believer or a greater expositor of God's Word. No one has ever heard him express a word that I believe he would not say in the presence of Christ.

Yet, in the association in which the church participates, Fundamentalists just cannot leave him alone. The delight of some is to continuously whisper that he is a "liberal." And staff members of some other Houston-area churches love to refer to Tallowood Baptist Church as "that liberal church."

I am sickened by lying tongues and those who call themselves Christians and Baptists, but purposely stir up discord among brothers. Possibly someday, I will tell you how I really feel about "Christian" slander!

Another
Villainous Action

Dr. Jerold McBride, a good and godly man, served for two years (1993-1995) as president of the Baptist General Convention of Texas. The church of which he is pastor gave more than 35 percent of its total 1995 receipts to missions enterprises. Yet, Fundamentalists hounded and reviled him during the two years he served as the BGCT president.

Whitewashing; Image Polishing:
"Conning" the Laypeople

Seemingly, it is appropriate to examine the Fundamentalist palette of pretense. To do so, one would:

- Peer beneath the "Whitewash" that has covered up the dark deeds committed against our Convention,

- Recognize the deceptive practices and devious actions that cast aside civility and publicly defiled Christian integrity,

- Strip away the veneer that veils Fundamentalist intent and

- Place on top of the table the wrongs that did not "just happen"—for they "happened" as planned!

I would prefer to use only healing words. But if a clear picture of "conning" the laypeople is to be painted, the Fundamentalist brush marks on the "takeover picture" must be examined.

What is Whitewashing and Why Does it Continue?

It is recognized that most readers, if not all, are familiar with the definition provided on the next few pages, but if not Webster's dictionary defines "whitewashing" as

> an attempt to gloss over or conceal faults and defects in an effort to exonerate or give the appearance of soundness; to gloss over or to cover up hurtful or biased presentation of data; an act or instance of glossing over a vice or reputation.

Whitewashing has proven to be an effective tool in Fundamentalists' hands. Fundamentalists have run roughshod over accepted Baptist principles. They have transformed the SBC into the largest and best-funded "Christian" politico-religious ideological movement in the nation. Future successes in political "cover up" will depend on whether the patient and considerate *mainstream* Baptists will allow it to happen. Unfortunately, we laypeople have shown ourselves to be incredibly gullible.

It seems that most *mainstream* Baptist "people of the pews" are just hoping that the controversy will end so we can "go back to the way it used to be." Seemingly, only relatively few have questioned if the spirit of Fundamentalism is morally bankrupt. The ambivalence of laypeople to demand honesty by SBC leaders has allowed Fundamentalists, uninhibited by Christian standards and unfettered by truth, to grow increasingly bold in their efforts to intimidate and harm men who refuse to yield to their rule. The SBC never can become "the way it used to be."

Mark Twain's Tom Sawyer made whitewashing and fooling your friends a popular pastime, but Fundamentalists have transformed whitewashing, along with its political corollaries—*propaganda* and *containment*—into political art forms. When applicable to political machinations, propaganda means:

> coordinated systematic efforts to persuade constituencies to accept, embrace, or not oppose, certain beliefs, postures or efforts to seize control of organizations or nations.

133

And containment is:

> the confinement or neutralizing of potentially hostile political thought, actions or force within cultural, intellectual, religious or geographical boundaries.

These carefully orchestrated functions have propelled the worldly Fundamentalist juggernaut along its sordid road to accomplish three things:

1) near neutralization of opposition to wrongdoing,
2) "justification" of hateful attitudes and unchristian actions and
3) reduction in size or complete elimination of any obstacles lying in the mass movement's inexorable course to further conquests.

Evidences and Effects of Whitewashing

Evil is evidenced in the hearts of men who allow political ambitions to crowd Christian character out of their lives and who permit obsessions to override Christ-principled conduct. It was such men who have exchanged the *power of Christ's love* for the *love of Fundamentalist power*. It was such men who seized control of the SBC.

Typical of the numerous examples of Fundamentalists' whitewashing techniques is one that occurred in February 1996. Bob Stephenson, a member of the board of directors of the *Associated Baptist Press* (ABP), responded to an article that appeared in *Baptists Today*. In his letter that was printed in *Baptists Today* on February 22, 1996, Stephenson stated that the trustees of the Louisiana state Baptist paper, The *Baptist Message*, had voiced concern about the amount of money that the ABP was receiving from the Cooperative Baptist Fellowship. The trustees suggested that ABP trustees "reconsider accepting support from any source which might compromise its ability to remain objective in news gathering and reporting."

This sounds innocent enough. However, as Stephenson pointed out, "the trustees of *The Baptist Message* make no mention of the fact that *Baptist Press* (BP) receives all of its funding from Cooperative Program funds administered by the Fundamentalist leadership of the SBC. This is the same leadership that fired editors Al Shackleford and Dan Martin because they refused to buckle under to the Fundamentalist edict that says, 'We pay your salary and will tell you what to say.'" That is how Fundamentalist whitewashing is done!

Fundamentalism:
Where Is It Leading Us?

Fundamentalists' whitewashing to cover up evil has been alarmingly successful. Many good and honest laypeople have turned deaf ears to calls for the restoration of Christian integrity in the SBC. Thus, Fundamentalists' secret planning sessions, dishonest methods, deceptive utterances, disturbing alliances, disarming piety and disquieting deeds largely go unheeded. One must assume that Fundamentalists' use of millions of dollars of Cooperative Program money for "image polishing" pays off for Fundamentalism!

Perhaps it is now appropriate to ask: "To what destiny is Fundamentalism's consuming passion for power—absolute worldly power—propelling the Southern Baptist Convention?" Inasmuch as Christian conscience prohibits our joining in that destiny, we also ask ourselves a pointed question: "What are the best ways for authentic Baptists to enhance their ministries and witness for Christ?"

Mileposts Along the Trail of Travail

As we seek answers to those questions, it might be useful to note some of the mileposts passed along the twisting trail blazed by fanatical Fundamentalists.

- **1963:** Adoption of the Baptist Faith and Message statement by the SBC. (Fundamentalists were greatly displeased that a straightjacket creed of controlled belief was not imposed on the Southern Baptist people.)
- **1967:** The converging ambitions and activities of two incredible personalities—Paige Patterson and Paul Pressler.
- **1972:** Political setback to the Fundamentalist thrust to take over the SBC annual meeting held in Philadelphia—and the beginning of six years of planning to overcome this hurdle.
- **1978:** 1) During the SBC Pastors Conference in Atlanta, there was extensive discussion of the power to be gained by shrewd politicking.

2) Four months later, in the fall of 1978, the secret meeting of approximately twenty-five men—Patterson, Pressler, and twenty-three Fundamentalist preachers—at the Airport Ramada Inn in Atlanta.

    3) Intensification of the Patterson/Pressler propaganda mechanism that had been functioning since the late 1960s.

- **1979:**   1) Initiation of endeavors that led to the ultimate "poisoning" of the SBC Pastors Conference.

    2) Seizure of the Southern Baptist Convention by:

        a) Intentional thrusting aside of God's commandments and other admonishments that constituted the holy ground over which thundered the political juggernaut at the annual SBC meeting in Houston.

        b) Wanton abandonment of civility and time-honored Christian proprieties, and

        c) Premeditated violations of the SBC constitution.

Baptists have been divided by the double-talk of skilled spinmasters. They are the same Fundamentalist spinmasters who have sought to rationalize and justify the nefarious schemes of "plunder politics."

Misuse of Laypeople's Tithes and Offerings

Paige Patterson and Paul Pressler, as well as each man who has served as president of the SBC from 1979 to 1993—Adrian Rogers, Bailey Smith, James Draper, Charles Stanley, Jerry Vines, Morris Chapman, and Ed Young—as well as Mark Coppenger, Al Mohler, Richard Land and other Fundamentalist leaders are effective articulators. Over the past seventeen years, as members of the Oligrachy of Eighty have captured leadership roles in the SBC, some of the tithes and offerings of Mainstream Baptists have been utilized to support spinning the yarn of propaganda and containment in an effort to whitewash the tarnished fabric of Fundamentalism.

In all of the recent SBC "Restructuring to save money," "downsizing" and other forms of "economizing," more of *mainstream* Baptists tithes and offerings are being used in the SBC and Fundamentalist-ruled mega churches in public relations, advertising, whitewashing and other forms of "justifying" Fundamentalism's practices.

"Gutter Politics" Propaganda

Following the secret 1978 meeting of the elitist inner-circle of Fundamentalists, there was widespread denial that any political organization was in existence.

Yet such an organization—the Baptist Faith and Message Fellowship—already existed and it was headquartered in Atlanta.

On January 20, 1978, Paul Pressler wrote a two-page letter in which he describes the "Baptist Faith and Message" Fellowship political organization.

It has an outstanding Board of Directors including Adrian Rogers of Bellevue Baptist Church in Memphis, Charles Stanley of First Baptist Church in Atlanta, and LaVerne Butler, pastor of Ninth and O Baptist, the second largest Baptist church in Kentucky. The names of others on the Board of Directors would also be familiar to you. I am also serving on the Board of Directors.

Pressler's letter continues,

The Baptist Faith and Message Fellowship has a full-time director. He is Bill Powell, whom I knew when he was the Associational Missionary for the Chicago Southern Baptist Association . . . . Bill is also editor of the *Southern Baptist Journal*, an excellent publication directed towards being of assistance to Southern Baptists and maintaining doctrinal stability.

At my request, Bill Powell is coming to Houston for a luncheon meeting on Monday, January 30, which will be held in the banquet room of Felix Mexican Restaurant, 904 Westheimer. . . . I feel that information will be given there in which you as a concerned Southern Baptist will be vitally interested. The Southern Baptist Convention will be held in June of 1979. This year's convention is in Atlanta. Some very tangible actions will be taken at these meetings.

An astonishing irony is that Fundamentalists, who vehemently reject the Baptist Faith and Message statements on the Scriptures—preferring the word "Inerrancy" to describe God's Word—artfully exploited the "Baptist Faith and Message" name to identify their political organization! Such artful conning of the people!

"No Takeover" Propaganda

Paige Patterson stated in 1980 that "No political party will emerge from among the various groups of concerned Baptists. No 'take-over' is planned, desired or possible."

Patterson further proclaimed, "How is it possible for men and women committed to historic Baptist belief in the scriptures to 'take over' a convention which is committed to the historic Baptist belief in the authority of scripture?"

"Heresy File" Propaganda

In 1984, Patterson stated to Jim Jones, the venerable reporter for the *Fort Worth Star-Telegram,* that he had a "heresy file" on professors, pastors and others whose beliefs vary from traditional Baptist beliefs. He said the file included tapes, letters, books, magazines, research papers, news stories and other items.

"We've kept all that against the day when the Southern Baptist Convention decides to say, 'Let's really look at the evidence.' We've gathered quite an archives during the past fifteen years." He said he had begun gathering the materials long before the start of the theological power struggle, then in its fifth year. Patterson then said that he hoped the files would only be used for history and research, "But they certainly could be used otherwise."

(As noted earlier, when the president of the Baptist General Convention of Texas reviewed Paige Patterson's vaunted "heresy file" he stated that all the people in the file who had any possible connection to the Southern Baptist Convention could fit into a single Volkswagen.)

Paul Pressler Propaganda

During a 1986 Houston area CBS television program in which Paul Pressler, Richard Land and Ed Young were participants, Pressler stated, "Our SBC institutions were devoid of persons who believe traditional Christian beliefs." Neither Land nor Young demurred or questioned the accuracy of Pressler's false statement that denigrated the Southern Baptist people.

Mark Coppenger's Propaganda

Mark Coppenger is an astute Fundamentalist spinmaster. He has been elevated to the presidency of Midwestern Baptist

Theological Seminary. In the mid-1990s the SBC Executive Committee provided Coppenger with some of the tithes and offerings dollars that Baptist people gave to the Cooperative Program. With these funds, Coppenger produced the slick propaganda magazine, *SBC Life*. In this publication Coppenger criticized and attempted to discredit individuals, state conventions and associations as well as various colleges and universities that would not yield to Fundamentalist domination.

He also hammered away at state convention paper editors and took unyielding positions against the WMU, the CBF and all others who could not be brought under Fundamentalism's control. Particular delight was evident in *SBC Life's* presentation of the Dr. Russell Dilday massacre. Coppenger readily admitted that he used the Cooperative Program money to obtain what he called "balance" in political reporting.

James Watters, president of the Southern Baptist Press Association, commented that Coppenger's writing in *SBC Life*

> . . . comes across as the work of a partisan spin doctor, rather than the effort of a journalist committed to presenting the news about the Good News. . . . nor does his attempt to make scapegoats of news journals for the uproar which Southwestern trustees' actions have caused among Southern Baptists across the nation.

Truth
in Crisis

Fundamentalists' expertise includes the use of misleading or slanderous innuendoes.

James C. Heffley is the author of the *Truth in Crisis* series. His book, *The Winning Edge,* with the foreword by Mark Coppenger, was released just prior to the 1990 SBC meeting in New Orleans.

The level of hatred that some Southern Baptists harbor against fellow believers reached new heights at that meeting. It was a travesty against God. Publicity about these events was unprecedented across America. Such hatred and distrust as demonstrated at that occasion can be cause to overcome reason, destroy democratic principles, displace love, and for a time, distract the fulfilling of commitments previously made to God.

Included in the contents of *Truth in Crisis* were the following statements.

The Executive Committee met in Nashville, February 19-21. Al Shackleford, the designated manager for the New Orleans convention, noted that the Super Dome where the convention was to meet in New Orleans would seat 71,000. Shackleford stated that "he hope(d) when we leave New Orleans we will feel as good about the Super Dome as the San Francisco 49ers [who recently won the Super Bowl there]."

'There are 27,000 hotel rooms in New Orleans,' he noted. 'All have been (reserved).' Shackleford couldn't answer the big question, who had reserved all of those rooms? Speculation centered on John Baugh, the millionaire food processor in Texas. Baugh had reserved rooms for moderates at previous conventions. But could he fill 27,000?

I wrote to Heffley saying,

As you are aware, other publications that support both the methods and goals of Fundamentalism have subjected many good and honest men to the movement's acrimony. Some of the periodicals also mentioned my reserving New Orleans hotel rooms. I view these matters with some objectivity, for I am not given to hate in return. Instead of this being a virtue, it is one of God's gifts that provides freedom from a spirit of animosity. You know that I was in New Orleans in June 1990 during the SBC annual meeting. Mrs. Baugh and I occupied one hotel room. We paid for one hotel room. Neither were other hotel rooms reserved for us nor did we pay the costs of rooms occupied by others.

Many of us have come to realize that in order to renew fully our witness for Christ, we should, once and for all, disengage ourselves from Fundamentalism. Yet quite a number of us still shrink from putting into practice what our hearts tell us to do.

I pray that God will grant the special gifts of heightened perceptions and steel-ribbed courage to all Mainstream Baptist laypeople. They are the only Baptists who can restore the practices of our birthrights—Christ-centered principles, Baptist distinctives and integrity in Baptist life.

8

Is Religious Freedom at Risk?
Yes, Even as Is Democracy in America

✳✳✳✳✳✳✳

In all things, be of good report—

"As Adolf Hitler said in the early days of the organization of the Third Reich, 'the masses do not want freedom of choice. They want a simple doctrine and an enemy, preferably just one enemy. Truth is irrelevant: emotional appeals are better than intellectual arguments' . . . and with his propaganda chief, Joseph Goebbels, Hitler made it clear that if the Jew had not existed, they would have had to invent him. And they also understood all too well that 'any lie, frequently repeated, will gradually gain acceptance.'

"You see, the Hitlers and Goebbels of all eras know that the "big lie" will work because most people are innately trusting and, therefore, have a limited capacity to fathom the deception on a grand scale."

Is Religious Freedom at Risk?
Yes, Even as Is Democarcy in America

Is religious freedom in America at risk? Yes, religious freedom is at risk—at grave risk—and its loss could adversely impact other rights that Americans cherish.

Since Religious Freedom is at Risk

It is the Oligarchy of Eighty, not the executive committee or the president of the Southern Baptist Convention, that determines all matters vital to each of the convention's ultimate goals.

The Baptist people have a right—and the need—to know details of the plans for the Southern Baptist Convention's further engagement in secular political and other non-traditional activities.

Therefore, it is obligatory that the Oligarchy of Eighty hold public meetings—to include unlimited question and answer sessions with editors of the state convention papers—in which to review SBC leadership's past actions and to examine the convention's planned long-term objectives, particularly as related to religious freedom, the separation of church and state and other factors to impact individual rights and religious liberty.

Thoughtful Americans are recognizing that the nation, most likely, will be caught up in a political crisis. I believe the many individuals who are fomenting hate against the U. S. government—regardless of who will serve as the nation's president or which political party will command a majority in the U. S. Congress—fail to recognize the dangers to which our democracy can be subjected by an unprecedented political crisis.

I believe also that men of dictatorial mindsets are savoring the nation's growing political turmoil.

143

Three constitutional safeguards protect democratic rights in America—1) the separation of church and state, 2) religious freedom, and 3) the citizens' rights accorded in the First and other amendments.

The loss of religious freedom could create far more turmoil in America than has the ungodly "Baptist Mess" already caused in Southern Baptist life. The loss of religious freedom also could impose upon our children, grandchildren and generations to follow, the mind control, persecution, physical hardship and tyrannical oppression suffered by individuals and groups of all nations where democratic rights are denied. Consider the plight of people whose lives are controlled by Fundamentalism in Iran, in some of the African and Asian nations and elsewhere in the world.

It is unlikely that the heirs of American men and women who turned their eyes from the ongoing fight to retain religious freedom—or who blithely "slept it off"—could ever again sleep in peace should they become victims of Fundamentalist rule in the United States.

It is recognized that some Baptists, even non-Fundamentalist Baptists "don't want to be involved" in ending the controversy in Baptist life. However, it is inconceivable that there would be even one freedom-loving American who would not raise his/her voice against Fundamentalist-spirited men who would strip from the citizens of this nation the church/state safeguards that protect the rights of democracy.

Those of other faiths, who are unable to "see" the safeguard that separates church from state, also are exposing themselves to the possible loss of their freedom as Americans. Indeed, all persons not willing to be involved in honoring, protecting and cherishing the constitutional church/state separation place themselves at grave risk.

Old World Fundamentalism

That which Southern Baptists are experiencing is classical Fundamentalism, the spirit of which seeks to "seize an inch, then a mile, a nation and possibly beyond."

To gain a foothold Fundamentalism makes inroads in times of discontent, always building upon the base of growing disaffection, regardless of whether fomenting of the discontent is religious or political in origin.

Upon gaining its foothold, Fundamentalism intensifies its systematic pursuit of its increasingly aggressive course.

Eventually, men who would unwittingly allow the wrecking of the wall of liberty that protects them from dictatorial rule will not have an "instant replay" opportunity to reverse the loss of their religious freedom and personal liberties.

It needs to be said again: individual liberties and religious freedom are among Americans' most cherished rights.

Yet, seemingly, some fellow Baptists give little thought to the protection and perpetuation of those blessings that so signally enhance the quality of all Americans' lives.

"The *Baptist*" Brand of Fundamentalism —A Hybrid Religion

Luther Burbank, the remarkable early day horticulturist, demonstrated the exceptional vigor that can be obtained by combining one strain of fruit, vegetable or flower with another.

He gained universal recognition for having developed the Burbank potato that revolutionized the growing of that important food in much of the world.

The work of modern day geneticists is directed toward creating hybrid organisms that can amass greater strengths and obtain economic and other benefits.

- *"Baptist"* Fundamentalism is a hybrid religion created by combining certain Southern Baptist assets and strengths with the personal ambitions of men obsessed with visions of unprecedented worldly power.
- *"Baptist"* Fundamentalism's hybrid vigor arises from the blending of its strongest component—traditional Southern Baptist churches and related organizations—with the ideological movement at large in the SBC.
- *"Baptist"* Fundamentalism relates to Reconstructionism, Calvinism and among other things, a desire to control governmental entities.

Money is the Mother's Milk of Baptist Fundamentalism

Reflective of the obsessive methods used in the seizure of the SBC, Fundamentalist leaders feel that neither church members nor organizations standing in the way of their money-driven objectives are to be spared from being brought under absolute control.

With regard to governmental funding, Fundamentalists want only "a little public money" with which "to do good:" fund child-care centers, pay Christian school operating expenses, feed the poor and other "just causes." Then, Fundamentalists will want "a little more government money" to improve things such as public schools—that could be turned into their political indoctrination centers—and public welfare—that could become the battleground of civil war resulting from Fundamentalism's *Imperial Ruler Syndrome* style of mind control.

The Gold Mine

To those committed to visions of worldly power—an irresistible temptation to many men—the Southern Baptist Convention in the late 1970s must have appeared to be an incredible gold mine, one that always replenished itself even through the Great Depression of the 1930s. Its mother lode since 1845 was fully exposed to view. What an incredible gold mine, especially since no one had felt the need for it to be guarded!

• In 1979 the SBC was comprised of more than thirty thousand churches with a combined membership of approximately fifteen million gentle, kind and unsuspecting Southern Baptists.

• If not gullible, those laypeople were trusting.

• If not naïve, they were unsophisticated regarding Fundamentalism's desire and drive for powers never before gained in America.

• The "people of the pews" simply could not believe—and many still cannot believe—that some "men of the cloth" would violate their vows to God and exploit all that Baptists had held to be sacred—merely to gain prominent positions, personal wealth and worldly powers.

• These kind and gentle Baptists could not believe—and many still cannot believe—that some men who speak so piously and are so persuasive while standing behind powerful pulpits on

Sundays could have any motives other than those of genuine Christians.

• Some laypeople could not believe—and many still cannot believe—that "the sweet men talking about God on television" could have any motives other than those espoused by traditional Southern Baptists! However, some of their Mondays-through-Saturdays time is devoted to crafting the Oligarchy of Eighty's schemes.

Vision of the Grandest of Treasures, Merely Awaiting the Taking

Forty thousand churches. More than fifteen million ready-made and easily swayed followers. More than $500 million in annual income—with more money rolling into the gold mine each day.

• Images of ever-greater worldly powers,
• The possibility that even the United States government could be absorbed into the ideological movement,
• The incredibly rich—and unguarded—Baptist gold mine,
• The possibilities of grandeur to exceed Caesar's most ambitious dreams!

A Vibrant and Uncontaminated Republican Party, As a Strong Participant in the Two-Party System, Is Vital to Freedom in America

---

Throughout many decades, the Republican Party has stood for sound economic concepts and for honest and logical responses to philosophical and social issues. No doubt leaders of the Republican Party, at least in part, recognize the risk to which it is being subjected in order to retain the support of the Fundamentalist Religious Right. Seemingly, at least some Republican leaders are aware of the dishonest means Fundamentalists used to seize control of the Southern Baptist Convention. The same strategy is being employed to gain control of the Republican Party's precinct, county and state organizations.

The Name "Christian"

Do you remember when the word "Christian" denoted a follower of Christ or described a program or institution whose purpose was to lead people in Christlike paths? Today, those who

147

lead some popular endeavors unabashedly plagiarize the term for less than true Christian purposes.

The name "Christian" identifies men and women who are believers and followers of Jesus Christ. If they are sincere followers, they seek to apply the teachings of Christ to their personal lives, as well as to their academic, professional, vocational and other pursuits. When enough of these good folk practice the moral and ethical tenets of their faith within a human enterprise, a positive impact always is made on society. When that happens, we would tend to call that enterprise a Christian undertaking.

On the other hand, the name "Christian" often is used as an adjective rather than as a noun. From time to time, the name "Christian" is plagiarized for various reasons. As an illustration, the "Christian" in Christian Coalition is a descriptive adjective. It follows, then, unless the Christian Coalition's leadership and their operations conform to the teachings and life of Jesus, then, seemingly, the name "Christian" could have been misused.

Inexorable Fundamentalist Pressure
Is Difficult To Resist

On April 18, 1989, President Bush met with twenty leaders from evangelical circles. Among the group were SBC president Jerry Vines, immediate past SBC president Adrian Rogers and Paul Pressler.

- An informal press conference was held after the meeting at which Rogers was reported to have expressed his "pleasure that President Bush had reaffirmed his support for tuition tax credits."

- The next day a special assistant to the president told the SBC Public Affairs Committee that "part of his job was to make sure Southern Baptists get their share of tax monies back because Southern Baptists are a large and powerful body."

- Then, it was suggested that one of the most vigorously ambitious Fundamentalist Baptists would be awarded a powerful but nevertheless a political plum position in the U. S. Government. However, the U. S. Office of Government Ethics remained unoccupied.

148

- Nevertheless, the persistence of Fundamentalism has paid off. Between the April 1989 meeting and August 1996, Fundamentalist pressures were applied to members of the U. S. Congress. A proposed new federal law calls for the first of government funding of churches!

(Update: Even though the Religious Right's exceptional political clout is recognized, it is nonetheless amazing that the U. S. Welfare Reform Bill that was signed into law in mid-August 1996, contains a well-concealed provision that, for the first time in history, will give specified federal funding to churches.)

The Southern Baptist Convention leaders who are now pressuring members of the United States Congress to create a law that would "prohibit the denial of government benefits" to churches should inform the Baptist people, and disclose to all citizens of this nation, what the *official* Southern Baptist Convention envisions to be the ideal form of government for America. The statement also should include SBC leaders' views regarding who should be in charge of that particular form of U. S. government.

I have far more confidence in the potential for the genius of well-informed rank and file freedom-loving Americans to cherish and protect democracy in the nation than to trust in the alliance of power-hungry Fundamentalists to do so. But many people continue to sleep!

Fundamentalism and the Religious Right

Knowledgeable observers of the nation's political scene could not fail to recognize that the intelligent, energetic and exceptionally clever Jerry Falwell is one of the most forceful, astute and effective of men among all power politicians.

It has been demonstrated that Falwell, who has an engaging charismatic personality undergirded by a consistently smiling public posture, also possesses a consuming ambition to gain exceptional power—power over men and money. His desire to exert extraordinary influence over the nation's affairs is augmented by the credibility generally imputed to religious leaders.

The Southern Baptist Convention's Fundamentalist leaders are the embodiment of the Religious Right that has veered from its initial "biblical course"—ostensibly to "elevate morality" in the nation. Many believe Falwell was one of the consulting engineers of the SBC takeover by Fundamentalists. Today, the Southern Baptist Convention's Christian Life Commission and other official agencies work in concert with Falwell and his other political allies.

Inordinate Pressures Imposed
on Members of the U. S. Congress

I believe that both religious freedom and the separation of church and state have been placed at growing and grave risk by the *"Christian Coalition"* brand of Fundamentalism as well as the *"Religious Right"* brand of Fundamentalism.

Without specific major efforts dedicated to generate new and far reaching support of religious liberties and separation of church and state, Fundamentalism's avaricious appetite for worldly power—and its lusting after unfettered governmental funding of Fundamentalist causes—ultimately can contribute to the demise of individual rights and the liberties guaranteed by this democratic nation.

In the meantime, the doctrines of religious liberty and the separation of church and state, as well as America's public school systems, are being subjected to grave risk—as is the Republican Party.

Who Is For and Who Is Against

The Baptist Joint Committee on Public Affairs stands immovable in its attempts to block the road Fundamentalists would travel to raid the U. S. Treasury.

Seemingly, the Fundamentalist-controlled SBC Christian Life Commission would use its considerable influence—and some of *mainstream* Baptist's tithes and offerings—to pry open the government's money vaults.

The Valuable Influence of Honest Editors' Truthfulness

Dr. Bob Terry is one of several competent, capable and conscientious state paper editors. In 1995, he "went back home" to become editor of the Alabama State Convention paper, *The Alabama Baptist.* But in 1989, Dr. Terry was editor of the Missouri Baptist paper, the *Word & Way.* In the May 25, 1989, issue of that publication, Dr. Terry wrote an article about religious liberty. These are some of the thoughts excerpted from his material (subheads are supplied by this author):

"Our history is filled with accounts of faithful witnesses who were flogged and jailed for preaching the gospel. Baptists were banned from towns and barred from pulpits. Baptists paid taxes that, in turn, were used to provide salaries for the clergy of the state-approved churches.

"Out of persecution grew a consensus that religious liberty meant that the church should not use its power of the state to further its religious mission. Conversely, the state should not use the spiritual authority of the church to coerce compliance with its policies.

Get God Out of Government?
"Baptists never advocated 'getting God out of government.' Only the most secular mind would ever think of such a thing. Baptists know that moral and ethical teachings of the gospel impact every part of man's life. Getting God out of government is impossible.

"Nevertheless, Baptists preached from their pulpits and voted at the ballot boxes that the church must be free of civil control and the state free of ecclesiastical control.

"Today that consensus is breaking down . . . . In the South, Baptists are the largest and most powerful religious body. Southern culture reflects many Baptists' understandings and certain church-related experiences are expected to be a part of a child's rearing.

Politics to Advance Work of the Church
"Baptists are the largest non-Catholic Christian group in the United States and that means Baptists are a politically powerful body. Now, some Baptists would use their newly discovered political power to advance the work

151

of the church. Once that is attempted, conflict is inevitable. The issues are the same argued 200 years ago, but this time Baptists are fighting Baptists.

"Nowhere is the conflict more clearly demonstrated than on the tuition tax credit issue. Southern Baptists' historical position is clear. Public tax money should not be used to help a church accomplish its religious mission through parochial schools.

Southern Baptists Spoke Twice
"Twice Southern Baptists officially proclaimed this position. In 1978 messengers to the SBC adopted a resolution 'registering our opposition to all tuition tax credit legislation pending in Congress' . . . . In 1982 the convention adopted a resolution calling on 'President Reagan to reconsider his support of tax credit legislation now under consideration.' Again Baptists labeled such proposals 'threats' to religious liberty and declared their opposition in unmistakable terms. The Baptist Joint Committee on Public Affairs (BJCPA) was asked to oppose tuition tax credits, vouchers and any similar legislation designed to assist churches accomplish their religious mission." (This was, of course, before Fundamentalists had completed their full capture of the SBC.)

But opposing tuition tax credits (federal voucher payments for the benefit of private and religious schools) has meant incurring the ire of some prominent and powerful Southern Baptists. The BJCPA was defunded by the Fundamentalists.

Government Support of Religion: Death Knell To Religious Freedom
Support to obtain government assistance to advance religious causes grew in the late 1980s. During that time, a Baptist congressman introduced a tuition tax bill in the House of Representatives.

Shortly after its defeat and the subsequent failure of the congressman's bid for reelection to the House of Representatives, he was placed on the SBC Public Affairs Committee. From that position he frequently criticized the Baptist Joint Committee for its positions on religious liberty.

Members of the SBC Executive Committee publicly stated "the BJCPA has worked against religion while supposedly being advocates of religious liberty." Dr. Terry responded to that statement in his article with these questions:

- Are the religious liberty positions of the BJCPA too narrow for today?

- Should Southern Baptists publicly support efforts to channel public tax money to help finance church related schools?

- Are such programs no longer a threat to religious liberty?

- Should distribution of tax money be based on religious affiliation, as the president's aide suggested?

- Are past principles of religious liberty inappropriate for Baptists today?

The editor then wrote, "Until Southern Baptists reach a consensus about their understanding of religious liberty for this generation, tensions will continue."

The Fundamentalist SBC leaders are working the halls of the U. S. Congress. They want the proposed legislation that would "prohibit churches from being denied government benefits" enacted into law.

Should the Fundamentalist effort be successful, Separation of Church and State and Religious Freedom will have been sacrificed on the altar of greed for even more money and lust for ever-greater worldly power.

And mainstream Baptists could add, "Should Fundamentalism seize control of the United States of America, its citizens will have surrendered their religious liberty to the most artfully deceptive propagandists that could be bought by the Baptist people's tithes and offerings!"

Has Reconstructionism
Invaded the SBC, Texas or Tennessee?

Only the Oligarchy of Eighty can provide a truthful answer to that question. But do not wait for that elitist band of fanatical Fundamentalists to reply.

Some of the most prominent Fundamentalist preachers are not encouraging Baptists to seek the Holy Spirit's guidance concerning what is best for the nation. Nor have SBC leaders revealed to the nation or to fellow Southern Baptists the ultimate goal of their one brand of power politics.

Can one believe they will openly share their secret—possibly, the "mother of all secrets"—with all Southern Baptists?

More and more, many people perceive that Fundamentalists' obsession is to establish a church-state government to replace our democratic system. If this is realized, will not even the most fanatical cults rebel against America and seek to control the nation in the same manner?

It is incredible that Southern Baptists would blindly follow Fundamentalism without knowing where it is taking them. However, it is equally unbelievable that some of the Baptist people have allowed themselves—without asking any questions—to be delivered into the hands of a politico-ideological movement.

One would think Southern Baptists would resist—kicking and screaming—every attempt by Fundamentalists to separate them from religious freedom and the individual rights and liberties afforded by this democratic nation—especially their God-given rights to exercise decisions that would impact the lives of their children and grandchildren.

What is Reconstructionism?

What is Reconstructionism and how can it affect each of us? No more than any other responsible person would I vote to convict a man on evidence limited to that of "guilt by association." Yet, the Baptist people have a right to know—and a need to know—all the information that can be made available regarding events that could encroach upon their work and could control the destiny of their churches.

I am not saying that the Southern Baptists mentioned in the following paragraphs are Reconstructionists. Only they could tell you of their ambitions.

An article contained in the February 20, 1987, issue of Christianity Today included several quotations from Reconstructionist leader Gary North. Among the comments were, "When Christians come to dominate a culture, they no longer need to turn the other cheek to the aggressor, but may 'bust him in the chops' . . . . The so-called underdeveloped societies are underdeveloped because they are socialist, demonists and cursed." This was the same Gary North whose interview of Paul Pressler created such a stir in Baptist circles in the mid-1980s.

R. J. Rushdoony, formerly Gary North's father-in-law, is the father of Christian Reconstructionism thought. In If *The Foundations Be Destroyed*, co-authors James Draper and Forreste Watson stated, "We gratefully acknowledge the assistance of R. J. Rushdoony, Adviser/Historian."

In a September 6, 1984, interview of W. A. Criswell by Bob Schieffer of CBS Evening News, Criswell said in effect, "I believe this notion of the separation of church and state was the figment of some infidel's imagination."

Free Gift from SBC's Public Affairs Committee

The Southern Baptist Public Affairs Committee was officially established as an SBC agency in the late 1980s. The inaugural issue of the Southern Baptist Public Affairs Committee magazine coincided with the SBC annual meeting in Las Vegas, Nevada, in June 1989.

In this magazine was a special offer of a free gift to the first one thousand new subscribers. The gift was the book, *The Reconstruction of the Republic*, by Harold O. J. Brown, for which Senator Jesse Helms wrote the foreword.

Prominently displayed on the back cover of the book were the comments of Jerry Falwell who wrote, "Harold O. J. Brown has written a thought-provoking book on the problems that face America. We may differ on minor interpretations of data, but we both believe our country faces a crisis."

Shortly thereafter, the Southern Baptist Public Affairs Committee was put out of business. Baptists do not know (and will not be allowed to learn) if the committee's demise was related to it being the first official mention of Reconstructionism by an SBC agency. We also do not know if SBC leaders frowned on the agency's public endorsement of the book or if the timing of the proposal was premature. Nevertheless, the Public Affairs Committee was rather summarily taken over—along with its entire budget—by the SBC Christian Life Commission.

I do not know who are—or who are not—Reconstructionists within Baptist life. Even so, whoever they are—and wherever they are—one can be certain SBC leaders will not allow the public admission of such politically-sensitive information.

Reconstructionism Is Not Religious Liberty

Now that we have looked at some aspects of Reconstructionism, let us think about what it is not! Reconstructionism is not religious liberty. The ideological, political and spiritual positions reflected in the concepts of Reconstructionism and those of religious freedom cannot co-exist. Only one such controlling belief can prevail over a nation's people.

The history of nations proves beyond doubt that religious freedom and governmental sponsorship—or other government involvement with religion—leads first to government control and then to dictatorship.

Certain Fundamentalist SBC leaders, without doubt, are seeking funds from the U. S. Treasury. They are demanding government money! They are salivating over the possible opportunity, through the leadership of the Religious Right, to wedge their political boots into the aperture of a slightly ajar U. S. Treasury door that protects the nation's money vaults.

Understanding Reconstructionist Philosophy

Reconstructionists anticipate a time when Christians will govern, using the Old Testament as the law book. In the March 1996 issue of *Church & State*, a publication of the Americans United for Separation of Church and State organization, information is provided about activities at the January 1996 National Affairs Briefing held in Memphis, Tennessee. The "briefing" was supported by virtually the entire spectrum of the Religious Right, including SBC leaders and several Republican presidential candidates who attended portions of the event.

The program featured a parade of speakers who bitterly attacked church-state separation, religious pluralism and public education. The program also was highlighted by other Fundamentalist denunciations of the American way of life.

According to the editorial in the bulletin, activists in the movement that was founded by theocrat R. J. Rushdoony,

> insist that the American government conform to their vision of "biblical law." Rushdoony and his followers want to abolish all public schools, ban all abortions and end all government programs that help the poor. They believe the Bible condones some forms of slavery and requires the death penalty for 14 different categories of offenders, including not only murders and rapists, but also blasphemers, idolaters, fornicators, homosexuals, adulterers, witches and 'incorrigible' juvenile delinquents. (Some Reconstructionists even argue that stoning remains the most biblically correct version of execution.)

Dictators And Their Insatiable Ambitions Do Not Change

Dictators who rule over nations make the claim that *all is done for the glory of the Fatherland.* Despots who rule over politico-religious movements make the claim that *all is done for the glory of God.* Typically, dictators have the active support of fewer than 5 percent of a nation's people.

Whether undergirded by propaganda chiefs and panzer divisions or by men whose obsessions are to hate and harm, dictators always seek more turf to conquer. As unprecedented despotic powers are gained, dictators are able to impose tyranny over nations and organizations. But this is possible only when the people acquiesce to the dictator's demands.

Patient Revolutionaries

The spirit of Fundamentalism disallows defeat! Capture of the target might be deferred or delayed even for a number of years but as long as there is life, a Fundamentalist's eyelock on a specific target never wavers.

Understandably, the compulsion of Fundamentalism to control all that it covets gives rise to disparaging but deserved observations about its grasping spirit. Christians' disagreements with Fundamentalist practitioners are inevitable. Nevertheless, Fundamentalists are neither discouraged nor deterred by criticism. The certitude of one's "true believer" self bolsters the "righteousness" of his commitments. Being "righteous," Fundamentalists never doubt they will get what they covet—in some way—sooner or later.

Above All Things, Mind Control Is Essential

How can one gain prominence and ultimate domination over a nation without obtaining mind control over millions of its citizens? How else can men become rulers of nations and gain absolute control of their treasuries?

I know of a few Fundamentalist preachers who feel they could easily manage IBM, General Motors and AT&T at the same time with one hand tied behind their backs!

Indeed, many Fundamentalists are highly gifted, have piercing intellects and engaging personalities. In combination, those gifts allow a Fundamentalist to arrogate exceptional powers unto himself. Many also are students of psychology and are very proficient in the practice of its disciplines.

Given All of the Above, Please Think on These Things

- Was it religious freedom and other rights inherent in democracy that failed the American people, or have Christian leaders failed the nation?

- There are many who believe that the failure of certain segments of Christianity contributed to the loss of "family values" and led to the "moral decline" of the nation. Did this failure occur because Fundamentalists believe that the ways of Christ are no longer effective in a more complex world environment? Or, was it because the Oligarchy of Eighty failed to adhere to the tenets and principles that Jesus taught and demonstrated to His disciples while on earth?

- Why have Reconstructionist-minded men been named to serve as trustees of SBC institutions, boards and agencies?

158

- Why should some Baptists be constrained to merely mutter timorous support of "separation of church and state" rather than speak out against the evils of Reconstructionism?
- Why should we not mention the suffering that would be incurred by the citizens of this nation under Reconstructionism? Please reflect on the fate of citizens subjected to dictatorial rulers as recorded in the history of mankind.

These are but a few questions we must ask as we seek to protect ourselves from being swallowed up by a Fundamentalist ideological movement.

Those who wish further information regarding Reconstructionism and other dangers to religious freedom may obtain it by contacting the Baptist Joint Committee on Public Affairs, 200 Maryland Avenue, NE, Washington, DC 20002-5797; (202) 544-4226; FAX (202) 544-2094.

The Nation's Citizens Further Endangered

- It is recognized that a growing number of Americans are turned off by the dishonesty and hypocrisy of secular political campaigns.
- However, even if the nominees for national, state and local elections have become disgustingly repulsive in their use of gutter practices, each citizen would be well advised to vote in every election.
- Vote, anyway. If not otherwise led, vote for the lesser evil.
- The greater evil is that which is imprinted on the hearts and minds of men who would destroy religious freedom and individual liberties that the American people have enjoyed for more than two hundred years.

Should the Oligarchy of Eighty refuse to hold the suggested public meeting, possibly the much maligned "liberal" media will serve all Americans as one of the most effective of safeguards against the loss of liberty!

9

Seizure of State Conventions
Vital to Fundamentalism's Total Control

❊❊❊❊❊❊❊

In all things, be of good report—

> " . . . there is always a continuation of doctrinal purification, use of slogans and an interpretation of 'historic new days' to try to reinvigorate those involved in the Fundamentalist movement and to attract new adherents.
>
> "There will also be increasing attempts to discredit prevailing beliefs and institutions and to remove them from the love and allegiance of those not involved in the mass movement."

Seizure of State Conventions
Vital to Fundamentalism's Total Control

It is not absurd, indeed, it is rationally prudent to inquire if the massive Fundamentalist politico-religious movement in control of the SBC has its sights set on controlling the destiny of the United States government.

Seizure of each Baptist state convention is a living, breathing Fundamentalist objective that is of paramount importance to the Oligarchy of Eighty's master plan.

Seizure of the Southern Baptist Convention by the spirit of Fundamentalism would have been impossible had not men, infected by its vital essence, employed its evil means to mislead and inflame Baptist brother against Baptist brother and Baptist church against Baptist church.

State conventions must be shielded from similar untruths, slander and outright lies that are being employed to seize them. It is needful to identify the perpetrators of such unchristian acts. Therefore:

> The work and witness of each state convention and every association could be greatly strengthened by an active no-nonsense Christian Principles Review Board.

Fundamentalists have at their disposal a great number of pulpits and they control more than $500 million in tithes and offerings that Baptists send to the SBC each year. Their ability to spend millions of dollars annually in "public relations" and image-polishing processes weigh heavily on *mainstream* Baptists and their state conventions.

Dear to Hearts of Baptists

Most of the Baptists whom I know and I are alike in many ways. These three things are dear to our hearts and are on our minds:

161

1) *The members of our families*—We wish that they receive salvation and be free under Christ and we want opportunities for them to lead useful, productive and otherwise rewarding lives as followers of Christ.

2) *The churches of which we are members*—Fostered under the freedom of Christ and with the guidance of the Holy Spirit, we are grateful for each opportunity to teach, hear and reflect upon God's truths; to study the Bible, both for enrichment and as the road map for life; to begin everyday, as our pastors encourage us to do, with thankfulness for God's forgiveness and with a commitment to be more Christlike.

3) *The United States of America*—We want to retain our individual rights and liberties as citizens of the nation; we cherish our religious freedom to exercise our consciences under Christ.

Ongoing relentless Fundamentalist assaults on state conventions will affect additional matters that we cherish as gifts of God:

- The freedom of one's mind to determine individual decisions and the autonomy of our local churches to serve Christ,
- The autonomy of each church will have a bearing on the state conventions' abilities to retain or regain their own autonomy and
- The autonomy of state conventions can foster associations' commitments to resist the spirit of Fundamentalism.

State Conventions Will Determine Outcome
Poles Apart—Fundamentalism and Christian Integrity

Fundamentalism and Christian integrity are poles apart. Since the days of Jesus's sojourn on earth, people have been drawn to one or the other. Today, the tug-of-war over our minds and hearts is intense. It is as if a line has been drawn between contrasting commitments. Indeed, it is as if a flag on one side of the line bears the words *Christian Integrity*; on the other side is emblazoned *The Spirit of Fundamentalism.*

You and I, along with many other Baptist laypeople, are privileged to participate on the side of genuine Christian and authentic Baptist work. Yet, some "people of the pews" seem blithely determined to ignore the further damage that can be

162

done to Baptist work by the spirit of Fundamentalism. Others merely long for the controversy in our denomination to go away without their personal involvement. Unfortunately, as you and I now know, that will not happen.

Unless you commit yourself openly to oppose Fundamentalists' worldly-powered activities now underway in our state conventions and local associations, the principle of church autonomy is subject to erosion and possible termination.

Fundamentalism in the SBC is demonstrated to be powerfully intimidating and viciously vindictive when an association's Fundamentalist director of missions says to a young man who has felt the call to preach God's Word, "Unless you obtain your theological education from a SBC seminary, you will be blacklisted all over the nation."

It will be well for *mainstream* Baptists to verify if such threats are being made in their associations and then to consider withholding further contributions to those associations as long as the offending directors of missions remain in their positions.

Authentic Baptists are dependent upon the Lord for strength and the Holy Spirit for guidance. They are committed to religious freedom. They are sickened by the worldly evil lurking at every turn in Baptist life. Each of us is free to make a difference by doing something, or we may lose such an opportunity to take a stand for Christ if we choose to do nothing at all. But none of us will be able to escape the ultimate consequences of our decisions.

In One Way Or Another

All *mainstream* Baptists are involved in the battle over Baptists' integrity in living by—as well as in proclaiming the Gospel of Christ. What do you consider to be your role in this struggle for lives and souls? Where do you place yourself in the tug-of-war? Are you on the side of truthfulness, love, servanthood—the stalwarts of Christian integrity? Or, are you on the side of slander, hate and mind control—characteristics of the spirit of Fundamentalism?

As I see It

• The Fundamentalist movement in the SBC has taken control of Baptist minds in sufficient number to overwhelm the decorum and decency in conduct of the convention's annual meetings. Thus, the SBC was seized—even as its constitution was violated.

• However, the Southern Baptist Convention's fate is still in the hands of millions of Southern Baptist people. I am referring to the millions of Southern Baptist people who continue to passively tolerate Fundamentalist evil.

As Others See It

I have just received a letter from a fine Baptist woman who has devoted much of her life to ministries and missions through her church, her association, her state convention and the SBC. In the letter she says, "As the SBC leadership continues their headlong drive toward absolute control over the minds, spirit and properties of Baptists, I am in amazement that so many stand silently by and let it happen! It is impossible for me to understand how dedicated and sincere people of God can continue to support such evil."

Crossing
the Line

Propriety, Christian Principles and Baptist Polity

Fundamentalists are not uncomfortable with who they are, what they say, what they do or the evil they have unloosed in the SBC. But are sincere Christian and authentic Baptists disturbed by sordid attitudes and worldly actions? Are they concerned when the lines of propriety, Christian integrity and Baptist polity are crossed in attempts to seize state conventions?

Yes, *mainstream* Baptist laypeople *are* concerned. They do not want their pastors and young people to be infected by the spirit of Fundamentalism! They do not want its rancorous spirit to damage our state conventions or the nation!

Straight Talk

My intent is not to be rude, but I feel the seriousness of the Baptist situation requires straight talk. So many Fundamentalists have "crossed the line" so often that it is difficult to keep track of the incidents. Here is just one example of the line having been crossed:

At a recent year's meeting of Fundamentalist fractionaries at a restaurant in South Central Texas, the principal topic of discussion related to methods that could be used to capture the Baptist General Convention of Texas. Specifically, it was said "If it takes dirty tricks to take over the BGCT, we will use dirty tricks." I wonder if some of those men would like to hear a recording of the times the vulgarity line was crossed, the truthfulness line was violated and the obscenities line was almost obliterated?

In that meeting good men were slandered and the Woman's Missionary Union vilified. One of those Fundamentalist nominees for high office in the BGCT is reputed to be a good man. I regret he was "running with the wrong crowd."

There are many examples of crossings of the line already mentioned in this publication; please recall with me:

- The massive 1979 Fundamentalist luncheon at the Colonnade Cafeteria in Houston where Patterson and Pressler preempted the Holy Spirit by *their selecting* Adrian Rogers and Bailey Smith as potential SBC presidents.
- Massive voting irregularities at the 1979 SBC annual meeting.
- Patterson's misstatements including responses to specific questions asked by the editor of the *Baptist Standard*.
- The absence of sincere efforts to foster reconciliation and achieve peace through the Peace Committee.
- Rogers' hawkish 1995 sermon on Spiritual Warfare.

BGCT Leaders Segregated for "Special Treatment"

Does any Baptist who resides in one state have a right or the authority to tell Baptists in another state how to designate their gifts? In 1995 when Texas Baptists were considering a reduction in the percentage amount of Cooperative Program money to forward to Nashville for SBC purposes, no less than seven SBC leaders attempted to tell Texans to vote against the reduction. Inordinate pressures were imposed on the Baptist General Convention of Texas not to reduce the percentage of its disbursement to the SBC.

An issue of the Indiana State Convention paper was widely distributed in the Lone Star State. It was highly critical of Texas leaders' decision to reduce slightly the future percentage amounts being freely given by Texans to the work of the SBC. Was there any legitimate justification for this? Or was it done in complicity with other Fundamentalists?

165

Texas Baptists' tithes and offerings were partially used to defray the cost of *SBC Life,* the publication that was openly critical of Texas Baptists' decision. Even Morris Chapman, president of the SBC Executive Committee, a portion of whose compensation is also provided by Texas Baptists, had unkind things to say about the decision of the BGCT. Such intrusions into an autonomous convention seemingly were arrogant, malicious and unprecedented.

Upon what authority, according to Southern Baptist polity which governs the operation of our denomination, were these actions taken? Our Baptist polity protects the autonomy of our state conventions. Each Baptist church is autonomous and voluntarily joins in the work with other churches in associations, state conventions and the Southern Baptist Convention. None of these groups has any "control connectionalism" with any of the others, including churches, as Southern Baptists have never approved any hierarchical arrangement.

Associations, state conventions and the SBC do have administrative authority over the agencies and institutions that, separately, they have created. However, all financial support of these institutions comes from Baptist men and women who make contributions through their local churches. In turn, the churches distribute some of the funds to the association in which they participate, as well as to their state conventions.

The state conventions then make disbursements to the SBC of a portion of the money that has been received from the churches in their particular convention. State conventions possess *sole authority* to decide the amount of the tithes and offerings to be forwarded to the SBC Executive Committee in Nashville.

Thanks—But No Thanks

Texas Baptists were determined to respond to a very real need to reach the millions of lost souls flooding into the state, and thus, at the 1995 BGCT annual meeting in November, they voted their consciences. They had seen what happened to Bold Mission Thrust when Fundamentalists effectively stymied it. Texas *mainstream* Baptists could not allow Indiana Fundamentalists to torpedo the state convention's bold new plan—"Texas 2000."

The Use of Worldly-Powered Baptist Politics

Another crossing of the line by Morris Chapman occurred earlier this year. The Northwest Baptist Convention is one of the smaller regional conventions that supports the SBC. According to a February 21, 1996, *Associated Baptist Press* news release, convention messengers unanimously approved a budget that channeled $50,000 of their Cooperative Program funds as a special gift to Golden Gate Theological Seminary.

Instead of praise for their benevolence in assisting the seminary whose financial support had been reduced by the SBC, Baptists of Washington, Oregon and part of Idaho were chastised by Morris Chapman, president of the SBC Executive Committee. He sent a letter to Northwest Baptist Convention Executive Director Jeff Iorg on January 8, 1996, in which he stated that the Convention's action

> is in violation of a principle that has been affirmed and reaffirmed by the SBC . . . That principle is that state and regional conventions will not attempt to fund national entities directly, but only through the national Cooperative Program budget as determined by the Executive Committee. . . . It is not the prerogative of the Northwest Baptist Convention to spend $50,000 of the money allocated to the SBC, not even if the state convention messengers vote unanimously.

Does Morris Chapman realize how seriously he crossed the lines of Christian propriety? One would think the messengers seated at the Northwest Baptist Convention annual meeting had the right to make their own decisions. I am unaware of any basis for Chapman to also tell Mr. Iorg "I encourage you to discuss with me in the future any such actions under consideration . . . ."

Mainstream Baptists will seek guidance of the Holy Spirit rather than the approval of the SBC Executive Committee's president in matters related to the Cooperative Program and in their state conventions' affairs.

Under Attack

A Baptist friend who lives in another state, a gentleman whom I respect and greatly appreciate, remarked to me, "We want our state convention to retain its autonomy." I responded, "If your state convention is to retain its autonomy, it will be necessary for other sincere Christians and authentic Baptists to work toward that purpose."

I was tempted to ask my friend where he had been for the past seventeen years but I did not. I also thought about saying, "Your church also is being placed under increasing pressure to forsake its autonomy." Again I refrained from saying what I was thinking.

For seventeen years the Southern Baptist Convention has been subjected to radical changes, not by *mainstream* Baptists, but by the approximately eighty key Fundamentalist leaders imbued with the *Imperial Ruler Syndrome*. The Oligarchy of Eighty has orchestrated and implemented the major changes that have drastically altered the SBC. It is no longer *Baptist*; it is *Fundamentalist*, it is *creedalistic* and it is well on the way to becoming *totalitarian*.

Underlying Reasons for Changes

The changes being forced on *mainstream* Baptists are for reasons far beyond satisfying the incredible pride and obsession for aggrandizement evidenced in the lives of the elitist Fundamentalist leaders. I believe their intent was and still is to seize control of the SBC and use it as a stepping-stone for the gaining and consolidation of ever greater worldly power.

Establishing a church-state government is tempting to power-hungry men. Theocratic rule over the citizens of this nation is desired by some. Yet, I wonder about who would be chosen as "Theo the First!"

State Convention Control
is Vital

Fundamentalist leaders of the SBC are intent on capturing *every* state convention. From their point of view, it is an imperative!

The appointment of directors of missions is determined by each state convention's leadership. Whoever controls the state convention has the capability of naming individuals to fill all other highly influential positions. Directors of missions, in turn, possess the potential to coerce churches to "vote the Fundamentalist ticket" or face the possibility of exclusion from the association. If Fundamentalists gain control of all state conventions and place their puppets as leaders of the associations, they would be well on their way to transforming the *Southern Baptist Convention* into a politically powerful *Consolidated Southern Baptist Church of America*. They could thus anticipate that fifteen million Baptists would vote as a controlled bloc in secular elections.

Baptist Faith and Message Statements Kicked Out

Does this sound far fetched? As I write this I am looking at a letter written by the moderator of an association of Georgia Baptist churches in which the director of missions is a high-level Fundamentalist. The gentleman who wrote the letter is both the association moderator and chairman of the association's credentials committee.

He states that by the unanimous vote of the Credentials and Missions Committees, the Baptist Faith and Message statement regarding the scriptures has been rejected and will be replaced by Fundamentalist terminology concerning the Word of God. And, therefore, of course, every congregation that embraces the Baptist Faith and Message statement is subject to exclusion from the association.

It Is a Fundamentalist Ploy to Suggest Piously, "Let Us Not Be Divisive"— But Is It "Divisive" to Recognize Immoral Actions?

Excerpts of the following letter that I recently received show the effect of Fundamentalist influence on an association. The writer stated:

> I knew that Dr. Dilday had been under extreme pressure from his trustees for more than a decade before his dismissal. I also knew that in the last few years of his tenure both he and the trustees had given candid reports to the press about the tension and dissension taking place within board meetings, particularly over faculty appointments. I was not surprised that the trustees wanted to replace him. I was shocked, however, by the barbaric and uncivilized manner in which they terminated him.

169

I felt this dismissal was so indecent and degrading that men of good conscience would be compelled to cry out in protest. I wrote a resolution to present to the _____ Association's April 19, 1994, executive board meeting. The resolution censured Southwestern's trustees and commended Dr. Dilday for his years of faithful service. A couple of days before the meeting I phoned the _____ Association's executive director, _____, to inform him of my intentions and read the resolution to him. He asked me not to present the resolution. He was concerned that the resolution would pass, that several prominent Fundamentalist pastors would take offense at the resolution and would withdraw from the association. I advised him that this issue was a matter of conscience and that I could not remain silent. He then told me to expect the moderator to rule the resolution out of order. He spoke at length about the tenuous financial status of the association and its ministries and asked me to pray further about the matter.

I agreed to pray and promised that, with the exception of the associational moderator, I would not speak to anyone about the resolution before the board meeting. I then called Associational Moderator _____ to inform him about the resolution and advised him of the content of my conversation with _____.

After sincere and agonizing prayer, I continued to feel compelled to submit the resolution. I presented the resolution. The moderator ruled it out of order. I appealed to the board members to overrule the decision of the chair. I reminded them that Dr. Dilday was a man of integrity who had pastored in the association and that his dismissal had been conducted in an unconscionable manner. The associational board upheld the moderator's decision.

On June 7, 1994, I presented a similar resolution at an executive board meeting of the Baptist General Convention of Texas. BGCT Board Chairman Leroy Fenton did not rule the resolution out of order and the resolution passed by an overwhelming margin.

I hesitate to draw conclusions from these experiences. _____ and _____ are my friends. Both were doing what they thought was best for the association. In the short term, it was. In the long term, they have merely postponed what looks to me to be inevitable. It is inevitable that men of conviction, conscience and integrity will separate themselves from those whose consciences allow them to achieve their ends by any means.

Local Church Autonomy

A letter from an individual in a prominent church stated that, "Because the _____ Association wanted to interfere with our local autonomy as a church, due to our refusal to yield to Fundamentalist pressures, we were declared unacceptable for participation in the associational activities." Yes, it *can* happen. Yes, it *is* happening!

Dealing With Enemies

Baptists do not go about looking for enemies. However, Fundamentalists have segregated many authentic Baptists to be treated as enemies.

In September 1994, after instructing SBC agencies not to accept contributions from the Cooperative Baptist Fellowship, the SBC Executive Committee adopted a resolution suggesting state conventions establish equally presumptuous positions.

Jesus Calls Believers to Love

Jesus calls for us to love our enemies and those who persecute us. It is not difficult to pray for those whom you love, but it is sometimes difficult to love those for whom you pray, especially if they have not been treating you fairly or dealing with you honestly. Overcoming difficulty in loving those for whom you pray can be accomplished by sincere prayer, coupled with striving to learn anew how to love.

Laypeople Can Reclaim Autonomy

Seminary officers, pastors and people of *mainstream* Baptist churches and presidents of Baptist universities, along with a select handful of denominational leaders, have been the main targets of the Patterson/Pressler coalition. Laypeople also have been victimized by the onslaught.

- Laypeople have been subjected to the stigma and embar-

rassment of the public display of the ungodly political fight in their Convention.
- Laypeople have had their pastors muzzled by false Fundamentalist charges.
- Laypeople have had their churches taken away from them by Fundamentalist interlopers.
- Laypeople have seen their congregations purposely split so that Fundamentalists could become undisputed rulers of their churches.

Ironically, the tithes and offerings of *mainstream* Baptist laypeople have funded many of these quests for worldly power. That will continue until we take action to *designate* the use of God's money for which we are stewards and to see that it is invested *solely* in His Kingdom's work.

Overcoming Evils of Fundamentalism

The evils of Fundamentalism can be overcome. If laypeople want to retain the autonomy to work and witness in Christlike ways in their state conventions, truth about Fundamentalists' worldly-powered goals must be made known. The Baptist people must be given assurance that their designated missions' dollars will be used in their states, in this nation and throughout the world, as they believe their designated offerings should be invested.

Additionally, truths about the carnage that Fundamentalists have wreaked against the SBC and their desires to seize our state conventions must be taken to the editors of the state convention papers. The editors—"prophets with pens"—are exceptionally influential Baptists. They must remain free to tell things the way they really are within their states.

Even when Fundamentalists seemingly are defeated, that spirit so strongly imbued with evil is not vanquished. It merely expresses a willingness "to be cooperative." Like a thief in the night, Fundamentalism merely is awaiting the next opportunity to initiate another segment of its "diminish, divide and conquer" strategy.

Hope for the Future?

Fundamentalists may not be able to bully Baptist laypeople forever. Michael Clingenpeel, editor of the *Virginia Baptist Herald*, wrote on January 4, 1996:

172

Congregations are reclaiming their autonomy. Instead of franchisees of a national denominational program, manufacturing Baptists with a precision that McDonald's sling hamburgers or Baskin & Robbins dishes up ice cream, local churches are deciding what denominational programs they will or will not support.

State conventions are beginning to see themselves, not as regional distributors of a national corporation, but as independent denominational bodies rendering services to local Baptist congregations. Texas Baptists' choice to decrease Cooperation Program funds to the SBC and the Virginia Baptist General Board's decision to network with an independent capital fundraising firm, are illustrations of a new style of denominationalism spawned by changes in the SBC due to the restructuring. There are many more.

All of this is fueled by individual Baptists who are rediscovering their individual priesthood either because American society has exulted the virtue of choice or because Baptist controversy has driven them to reexamine the scriptural concept of soul competency . . . the future is promising to Baptists who can model creativity in approach to ministry and openness of spirit toward others whose style and approach is different. If we have any hope of reaching our changing society, Baptists must accept the reality that new containers are needed for the unchanging gospel.

Unacceptable Differences

With that in mind, whenever and wherever Fundamentalists are seen on television, behind pulpits or elsewhere—please think on these things:

- Fundamentalists seemingly disagree with Jesus about the basic precepts and tenets that He established to serve as models for His followers' conduct. Yet, Fundamentalists, as evidenced in their own behavior, will go to great lengths in attempts to "justify" the rejection of Jesus's life and ministry.
- *Mainstream* Baptists would not presume to believe that Jesus was in error regarding any matter. They believe the Bible is

true as specifically expressed in the Baptist Faith and Message statement regarding the Scriptures. *Mainstream* Baptists seek to honor Christ by adhering to His admonitions.

Please think on these things:

We pray that as *mainstream* Baptists choose like-minded Christians with whom to work in cooperative endeavors, they will use the wisdom granted by God to think on these ongoing Fundamentalist practices:

• In associational meetings, what is the true intent when Fundamentalists intensify whispering campaigns against *mainstream* Baptist pastors and churches?

• At "Pastors' Conferences" that precede state convention annual meetings, is there a more central objective of the "Conferences" than to seize control of the state convention?

• At state conventions, what are the actual, but undisclosed, motives of Fundamentalists who make emotional presentations of resolutions that have been crafted to achieve political advantage?

• What is the basic intent when Fundamentalists publicly express vilifying statements against specific individuals and institutions?

• Can the presentation of political diatribes at secret political strategy meetings held early in the day and the pious exhortations on Evangelism Conference platforms held later in the same day be indicative of anything other than Fundamentalists' intentions to seize control of the state convention?

• In trustee meetings at SBC seminaries and other SBC organizations, what is the psychological problem that causes Fundamentalists to be so fearful of their responsibilities—at least until the last person in the institution who could express a difference of opinion has been fired?

Return to Christ? — Who? How? When?

It is my prayer that those misguided Fundamentalists will regain their senses, rethink their personal commitment to Christ and return to His ways. I pray also that Fundamentalists will be led to dissolve their politico-religious movement that largely has negated the sincerity of virtues and values of Christian teachings and principles.

If these things were to occur, would it be possible for the intent to harm and hate "opponents" and "competitors," to be exorcised from the hearts of Fundamentalism's followers?

Could Fundamentalism's foot soldiers who have blindly engaged in "spiritual warfare" to "purify" the SBC change the direction of their steps and join in a march for missions?

Is it possible for those who have willingly obeyed commands to diminish or to destroy any person standing in the way of Fundamentalism's obsessive goals—to change their allegiances?

Could those whose actions have reflected the malice of leaders' hearts "do an about face," forsake their errant ways and return to the Lord?

We pray these changes will occur, and that those who have heeded the pungent call of Fundamentalism will seek to "overcome evil with good." We wait in hope. Yet, we stand in vigilance to shield our state conventions from further Fundamentalist evil.

10

Baptist Work and Witness *Will It Survive Fundamentalist Apartheid?*

✸✸✸✸✸✸✸

In all things, be of good report—

"Since it is doubtful that the involved mass movement extremist who deserts his holy cause, or is suddenly left without one, can adjust himself once again to an autonomous individual existence without incurring much self-hatred, then it is also doubtful that the leaders and many followers of the movement will change their behavior. It would be like the loss of life itself to those who are most psychologically afflicted."

Baptist Work and Witness
Will It Survive Fundamentalist Apartheid?

The Southern Baptist Convention is not the same organization it was when constituted in 1845. It is not reflective of its commitments—solely to Christ—that led to the growth and success that it experienced in its first 130 years, until 1979.

The Southern Baptist Convention has retained its corporate identity, but it has been starkly altered in purpose, operation and principal objective. Currently, it is little more than an extension of the Southern Baptist brand of Fundamentalism. In this book it is referred to as the *official* Southern Baptist Convention. It is composed of approximately 10 percent of the total number of men and women, all of whom traditionally had been known as Southern Baptists. In due course, it is felt this *official* Southern Baptist Convention largely will be the base of operations for the deployment of Fundamentalist forces bent on extending the politico-religious mass movement's ideology throughout America.

The remaining 90 percent of Southern Baptists—those who hold fast to their Christian witness and traditional Baptist distinctives—are called *mainstream* Baptists. The spirit of Fundamentalism has impacted the work and witness of *mainstream* Baptists to such a degree that their courage and commitment are challenged to serve and grow as a traditional Christian/Baptist enterprise

I believe authentic Baptist witness and work cannot survive in a significant measure as a cohesive force for Christ unless the non-Fundamentalist pastors inspire and lead the "people of the pews" to restore Him as head of the church in our denomination, as He was prior to the 1979 Fundamentalist onslaught. If they do not, the *mainstream* Baptists largely will be consigned to observe haplessly the ongoing relentless corrupting of our denomination by power-hungry men controlled by the spirit of Fundamentalism.

The Oligarchy of Eighty which is in absolute control of the SBC has not publicly identified the national or worldwide political objectives that seemingly consume its leaders' thoughts. But, of course, it is not necessary that Fundamentalists disclose their ultimate goals in order to continue use of the Convention's influence and assets. The Oligarchy of Eighty is composed of such powerful men that it is accountable only to itself.

Therefore, one cannot be certain concerning the ultimate objectives of the power-hungry ideological movement. Nevertheless, all Baptists have a right and a need to know details of its agenda, particularly as it relates to use of *mainstream* Baptists' tithes and offerings, capabilities, time and energies.

Mainstream Baptists' Legacy

Inasmuch as Fundamentalism has relegated Christian values to a secondary or lesser role in Baptist life; whereas Baptist distinctives, have, in some cases, been cast aside and in others completely nullified; and whereas the denomination's democratic principles have been overridden, it is, therefore, important for mainstream Baptists to decide whether these drastic changes can serve the cause of Christ.

Mainstream Baptists' legacy of Christian witness testifies to their desire, as far as is possible, to live in peace with all persons. Fundamentalism restricts cooperative relationships, allowing them only to men who are submissive to its spirit.

Mainstream Baptists' lives give witness to their belief that the Bible is the divinely inspired record of God's revelation of Himself to man; that it is without any mixture of error; that one of its principal purposes is to provide inspiration and instruction for serving in His Kingdom; that the Word is to be preached and taught with fidelity; and that its instructions and spirit of admonition are to be practiced.

On Sunday mornings, Fundamentalists usually give the proper appearance and present the words as do other Christians. On other occasions, seemingly any inclination to "practice what they preach" is overcome by the desire to reap the rewards of worldly power.

178

If a person is willing to flirt with Fundamentalism, that person will usually be caught in a trap—one that is mental, spiritual, personal, monetary and political—the key to which is kept in the hip pocket of the Oligarchy of Eighty.

Is There a Possibility for Reconciliation?

Fundamentalism in America continues to gain strength, adding to its ranks some of the varied groups that seek to profit from the broad-based political discontent currently at large in the United States. As a result, knowledgeable observers of the Southern Baptist and American scenes feel that triumphal Fundamentalism most likely will continue on its course—forcefully coercing others to reject God-honoring conduct—until it finally is crushed under the weight of its own evil. In the meantime, the form, substance and face of Christianity are being substantially altered by the power-mad political alliance that desires to control the United States of America.

Since sincere Christians have the responsibility of honoring Christendom by adhering to its tenets, can *mainstream* Baptists have fellowship with or knowingly yield to men who intentionally violate the Word as fellow believers are persecuted? Is reconciliation between Fundamentalists and *mainstream* Baptists possible? To answer these questions, one must remember that reconciliation can only begin when both parties *desire* to reach accommodation with one another. As previously mentioned,

1) Fundamentalists have no desire to be reconciled with *mainstream* Baptists; instead, they seek to silence them.
2) Fundamentalists do not wish to work cooperatively with other Baptists; they much prefer to intimidate rather than cooperate. Mind control is the key to Fundamentalism's expansion.
3) Fundamentalists do not want to engage in forgiveness; they want to be feared. Opposition cannot be tolerated.
4) Fundamentalists do not want reconciliation; they want obedience. Unquestioned obedience is tantamount to absolute control.
5) *Mainstream* Baptists' purpose in presenting the Gos-

pel of Christ is to lead people to become followers of
Jesus. Fundamentalists tend to conscript people to
become foot soldiers to fight for their politico-religious
movement's ideological "cause."

6) Jesus invested His all in us. As *mainstream* Baptists
we are privileged to commit ourselves in ministries and
missions in ways we believe He would have us do.
Fundamentalism's scheme is different—it demands
what it wants. It is a "Do as we say or suffer the consequences" mind control ideology. Those who withhold
allegiance from Fundamentalism are to be denigrated,
diminished or destroyed.

Thus, as a matter of conscience, it is evident that *mainstream*
Baptists cannot yield their lives and God's gifts to any group
that rejects Jesus's teaching—wholly or in part.

Nevertheless, Does Any Possibility of Reconciliation Exist?

One cannot foretell if at some distant time reconciliation
among Baptists is possible. It will depend largely on whether
the spirit of Fundamentalism will be overcome and its adherents choose to embrace Christ alone and to follow His teachings. At this time, there are few similarities, if any, in what is
deeply embedded on the hearts and minds of *mainstream* Baptists and what is of compelling import to those obsessed by the
ideological movement.

Mainstream Baptists are committed to ministries of mercy
for those in need wherever they might be, to evangelism at home,
to preaching the gospel in all nations and to Christ-centered
theological education.

In stark contrast, it seems evident the Oligarchy of Eighty,
which is in absolute control of the *official* SBC, is committed to
the political alliance that includes the Religious Right, the Christian Coalition and other participants in that massive broad-
based politico-religious movement.

Questions for Your Unhurried Consideration

It would be foolish to expect the Oligarchy of Eighty to provide straightforward answers to these questions. So, we ask
them of *mainstream* Baptists:

1) Can the subjects of "family values" and "the nation's moral

condition" be successfully addressed by men committed to the practices of worldly-powered politics? Can those values be advanced by a political movement allied with gambling, tobacco and liquor interests?

2) Can "family values" and "the nation's moral condition" actually be enforced without government control of religion— or without the politico-religious movement's control of the government? Please give careful consideration: Can "family values" be advanced by legislation, by force of law, by requirements and regulations? Can virtue be rooted in any force but faith?

3) Can "family values" and "morality" be reestablished and sustained by any force other than voluntary, personal commitments of genuine Christians?

4) After more than two hundred years of religious freedom, will the cause of Christ be better served under a state church or by a church state? How can the vitality of religion—American's widespread embrace of various religious beliefs and the peaceful co-existence of different faiths in the United States—be compared with conditions in Northern Ireland, Bosnia, Iran or Iraq or any other church-state on earth?

5) Would Christ be better served by a new form of national government? Would it be Classical Reconstructionism or a hybrid Calvinistic-Reconstructionism? Or, would it be still another "ism," along with the changes it would impose upon the nation's citizens?

6) Should the United States be designated exclusively as a Christian nation?

7) Would state subsidized religious institutions avoid monitoring, entanglement, government intrusion, questionable guidelines and regulations?

8) Would a politicized view of a specific religion lead to civil war? If not, how would other religions be controlled?

Will Southern Baptist Laypeople Abandon Their Rights?

It would be grossly unfair to state that all Southern Baptist laypeople have haplessly conceded their birthrights as Baptists to the spirit of Fundamentalism. Indeed, some laypeople have retained their freedom to believe and to act as sincere followers of Christ. They have held fast to the legacy of Christian principles and long-held Baptist distinctives by distancing themselves from Fundamentalism

However, many of the men and women who constitute a

181

majority of the Baptist laypeople have not raised a voice or finger in opposition to the creation of the state of Fundamentalist apartheid at the expense of true Christian fellowship, work and witness. Incredibly, many congregations of believers, even some not under Fundamentalist rulership, seemingly have seen much of the evil committed, but merely have "looked in the other direction."

Some Southern Baptists have joined other Christian denominations. Others merely have "dropped out" of the life that had meant so much to them—victims of the evils by which our denomination has been beset. The faith of many young people also has been damaged or destroyed by the spirit of Fundamentalism.

Baptist laypeople are not stupid nor without honor. They simply have not yet taken appropriate initiatives to correct violations of truth, fairness, honor, integrity and fidelity, nor have they attempted to restore the other virtues and principles by which the life of Jesus was exemplified. I find it difficult to believe that honorable people will be found to have "rolled over and played dead" in the face of the greatest evil that has ever beset their fellow Baptist believers in Christ.

State Paper Editors: Is It Too Late For The SBC To Be Baptist?

Editors of most state convention papers have sought to serve all Baptists; they have "tried to keep peace." Some "had friends on both sides," and/or have expected "the pendulum to swing back to the middle."

Perhaps some editors have not fully understood the true spirit of Fundamentalism. But, even so, the editors should have known better when, as a group, they recently appointed an emissary to request that Dr. Bob Reccord, chairman of the Implementation Task Force, hold open meetings of his committee. The Fundamentalists who comprise the dictatorial oligarchy that rules the SBC will not yield to any such requests. They do not have to do so—they are accountable only to themselves.

For various reasons, some editors have declined to put into print that lies are lies, that Christian principles have been repetitively violated and that evil is evil. Failure to do so, however, does not alter the fact that unopposed evil follows its malignant course to become absolute totalitarianism; in turn, tyranny reigns until families fail, until business organizations are destroyed, until nations fall. The Southern Baptist Convention is not immune to the ultimate ravages of despotism. Of course, the editors of the state papers are unable to function as a "truth committee," but can Fundamentalists who continue committing wrongful acts avoid public examination forever?

Pensions or Denominational Uprightness

Possibly, some pastors may have had their eyes on their pensions rather than on denominational uprightness. If so, they are probably unaware that if anyone tinkered with their pensions, those who violated the sanctity of their savings face incarceration in a federal penitentiary. Therefore, it is not necessary to compromise the integrity of a pulpit by accommodating Fundamentalism for the safety of one's pension.

Biblical Basis of
Fundamentalist Error

In order to understand the reasons Fundamentalists seek to discredit *mainstream* Baptists' Bible beliefs, one might consider the following:

- **Jesus chose not to be the ruler of nations.**

  Fundamentalists desire to rule churches, the Southern Baptist Convention and the nation.

- **Jesus chose to be the servant of mankind.**

  Fundamentalists vie among themselves and in contest with others over who is to be recognized as the greatest.

- **Jesus advocated and practiced love to fulfill the two great commandments.**

  Instead of leading the less sophisticated Fundamentalist preachers to love those who are different from themselves, SBC leaders employ hate to induce harm against those who will not bow to Fundamentalist domination.

- **Jesus reflected humility in His walk with men.**

  Fundamentalists' practices reflect the inordinate arrogance and pride in the power of rulership.

183

- *Jesus' custom was to reflect compassion.*

  Fundamentalists demand conformity and practice coercion to enforce the silence of those who disagree and thus compel submission to their rule.

- *In dealing with all persons, Jesus sought to elevate.*

  Fundamentalists are committed to denigrate to achieve control over persons who come under their purview.

- *Jesus referred to God's Word and led followers to understand it.*

  Fundamentalists interpret God's Word with finality, with an eye cocked toward harmful propaganda and political conquest.

- *Jesus used His strongest words to deal with the Pharisees' false teachings .*

  Fundamentalists' harsh words and hate are directed against all who will not submit to their rule.

- *Jesus was patient even with Thomas. The Lord granted an opportunity for Thomas to "see for himself" without being subjected to harsh treatment.*

  The spirit of Fundamentalism demands conformity. Should one not acquiesce to such demands, Fundamentalism eagerly seeks to impose worldly penalties against the "offenders."

- *About sinfulness (Paul wrote to the Ephesians 4:19-25) " . . . Assuming that you have heard about Him and were taught in Him, there is the truth as in Jesus. Put off your old nature . . . and be renewed in the spirit of your minds . . . then put on a new nature . . . therefore, putting away falsehood, let everyone speak the truth with his neighbor, for we are members one of another.*

  Prior to 1979, Southern Baptists' Christian code of moral conduct had been forged on the anvil of God's admonitions to His people. Since 1979 Southern Baptists' value systems have been tarnished and tattered by the spirit of Fundamentalism. It is both the opportunity and responsibility of *mainstream* Baptists to seek to re-earn the respect of a lost world so that the lost will listen to the gospel of Christ. We must seek to re-earn the credibility that has been largely forfeited by the *official* SBC leadership.

Smoke Screen

Dr. Richard Land wrote in 1993 that the challenge of Southern Baptist institutional leadership for the remainder of this decade will be to find ways to build bridges of cooperation between Fundamentalists (who are not mean-spirited) and Baptists who believe the Bible but also believe that the Fundamentalist course of correction in Southern Baptist life has gone too far.

Dr. Land's statement gives rise to certain questions, the honest answers to which could disclose the Oligarchy's worldly political goals. In turn, those disclosures could indicate the possible ultimate fate of the SBC. Some of the questions are:

- Within the Oligarchy, who are the mean-spirited leaders mentioned by Dr. Land and who are not?
- Was it not mean-spirited Fundamentalists who were shocked by Dr. Jim Henry's 1994 election as president of the SBC?
- Which among the Oligarchy of Eighty supremacists vowed to never again allow more than one man to be nominated for election as SBC president?
- How would another be nominated without encountering the Oligarchy's most severe retribution against any and all who would dare oppose their will?
- Who but those in control of the Oligarchy made decisions by which some of the radical and mean-spirited Fundamentalists serve as trustees, even heads of SBC institutions?
- Have any of the less mean-spirited Fundamentalists openly opposed those appointments?
- Has Dr. Land opposed them? If not, why not?
- Will the SBC largely be destroyed by the infighting of Fundamentalist Inerrantists?

Each little sect of Fundamentalists—from the most mean-spirited to those trapped in the ideological movements' evil enclave—imputes the highest priority of their lives to the control of others, even other Fundamentalists. Each small

185

sect of Fundamentalist Inerrantists holds its views of Inerrancy to be superior to those of other Fundamentalists.

Each small sect of Fundamentalists holds to its own power-hungry party line.

Fundamentalism and peace cannot coexist anywhere on earth, nor can Christian love prevail in Baptist life unless and until Jesus is restored as the head of God's Kingdom.

Alternatives to Total Ruin

The most ardent followers of the radical supremacists number no more than 10 percent of all Southern Baptists. The remaining 90 percent, some 14.5 million, are powerless to restore a modicum of civility in Baptist life or the practices of Christian love and honest voting.

The only human means by which voting could restore honesty and decency in the SBC would result in the renewal of expenditures that amount to millions of dollars to transport to the SBC annual meetings sufficient numbers of messengers to elect non-Fundamentalist officers. By then, the Southern Baptist Convention would be in total ruin.

Alternatives to the erroneous renewal of that evil conflict are clearly defined in Chapter Fourteen, *Clear-cut Choices*.

Dr. Jim Henry's Concerns
Regarding Broken Trust

Prior to his 1994 election as president of the Southern Baptist Convention, Dr. Jim Henry stated in an interview published in the May 14, 1994, issue of the *Florida Baptist Witness* that during the last fourteen or fifteen years, some people have "labeled" other people and this has led to misunderstandings and distrust.

As a result, he said, many have been pushed aside or ignored. Dr. Henry enunciated as a presidential principle to be "untiring in our efforts to build trust and love in our family of faith."

He further stated:

Really, when you talk and listen and get to hearing each other, you find you're on the same page. Let's see if we

186

cannot do some healing and some talking and focus on our main business, on what God's program is through Southern Baptists. That's the feeling I'm getting.

As to the future, Dr. Henry said he saw the Southern Baptist Convention on the verge of either a slow disintegration or on the edge of a fresh, bold, new reach into the future. He added, while describing the SBC as the strongest denomination in the country:

> I think God has used us. . . . The talent and resources in our laypeople and in our institutions are unbelievable. If it can be recaptured, I think the SBC will live. If not, then I think we will die a slow death.

I believe the spirit of Fundamentalism will allow the SBC to survive only as the vehicle to infect all of America with its totalitarian-fostered ideology.

I have met Dr. Henry only once, and he would have no particular reason to recall the occasion. We exchanged correspondence when I called to his attention that one of the good and godly leaders of our denomination was the ongoing victim of Fundamentalist untruths and slander.

The man who was wronged is a gentleman in every sense of the word. He is an outstanding Baptist pastor who most likely has baptized a greater number of lost souls than any other living Baptist.

Yet, his reputation was ruthlessly savaged because of his opposition to the spirit of Fundamentalism.

Some Fundamentalist supporters even sought to disrupt the church of which he was pastor.

It seems appropriate at this point to repeat what James Draper wrote:

> In the name of the Lord they will launch vehement attacks on individuals and churches. In the name of the Lord they attempt to assassinate the character of those whom they oppose. They direct their attack most often on other Christian leaders with whom they find disagreement.

Era of Dr. Henry's Influence Ended

The Patterson/Pressler elitist faction of Fundamentalism was adamantly opposed to the 1994 election of Dr. Henry to serve as the SBC president. The fanatical followers of this faction exerted typical Fundamentalist measures to prohibit his election. Indeed, formal arrangements had been made to hold a lavish "victory" reception to honor Fred Wolfe, their own nominee. Dr. Henry's election thwarted that plan, and as far as I know, it is the only Patterson/Pressler political scheme that has not been successful.

Dr. Henry seems to be in a terribly awkward position. If he publicly named the participants in the secret 1978 Atlanta meeting and identified the evil that has been imposed upon Baptist life, or even suggested repentance, confession and restitution, he would quite likely become subject to the fury of Fundamentalism. He could be called a "liberal" and otherwise slandered. Fundamentalist zealots could even be sent to join the church of which he is pastor in order to stir up trouble within the congregation.

Fundamentalist Propaganda Finally Laid Bare

On June 20, 1995, the *Associated Baptist Press* reported that Dr. Jim Henry, recognizing that mutual trust has been shattered in the Southern Baptist Convention, suggested that the "perils" facing the SBC were:

- Diversions and inertia,
- Tendency to "depend on Caesar to christianize our earthly colony,"
- Dedication to narrowness, and
- Tendency to be "biblically correct" but reflect a spirit that is not of our Lord Jesus Christ.

Integrity Sacrificed on the Altar of Fundamentalist Ambition

In his presidential address at the June 1996 SBC annual meeting, Henry stated, according to the June 16, 1996 *Fort Worth Star Telegram;*

Conservatives [Fundamentalists] have gone beyond the "battle for the Bible" and are still blatantly focusing on power. They want the high positions in denominational life and now have them. . . . Principles and integrity can be sacrificed on the altar of accommodation and blind loyalty to a temporal kingdom under the mask of continuing the conservative resurgence.

Jim Henry knows full well that power-mad politics has nothing to do with saving souls!

"Fresh Air" Silenced

Dr. Henry's two years of leadership were not allowed to provide hope for the future of the Southern Baptist Convention. With the unopposed election of the Oligarchy's hand-picked man, Tom Elliff, the Patterson/Pressler faction is back in control. Those who backed Dr. Henry's bringing "fresh air" to the denomination have been silenced. **One wonders if an appointment in 1997 will indicate the means by which the silence was accomplished.**

Violated Trust

Men and women who understand God's Word recognize that trust cannot be restored in the SBC until perpetrators of unchristian conduct, as well as their supporters, are led to repent publicly of all their wrongdoings. Realism suggests that repentance will not be heard.

The malignancy produced by *broken trust* has spread throughout our denominational body and has infected almost everything we do as Baptists. Quite likely, this will be evidenced in the latter of Dr. Henry's following predictions:

> The talent and resources in our laypeople and in our institutions are unbelievable. If it can be recaptured, I think the SBC will live. If not, then I think we will die a slow death.

Edmund Burke must have understood the Fundamentalist mindset. The following was attributed to him.

> **The only thing necessary for the triumph of evil is for good men to do nothing.**

The honest men and women who served as trustees of SBC institutions and held other offices in 1979 wanted the convention to be for all Baptists. Their hearts were right. But they

189

had not learned at that time about the spirit of Fundamental-ism.

You can be certain that those good and godly men and women who had served fellow Southern Baptists so well for so long now realize the only way to get on with the credible work and wit-ness of the Baptist family is to separate themselves from Fun-damentalists. The first step in this "separation" is for the good and godly men and women to work more zealously than ever before with like-minded Baptists in ministries of mercy and in missions and to devote their tithes and offerings to these pur-poses. This would be in lieu of forwarding their tithes and of-ferings to Nashville.

In another 150 years, possibly the surviving Baptists of that day will step forward and declare that the intentional sowing of the seeds of hate and distrust in the SBC was "a deplorable sin," even as in 1995 Southern Baptists finally addressed sla-very, which had been embraced 150 years earlier by their fore-bears, as having been grievously wrong. But was that Funda-mentalist declaration more than politically motivated?

When the Work of Fundamentalism Has Absolutely Nothing To Do
With the Witness and Work of the Gospel of Christ

I have wondered how honorable men, upon finally recogniz-ing that Fundamentalism's grasp is for ever greater worldly powers, can be at peace regarding the *official* SBC leadership. When will they finally recognize that such powers are devoted to the politico-ideological pursuits that have nothing whatso-ever to do with the Gospel of Christ.

I do not know of the ultimate price, if any, to be paid by Dr. Jim Henry for having spoken so forthrightly in his June 1996 presentation as SBC President. His courage is admired and appreciated.

Some of the SBC leaders seemingly have lost their biblically moral directions. They are not individual crackpots such as J. Frank Norris, but regardless, their chasing after worldly power to obtain secular political prowess can only harm the cause of Christ.

No doubt there are thousands of men who are made uncomfortable by their association with the evil directions that the Fundamentalist "cause" has taken. What do they think? What is to happen to them? Is spiritual schizophrenia contagious? Is it addictive? I do not know. But I wonder about it.

The Most Important Question

The most important question that *mainstream* Baptists continue to face is whether Christian principles will be restored as the hallmark of authentic Baptist life. If not, Christendom in America also will be diminished.

Conversely, will a rapidly growing number of valiant *mainstream* Baptists pay the price required to perpetuate Baptists' longheld principles? Will they continue to live by the teachings and examples of Christ? *Will they pay the full price to restore integrity in Baptist life.*

Mainstream Baptists who remain true to the teachings of the Savior will not attempt to repay evil for evil. They will strive to do what is right in the sight of God and what our fellow Americans expect of genuine Christians.

If it is possible *mainstream* Baptists will attempt to live in peace with everyone. They will remain confident in hope, patient in affliction and faithful in prayer. They will not attempt to take revenge but leave room for God's wrath for, "It is mine to avenge; I will repay," says the Lord.

Mainstream Baptists will pray for Fundamentalists, yes, even as they are.

11

The Body of Christ
The Model for Mainstream Baptist Churches

✳✳✳✳✳✳✳

In all things, be of good report—

> "Now you are the body of Christ and individually members of it. And God has appointed in the church first apostles, second prophets, third teachers, then workers of miracles, then healers, helpers, administrators, speakers in various kinds of tongues. Are all apostles? Are all prophets? Are all teachers? Do all work miracles? Do all possess gifts of healing? Do all speak with tongues? Do all interpret? But earnestly desire the higher gifts.
>
> "And I will show you a more excellent way."

The Body of Christ
The Model for Mainstream Baptist Churches

The word "church" evokes various images in the minds of peoples around the world. Some relate it to a particular faith, such as Christianity, or identify it with a specific sect, cult or religious group. Others equate "church" with ecclesiastical authority or simply as a building designed for worship.

Straight Talk About Southern Baptist Churches

There are more than 16,000 religious groups and denominations in the world for which the word "church" has a specific meaning. Baptists define church as "a body of baptized believers who gather together to worship and then scatter to serve Christ."

When the word "church" is used in our discussion, the designation is not to churches in general or to all "Baptist" churches. Rather, the reference is to congregations of *mainstream* Baptists who are fully committed to Christ and have a desire for their churches to become the mirror images of His life and work.

The Early Church, the Body of Christ

God's mission for the church—the body of Christ—has not changed. Jesus was the model for the early-day Christians and their churches. He also is the model for Mainstream Baptist churches whose members seek to serve as extensions of His life and ministry. They proclaim the Gospel in response to His command to make disciples of all nations to the end of time.

Until 1979, most Southern Baptist churches typified our current day *mainstream* Baptist churches. They were actively striving to fulfill their Christian responsibilities according to His will. They enjoyed fellowship and sharing in cooperative endeavors with like-minded believers. Jesus alone was their model of conduct.

Since 1979, however, it is apparent that the purposes of some Southern Baptist churches which are under Fundamentalist rulers have changed. Although they maintain denominational ties and Christian connections, the "modus operandi" of some Fundamentalist churches is more oriented toward obtaining worldly powers and secular political objectives.

But the question remains: Who will restore Christian integrity in Baptist life?

Of Course, Christ is the Head of Our Church, It's In the Bible

Since it is in the Bible that Christ is the head of the church, we need not question who is in charge of the Baptist congregations in which we worship, study, work and teach. Our churches *are* extensions of the *body of Christ*. He is the ruler of the church and has demonstrated to us His examples of servanthood.

The apostle Paul, in his epistle to the Colossians, stated this about Christ:

And He is before all things, and by Him all things consist. And He is the head of the body, the church: who is the beginning, the firstborn from the dead; that in all things He might have the preeminence. (Colossians 1:17-18 KJV)

Paul said further in his letter to the Ephesians, "And He gave some, apostles; and some, prophets; and some, evangelists; and some, pastors and teachers." The next verse says, "for the perfecting of the saints, for the work of the ministry, for the edifying of the body of Christ; until we all come in the unity of the faith, and of the knowledge of the Son of God, unto a perfect man, unto the measure of the stature of the fullness of Christ."

Paul continues, "That we henceforth be no more children, tossed to and fro, and carried about with every wind of doctrine, by the sleight of men, and cunning craftiness, by which they lie in wait to deceive."

He then admonishes, "But speaking the truth in love, may grow up into Him in all things, who is the head, even Christ." (Ephesians 4:11-15 KJV)

Southern Baptists, except Fundamentalist rulers, have the opportunity to insist that Christ be the unquestioned head of their churches. It seems likely, however, that Fundamentalists who have devoted much of their lives (and possibly have seared their souls to seize control of the SBC), will continue to fight even more fiercely to gain ever more power over all churches, associations and state conventions.

Mainstream Baptists
What Are Their Expectations?
What Are Their Responsibilities?

Are we truly committed to look upon Jesus as our role model for daily living? Or, are we willing to allow ourselves to be absorbed into Fundamentalism? Answers to these questions will disclose who we actually are and, to whom we belong!

God-Given Assurances Held Dear by Laypeople

Some of the experiences that have been wonderfully right in the lives of the "people of the pews" are:

- Certainty of salvation
- Power of prayer
- Availability of guidance
- Enrichment brought by godly pastors and by self-study of the Bible
- Fellowship
- The thrill of missions and service in ministries.

Characteristics that Laypeople Expect of Leaders

The characteristics that laypeople expect of leaders are:

- Truthfulness
- Maintaining a focus on that which is right in the sight of God
- Reasoned teaching
- By example, inspiring members of the congregation to be more Christlike, to exemplify servanthood in ministries.

Things that are Most Important to Laypeople

The matters that are the most important to laypeople—for which we are willing to "pay the price" for preservation are:

- Well-being of family members
- Autonomy of our Baptist congregations
- Seeking to conduct ourselves in a manner to honor Christ
- The religious freedom that can be maintained only in a democratic nation.

Our Responsibilities as Laypeople

Our children, grandchildren and even generations yet to follow can fulfill their potential *only* if our churches remain strong by seeking, discovering and carrying out His will. However, the trust and fellowship that formerly permeated what we attempted to do for the glory of God have been destroyed.

No longer do all Southern Baptists fellowship, minister, witness and work together harmoniously in God's kingdom. We are in conflict with one another in area associations, in state conventions and in the national organization.

> *No doubt the ongoing political infighting grieves our Lord. While we squabble with each other, approximately 50,000 people die each day in areas of the world in which the Gospel has not yet been heard.*

The leaders of some churches have apparently permitted their primary witness to Christ's love to be supplanted by the avarice of worldly power. In these churches, commitments to missions and ministries, seemingly, have been largely put aside. In their place, political schemes designed to gain the power to intimidate members of other Baptist churches and to dominate denominational organizations have been put on fast forward.

Why would men, knowing that Christ modeled a life of servanthood for each of us, seek ever greater personal acclaim and worldly power? Defying Christ's commandments can only lead to destruction of individual lives as well as that of a denomination which once was the most rapidly growing in the history of Christendom.

God's desire is for His love to be known throughout the world. If some who are called Christians fail His test of faithfulness, their responsibilities must be shouldered by others who *live to love*, even as Christ loved. Therefore, *mainstream* Baptists who desire to be faithful servants of Christ must take up the slack; there are so few to seek the many who are lost and there is so little time to reach them.

Denominational Relations Committees

There seem to be rather simple solutions for Baptists who cherish the autonomy of their churches. If a congregation, by freedom of conscience, determines not to follow in the footsteps of Fundamentalism, is there reason not to pursue every other conceivable means to work and witness to the cause of Christ? What would be the process?

When a pastor or church members feel careful study should be made of the cooperative relationships that exist between one's church and the local association, state convention and national convention, what are some of the best ways that this can be accomplished?

Many *mainstream* Baptist churches have benefitted from having a Denominational Relations Committee.

If a church does not already have such a committee, the formation of one would be helpful in the study and evaluation process as members of this committee

1) inform the congregation about important developments within the denomination;

2) suggest forums for discussion of Baptist distinctives and history;

3) recommend actions to maintain responsibility and integrity of voluntary association with churches of like faith and order to further missionary, benevolent and education ministries; and

4) consider other matters related to the church's participation in area associations and state conventions.

What If We Sought To Establish a New Baptist Church?

If we, as a group of sincere Christians and authentic Baptists, were planning to plant a new church, no doubt we would search the Bible for encouragement and for His guidance. Among His wonderful words:

> Remember not the former things, neither consider the things of old. Behold I will do a new thing; now it shall spring forth; shall ye not know it? I will make a way in the wilderness and rivers in the desert. (Isaiah 43:18-19 RSV)

We would have memories of the past and visions of the future regarding Bible study, teaching, witnessing, preaching, worshipping, missions and ministries.

We would remember business meetings of the past and anticipate those yet to be held and our intent would be to conduct all of the church's affairs as if Jesus were physically present in our midst.

Start a New Church? Why Not Begin Anew, Seeking to Excel in the Church We Already Love?

The message in William Easum's *Dancing With Dinosaurs*, merits consideration:

> Our task is to discern between present traditional practices and our Christian heritage. We must rediscover and reclaim our spiritual heritage. The emerging new world of the 21st Century may be new to us, but it is not new to our spiritual ancestors. They developed a Christian community in the midst of a very similar hostile culture. If by God's grace, they could do it, so could we.

Dr. Albert Schweitzer's oft quoted statement is also appropriate to consider. He said, "The only ones among us who would be truly happy are those who have sought and found how to SERVE." Jesus Christ said, "He who will be first among you must be servant of you all." Why not make the clear-cut decision that our churches will become more of what Jesus would have them be?

Redemptive Spirit

Quite likely many more Baptists are aware of the seriousness of the Fundamentalist problem in the SBC than is indicated by the limited responses to the wrongful actions that have plagued the denomination for so long. It is apparent that some choose to ignore the distress that the spirit of Fundamentalism has created in churches and denominational organizations, even within the immediate families of Fundamentalists.

We deplore the spirit of Fundamentalism. But we continue to pray that those who have succumbed to its evil will begin anew the steps necessary to please God and to seek renewal of fellowship with fellow Baptists.

Preservation of History

It is said that those who preserve the great moral principles of history are as heroic as the ones who fought to establish those tenets that have so greatly benefitted mankind. Therefore, possibly this book should be dedicated to younger adult Baptists. It is for good reason I beseech them—the Generation Xers and those in their forties and fifties—to provide patient, thoughtful consideration to the matters being discussed.

The reason? It is they who, almost single-handedly, will determine if Christian principles and Baptist distinctives are to be honored and preserved in our denomination. It is they, also, who will have a significant impact on whether democracy survives in the United States.

Wonderful Women and Committed Churchmen Make The Difference

Throughout my lifetime I have benefited from observing truly outstanding Baptist women and men who have served the church as they would had the Lord been physically present among them. One such man was a dear friend and valued mentor to many Baptists. His life exemplified those who make a conscious effort to begin each day seeking to be more Christlike in their own ways. Pastors call such a man a "churchman."

He was Owen Cooper. He was one of my heroes, and I tell you about him because he was one of the most outstanding Baptist laymen whom I have known. He was exceptional because of his love for others. He was outstanding because of his incredibly effective use of God's gifts to win the lost. In fact, he knew more about how to win the lost than any other layman about whom I have heard.

Owen Cooper was the last layman to be elected as president of the Southern Baptist Convention. He served consecutive terms in 1973 and 1974. Why did I not tell you about that earlier? Being president of the SBC was no "big deal" to Owen. But it was important to apply everything that he knew to winning the lost; that commitment consumed his every thought. Owen died in 1986. In the preceding year, he and I conferred with Charles Stanley who was serving as president of the Southern Baptist Convention. Possibly our discussion with Dr. Stanley could have made a difference regarding the SBC conflict, but it did not.

Loving Our Pastors

I tell you about Owen Cooper because of his love for every pastor whom he met, especially the pastors who preached and otherwise provided spiritual leadership for members of Owen's beloved congregation—the First Baptist Church of Yazoo City, Mississippi. Drs. Harold Shirley and Jim Yates were the last two of his beloved pastors, serving the church respectively from 1956 to 1960 and from 1960 until almost 30 years later. Owen Cooper had a special love for both men, especially for his twenty-six years with Jim Yates.

Owen was blessed with having the inspiration of great ideas and the commitment and energy to carry them out. First, the church was led to give one-third of its budget to the church's ministry and missions endeavors. Would not it bless the Kingdom's work if many churches sought to do likewise? It did not stop there. Dr. Yates and Owen came up with the idea of a 30-10 missions program. After adoption by the church, the 30-10 missions program was put into practice, and the First Baptist Church of Yazoo City established thirty new churches in ten years as planned. Would not it be inspiring if other Baptist churches sought out more effective ways to strengthen and expand Christianity in America?

Missions at Home and Abroad

I know of no person who was more deeply and personally committed to missions throughout the world than was Owen Cooper. Allow me to share with you one of his favorite stories about the promises of God.

After working seven years in Burma without a convert, missionary Adoniram Judson was asked about the future. His response was, "The future is as bright as the promises of God."

Subsequently, in a Baptist World Alliance meeting, a representative of Burma was heard to say, "The Baptist work in Burma is growing very rapidly. Three years ago, we baptized six thousand persons in one day—twice the number at Pentecost." Only five countries in the world now have more Baptists than Burma!

About "Doing Enough"

Among many other things, Owen Cooper taught me much

about ministry and missions. By his example, I was led to learn that life is increasingly joyful in relation to ever greater participation in ministry and mission efforts of the church. He taught me that when we thought we were "doing enough," we were limiting our own happiness. He taught me that "enough" is all that we have.

With Regard to Judgmentalism

Some of our fellow laypeople have simplistically taken the words of Jesus, "Do not judge, or you will be judged . . ." as recorded in Matthew 7:1 to mean that we should never exercise our discernment about others. That interpretation is contrary to the Scriptures that call upon us to be wise and to make the best of decisions.

In many ways, we make judgments every day. Weighing evidence mandates making decisions. Such decisions provide the basis of our judicial system. We decide whom we shall marry. We exercise judgment about the work that we are to do, how we are to spend our money, etc.

It is we, and we alone, who must defend the claim of freedom under Christ. It is we, and we alone, who must exercise the courage to hold fast to that freedom of conscience. Failure to make that specific decision and stand strongly to defend it will mean that ever more individuals and churches will be drawn into the Fundamentalist orbit.

The spiritual gift of discernment that pulsates in our hearts and courses through our minds is augmented by the prayerful seeking of His will to be enacted in our lives.

The subjects presented in Chapter Fourteen, *Clear-Cut Choices*, merit the best use of the gift of discernment which has been granted for our guidance. Always hanging in the balance are the vital matters of conscience, freedom and credible Christian witness.

Each of these significantly critical matters awaits our decisions. Indeed, every Baptist man and woman will make those decisions *as inspired by the Holy Spirit* to do that which is eternally right, *or by default,* choose ignominy until death.

Pulpit Search Committees
at Risk

Imagine the surprise of the church's pulpit search committee chairperson upon receiving an unexpected phone call from a highly prominent Fundamentalist preacher of a large Southern Baptist church.

First, it is well to recall that Paul Pressler stated he wanted a Fundamentalist placed in every Southern Baptist church. It is quite likely some Fundamentalists changed their church membership for that purpose.

Experiences of the past seventeen years indicate a considerable number of Baptist laypeople have been misled to support the Fundamentalist infiltration in all segments of Baptist life. And a greater number have been coerced to remain silent concerning the evil that has emerged during the unwarranted controversy.

The Unbelievable "Conning" of the Committee

Usually, the conversation is such as this, "I am Dr. ____, pastor of the ____ church, and I am phoning to share with you a vision that I experienced last night."

The prominent Fundamentalist preacher, having been prompted by a confederate, continues the hypothetical conversation, "I don't remember having met you and you might not have ever heard of me. But, as I said, I want to tell you about the vision that I had. Even though I have never been in your church—in fact, I have never been in your town—I felt that I was standing near the center of your church admiring the beautiful round stained-glass window high above the choir loft, and my emotions were particularly stirred when I saw the baptistry."

"While standing there, a voice came to me that said 'John Doe' would make an ideal pastor for your church. I'm not absolutely certain as to what the vision means but I wanted to share it with you."

Within a few days, the chairperson of the pulpit search committee receives a phone call from another person who also recommends the committee consider the name of "John Doe" to become pastor of the church. Of course, the name is the same as the one mentioned by the prominent Fundamentalist preacher.

Dr. W. A. Criswell Stated that "Preachers Should be Rulers of Churches."

The "John Doe" pastor who has been recommended to the pulpit search committee then receives a phone call from the prominent Fundamentalist preacher who "had the vision." The message is short and simple, "Tell the pulpit committee what they want to hear—and when you have been pastor of the church for a few months, you can become its ruler."

A Different Approach, but Still a Ploy

One can understand the reason that the following ploy is equally useful to Fundamentalists:

Another prominent Fundamentalist preacher, one of the several who are involved in such practices, is made aware of the church that is without a pastor. He calls the pulpit committee chairperson and says, "I was praying about your church last night and the Lord told me that you should have 'Dr. John Doe' as your pastor."

After that, the prominent preacher continues the conversation, making certain that the chairperson of the pastor search committee is aware the caller had formerly served as president of the Southern Baptist Convention or in another highly visible denominational office.

The Payoff—A Church's Misadventure with Fundamentalism

Many unsuspecting congregations have fallen prey to such pulpit committee scams. In some cases, it seems impossible to free themselves from a Fundamentalist interloper. Even so, some congregations have found it necessary to agree to a distasteful financial arrangement to divest themselves of a Fundamentalist preacher.

But, always, the preacher takes some of the church's members, and, of course, some of its money, and some of its heart and soul when he leaves.

Wise Words from Dr. R. G. Puckett

Dr. Puckett, editor of the North Carolina state paper, *The Biblical Recorder*, prepared a series of four articles entitled "Pas tor Search Committee's Role Indispensable." Dr. Puckett has generously offered to forward copies of the four articles to any person who requests them. His address is: Dr. R. G. Puckett, Editor, *The Biblical Recorder*, P. O. Box 265468, Raleigh, N.C. 27611.

Petty Potentates in the Making: The Lure

Fundamentalist preachers perceive themselves to be Chief Executive Officers of Baptist congregations. Church committees are a nuisance to the career of a Fundamentalist preacher. A finance committee not controlled by the preacher is anathema to him.

An "exciting church" gradually yields great power to a Fundamentalist preacher. Money is a necessity. It brings outstanding entertainers and public figures to speak to the congregation. Entertainment brings those who have never set foot in the church before. Big numbers that yield more money and power go hand in hand.

In Fundamentalist seminaries, the young men who heard God's call to preach the gospel, if not yet Fundamentalists, receive particular attention. Leaders persuade the younger men that they are destined to become rulers of churches. All that is required is to "tell the pulpit" search committees what they want to hear and then, in due course, take control of the congregation.

Taking the Bait

The bedazzled young pastors take the bait. They learn how to become rulers of churches. They begin climbing the ladder of power. They have been taught by Fundamentalist masters. In exchange, they are committed to the political "cause" of the extremists. In most cases, and for quite a time, the younger pastors are unaware of the depth of their commitments to the fanatical worldly objectives to be gained.

No doubt the younger pastors who have been corrupted had genuine early day encounters with God, praying while walking across a starlit campus or on another equally memorable occasion. But, by succumbing to the temptations of pride, power and personal aggrandizement, their spiritual gifts have been perverted, then yielded, to the gods of fanaticism and worldly power.

A Man in Every Church, A Man in Each Association

According to the September 24, 1980, issue of the *Virginia Religious Herald*, Paul Pressler's strategy to seize control of the Southern Baptist Convention was for "an organized chain of communications, including someone in each association and a layman in each church." If a Fundamentalist supporter could not be identified in every Baptist church, no doubt one would be expected to join that church. As is evident, Fundamentalists strategically positioned in churches and associations have performed their tasks with signal effectiveness.

A Baptist Leader's Comments: "Those Who Run for Cover."

"With regard to my making recommendations to pulpit committees, I am not comfortable with pastors who have not committed themselves to the most serious struggle that has occurred in Southern Baptist life."

Another Baptist whom I respect, a gentleman who understands the two positions in the SBC controversy, made a statement that I found to be quite interesting. In effect, he said, "No issue greater than the SBC controversy has arisen that is more related to our understanding of ourselves as a denomination. There are many major and critical issues that affect our witness as Christians, but the controversy is the most telling of all."

He continued, "I have far greater respect for the men who have taken a positive position—whether Fundamentalist or moderate—than for those who seemingly have decided to run for cover. Apparently, neither the ethical nor moral content of the controversy is of concern to such men. Surely, the conflict's potential impact on Baptist work and witness merits one's participation in the most substantive matter to surface since formation of the Southern Baptist Convention in 1845."

12

Our Tithes and Offerings
Resolution of the "Baptist Mess"

****

In all things, be of good report—

"Furthermore, it is a fact of history that when a mass movement begins to attract and reward people who are primarily ambitious in their personal careers, it has passed its most viable stages and is committed to preserving the power of the present.

"Hoffer has said that, 'It ceases to be a movement and becomes an enterprise' . . . . The more posts and offices a movement has to hand out, the more inferior stuff it will attract, and in the end these political hangers-on overwhelm a successful movement in such numbers that the honest fight of former days no longer recognizes the old movement . . . when this happens, the mission of such a movement is done for."

Our Tithes and Offerings
Resolution of the "Baptist Mess"

In Matthew 6:19-21, the Lord admonished His followers not to be unduly anxious regarding money matters. He told them not to have anxiety about their lives, about what to eat or about what to wear "for life is more than food, and the body more than clothing."

Repetitive Comments Regarding Our Tithes and Offerings

Throughout this book we search our hearts and minds to define the trustworthy enterprises that will make Christ-honoring use of our tithes and offerings.

The purpose for mentioning tithes and offerings in several different places in this book is to encourage *mainstream* Baptists:

1) to provide generous financial undergirding for their own churches' work and witness, and

2) to engage in and otherwise support other Christian ministries and Baptist missions with like-minded and trustworthy believers.

Godly Investment of Tithes and Offerings

Many *mainstream* Baptists are committed to the belief that all wealth belongs to God. Further, those who belong to Him are responsible for their lifetime use of the possessions of which they are stewards. Therefore, seemingly, they should be vitally interested in being fully informed about the Christian enterprises in which their tithes and offerings are to be invested. Our tithes can support the work and witness that we believe are looked upon with favor by God, or they may be used to accomplish no more than to pay for the political avarice of self-centered men.

Without Knowing It, Baptist Laypeople Paid Some of the Costs Incurred in the Seizure of The Denomination

As is evident, the SBC is under the control of men imbued

with the spirit of Fundamentalism. Only a "handful" of such "Baptists" voted to hand the Convention over to Fundamentalism.

> Typically, because of the Southern Baptist Convention's structure, no more than approximately one tenth of 1 percent of all Southern Baptists *can* vote on SBC matters.

A great majority of Fundamentalists have their expenses to attend the SBC annual meetings paid by churches, SBC seminaries, the Foreign Mission Board, the Sunday School Board, the Home Mission Board or other SBC agencies.

Seemingly, the rank and file—the 90 percent majority of Southern Baptists who pay their own expenses to attend the SBC annual meetings can do no more than read about Fundamentalism's ongoing stranglehold of their convention and misuse of some of its assets.

Please consider this paper trail of laypeople's tithes and offerings:

• First, their tithes and offerings are given to their churches,

• A specific amount is then sent to state conventions,

• The state conventions, in turn, forward millions of dollars annually to the SBC Executive Committee in Nashville,

• The SBC Executive Committee, at its discretion, allocates those vast sums of money to the SBC boards, institutions and agencies.

• Finally, the trustees of *each* SBC board, institution and agency are empowered to pay their own and others' expenses to attend the SBC annual meetings as well as the expenses required to attend their own board, institution or agency meetings, or to make other use of the money!

• All, then, are free to vote to extend Fundamentalism's grasp and misuse of worldly powers at the laypeople's expense.

Laypeople should remember one particular misuse of their tithes and offerings: Fundamentalist "spinmasters" are handsomely paid by the people's tithes and offerings to "manage" all of the SBC's "public relations" and to cast Fundamentalism's evils in a favorable light at a total annual cost of millions of dollars.

The rank and file of Southern Baptist people are not yet up in arms against Fundamentalists. The people simply do not know how to rectify Fundamentalism's wrongful deeds.

The Only Way?

Laypeople want Christian integrity restored in the SBC. When they realize that something is terribly wrong in their convention, they will insist that only godly use be made of their tithes and offerings. However, Fundamentalism's fanatical Oligarchy of Eighty has shown no inclination on its own to surrender its worldly power, the pursuit of which brought dishonesty and dishonor to the denomination.

Since the traditional Southern Baptist witness and work will not return until the fanatical Fundamentalists' grip on the Southern Baptist Convention is broken, I believe the way for *mainstream* Baptists to start righting the Fundamentalist wrongs is for them to stop sending their tithes and offerings to Nashville.

The Cooperative Program

The Cooperative Program is an exceptionally politicized and emotionally charged topic of conversation in the Southern Baptist Convention. Inasmuch as it is increasingly controversial, the Cooperative Program *must* be discussed.

Pulling Together

A remarkable book that provides unique insights about Baptist missionary work in the past three centuries is entitled *Pulling Together!* It is co-authored by Dr. Daniel G. Vestal, Jr., pastor of Tallowood Baptist Church in Houston, and Dr. Robert A. Baker, the late Baptist historian who taught church history at Southwestern Baptist Theological Seminary for many years.

This highly informative volume provides historical information about missions and missions support. It also serves as a practical guide to the Cooperative Program that Southern Baptists created in 1925 as they sought ways to fund mission enterprises more efficiently and effectively. The introduction, written by Dr. William M. Pinson, Jr., the respected Executive Director of the Baptist General Convention of Texas, also is most inspiring and encouraging.

Whom Do We Serve?

Since the following comments obviously are critical of the Fundamentalist politico-religious movement, I preface them with the statement that Fundamentalists have the right to think, speak and act as they wish. That is their business. However, it is the laypeople's business to understand and act on matters that can have a major adverse impact on Baptists' opportunities and responsibilities to share with a lost world the good news about Jesus Christ.

After observing Baptist life for many years and studying Baptist history to some extent, it is fully apparent to me that something is quite different about the controversy that has marred Southern Baptist work since June 1979. Baptists' disagreements in the past have usually arisen over "what to do and how to do" church ministries, evangelism and missions.

As I perceive it, the controversy that continues to wreak carnage on Baptist life today is not merely about *how mainstream Baptists are to work together.* It is about *to whom we belong and how we shall serve Christ.* It is about whether we shall capitulate to Fundamentalism's pressures. It is about the grave risk, at the least, of being partially responsible should we be associated in any way with the grievous damage that can be caused to Christendom and to the nation by Fundamentalism's politico-ideological movement.

Many believe that genuine and ongoing commitments to the one true God, instead of to the gods of worldly power, would have precluded the current controversy among Southern Baptists.

Cooperative Program to Southern Baptists—
Money and Mind Control Program to Fundamentalists

The controversy, including managed machinations of the Cooperative Program, is closely related to men who would presume to usurp the power of God. Please recall the 400-man

Fundamentalist luncheon in 1979 and the two presidential candidates *approved* by Patterson and Pressler as discussed in Chapter Four.

If you believe, as do I, that the controversy would not exist had Jesus been physically present among us in 1979, then you might want to ask this question: "Do the attitudes evidenced to gain personal ambitions and the use of worldly powers to seize control over the SBC reflect the expectations that Jesus has for His followers?"

Two other questions of interest: "Was the seizure of the SBC an act of Christians?" "Was the commandeering of the denomination for the glory of God or for the personal aggrandizement of power-hungry Fundamentalist men?"

Survival of the Cooperative Program

The possibility of restoring cooperative relationships among Southern Baptists, in light of human experience, is remote. Working together requires mutual trust, love and respect. These virtues have been destroyed. Reality suggests the rekindling of these precious ingredients, upon which treasured relationships are built, must await the passing of several generations of Baptists.

Reshaping of the Cooperative Program is inevitable. Sooner or later, the Baptist laypeople will recognize they have subsidized the plans to strip state conventions and local churches of their autonomy. The most effective way for *mainstream* Baptist laypeople to protect their churches and state conventions is to stop forwarding their tithes and offerings to Nashville.

Some Fundamentalist leaders anticipate giving through the Cooperative Program to decline. They know that as Baptists become increasingly aware of Fundamentalists' intent to seize control of all state conventions, the Cooperative Program could experience a reduction of some $50-$200 million in annual giving. Even this would not be catastrophic to Fundamentalism's worldly-power ambitions. However, if state conventions maintain their autonomy, this could thwart the achievement of Fundamentalists' national political goals.

There are many Fundamentalists who have demonstrated themselves to be untrustworthy, belligerent and mean-spirited.

Even so, some also are remarkably gifted; they possess piercing intellects and mesmerizing personalities.

Most Fundamentalists count on the naive and gullible—but honest *mainstream* Baptists to continue funding the Convention's politico-religious ideology through their gifts to the Cooperative Program.

Individual Rights and Responsibilities Related to Our Offerings

Baptists who have not surrendered control of their minds to Fundamentalism can exercise the right and responsibility to seek the Holy Spirit's guidance regarding the amount of their own tithes and offerings to be designated for specific missions enterprises.

Therefore, I believe churches should accept and use such designated gifts as made by its members. If a church declines to do so, then that church is attempting to exercise an inappropriate control over the Holy Spirit's guidance of individual members in the matter.

Were I a member of a church that had not yet voted to accept and forward gifts as designated by its members, I would still support the church's operating budget, but I would continue to request the right to designate my missions offerings. However, should that request be unduly denied, I would send my missions offerings directly to the ministry and mission enterprises of my choice.

In the event the state convention would not accept and forward gifts as designated by my church, I would vote to send those designated gifts directly to the organizations for which they were intended.

The congregation of which I am a part does not attempt to control the minds of its members. Quite simply, each member designates his/her missions gifts, for the Southern Baptist Convention, for the Cooperative Baptist Fellowship or for other entities. The missions gifts of members who have not chosen a plan of designation are sent either to the SBC or the CBF in the precise percentage of total missions gifts forwarded to those entities.

Choosing the entity to receive designated offerings is made

convenient for the church's members. The offering envelopes are printed with CBF, SBC and "Other" designations, any of which can be easily selected.

Transcriptions of the earlier year discussions that preceded the church's vote to honor its members' rights to designate their missions offerings may be obtained by writing to Tallowood Baptist Church, 555 Tallowood, Houston, Texas 77024.

It goes without saying that Fundamentalist rulers of churches will continue their attempt to deny members' rights to designate missions gifts.

Taxation Without Representation

Obviously "taxation without representation" already prevails in the denomination. In many cases, the tithes and offerings of *mainstream* Baptists are being used for purposes other than those perceived to be worthy of the givers' support. As more *mainstream* Baptists realize this, no doubt they will *designate* portions of their tithes and offerings for use by chosen enterprises or else they will yield to the alternative—Fundamentalist mind control.

Cooperation requires mutual honesty and constant nurturing. Without abiding trust and respect, cooperative endeavors cannot be sustained.

What Fundamentalists Are Doing about the Cooperative Program

In the mid-1980s, no one could disagree that the Fundamentalist quest for worldly power had created a great gulf between Baptist brothers and sisters. During this time, Charles Stanley was elevated to the highest office in the Fundamentalist hierarchy—the presidency of the Southern Baptist Convention.

With formation of the Peace Committee in 1985, there loomed on the horizon the possibility that a "mantle of peace" would settle on all Southern Baptists. Many thought the spirit of "pulling apart" would be replaced with the spirit of "pulling together" once again.

During this period, several state Baptist papers published information regarding Cooperative Program giving by Fundamentalist-controlled churches. It was difficult for many laypeople to fathom the revelation that the First Baptist Church of Atlanta, of which Charles Stanley was its pastor, was reported to have contributed only a paltry sum each year to the Cooperative Program. One of the largest and most influential churches in the Southern Baptist Convention was giving less money per year than many of the smaller churches in the denomination! (One is caused to wonder if the minuscule Cooperative Program gift that was reported even qualified the church to have messengers at the 1985 SBC annual meeting.)

That was more than ten years ago. Have times changed? Are Fundamentalist-controlled churches now generously giving to the Cooperative Program? Unfortunately, it appears that little has changed. In the February 29, 1996, issue of the Georgia State Convention paper, *The Christian Index*, the First Baptist Church of Atlanta (still one of the largest and most influential churches in the denomination) is not listed among the top 100 Georgia churches in total giving to the Cooperative Program.

Are Old Habits to Exist Forever?

It is sometimes difficult for me to understand how or why we do things as Baptists. For example: In a recent year's annual report of the Baptist General Convention of Texas, it was noted that Texas Baptists were contributing $1,058 per student enrolled at the Paige Patterson-controlled Southeastern Baptist Theological Seminary. As if that were not perplexing enough, the budget also indicated that Texas Baptists were providing less than half that amount per student enrolled in some of their own Texas Baptist colleges and universities.

Is it the intent of Texas Baptists to deny opportunities for higher education to some of their own young people so that students in other states may be subjected to Fundamentalist indoctrination? More specifically, is that the way for Texas Baptists to restore Christian integrity and treasured Baptist distinctives in Baptist life?

A Texas Footnote: Texas Baptists have the right to ask if some of their Cooperative Program money forwarded to Nashville was used to defray costs of several issues of the Fundamentalist Indiana state paper that inundated Texas prior to the 1995 meeting of the Baptist General Convention of Texas.

It is a fact that some of Texas Baptists' Cooperative Program money *was used* to pay for the Fundamentalist-controlled *SBC Life* that "trashed" Texas Baptist leadership. The publication is sent largely to pastors throughout the nation.

Recognizing the Folly of Lose-Lose Involvement

Many sincere Christians and authentic Baptists no longer attend the SBC annual meetings where the women they love could be called "whores of Satan"—as has been done in the past.

What would the answer be should *mainstream* Baptists, through their state conventions, advise the SBC Executive Committee that election of trustees of all SBC seminaries, boards, agencies and commissions will be based on the amount of money contributed by the state conventions? For example: If a state convention provided 10 percent of the money for the operation of the SBC, then Baptists of that state should demand the right to name 10 percent of the various trustee boards.

Should the SBC Executive Committee respond, "We will think about it and pray about it," then would it not be appropriate for *mainstream* Baptists in state conventions to reply, "That's fine with us. We will keep the money *in escrow* until you are through thinking about it."

Why should *mainstream* Baptists' tithes and offerings be used to perpetuate Fundamentalist abuse? The straightforward message needs to be—no vote, no money! If *mainstream* Baptists in state conventions are going to pay for the band, then they should be allowed to call some of the tunes and sing along if they want to!

Fundamentalism's Control Program—Not Cooperative Program

Again, it is recognized that Fundamentalists have the right to say and believe as they please. But I have the same rights and I am weary of the shedding of crocodile tears over the Cooperative Program especially by men who give little or nothing to it themselves. The Cooperative Program has been stripped of cooperation. Because of worldly power practices that have engulfed our denomination since 1979, Southern Baptists' *Cooperative* Program has been transformed into Fundamentalism's *Control* Program.

Many *mainstream* Baptists are recognizing the foolishness and impropriety of sending money to the SBC Executive Committee through the Cooperative Program. Fundamentalists are using some of those monies to subject Baptist people to attempted intimidation and interference in the conduct of their state conventions.

Personal Perspective

I believe that most *mainstream* Baptists want to get on with their spiritual lives. I also am convinced they want their work for Christ to be protected from further Fundamentalist interference and manipulation. *Mainstream* Baptists wish to move forward with their ministries of mercy, evangelism and missions!

Is it possible some are waiting for a *mainstream* Baptist ship to come in? If so, my prayer is that they will be encouraged to be like Noah. He did not wait for a ship to come in—he built one!

13

Mainstream Baptists' Christlike Pastors
Unprecedented Opportunities

✳✳✳✳✳✳✳

In all things, be of good report—

"And his gifts were that some should be apostles, some prophets, some evangelists, some pastors and teachers, to equip the saints for the work of ministry, for building up the body of Christ, until we all attain to the unity of the faith and of the knowledge of the Son of God, to mature manhood, to the measure of the stature of the fullness of Christ; so that we may no longer be children, tossed to and fro and carried about with every wind of doctrine, by the cunning of men, by their craftiness in deceitful wiles.

"Rather, speaking the truth in love, we are to grow up in every way into him who is the head, into Christ."

Mainstream Baptists' Christlike Pastors
Unprecedented Opportunities

A *mainstream* Baptist pastor is one who serves Christ by providing spiritual insight, knowledge, guidance and encouragement to his congregation as part of his leadership, and in so doing reflects the servanthood of Jesus.

Opportunities to serve Jesus Christ with our pastors are limitless. However, over the past seventeen years, extraordinary, even bizarre, political barriers have challenged our abilities and interfered with the fulfillment of our commitments to Christ. Yet, to work and witness in ways that reflect the life and ministries of Jesus Christ is *mainstream* Baptists' ongoing quest.

God has granted to us the power of prayer and the leadership of many good and godly pastors. In the years ahead we must earnestly seek to circumvent the political intrusions by which our lives and work have been beset. We must faithfully strive to minister to the needs of people with whom we come in contact and otherwise attempt to fulfill the call of the Great Commission. Therefore, laypeople may be well-advised to listen to the pastor until the sermon is over, and then get out and do something about it.

Our Pastors' Burdens Have Grown in Scale and Severity

Over the past two years, several Baptist friends have arranged for me to "listen in" on numerous discussion sessions with groups of pastors and separately with laypeople who are among the spiritual leaders of their respective churches. The size of the congregations so represented ranged from fewer than 200 to more than 10,000 members.

In the open and frank discussions involving more than 200

pastors and a much larger number of laypeople, it became evident that confidence in the denomination's integrity of purpose is continuing to erode.

Furthermore, pastors and laypeople increasingly wonder if the vast, complex and pervasive problems by which the SBC is beset, can be corrected.

As I took notes on the pastors' discussions, I was deeply touched by their sincerity of purpose and depth of concern. Some of the matters said to be disquieting to them:

- **_The Loss of Truth._**

Truth within the SBC has been stretched to reflect largely the worldly perspectives of Fundamentalist leadership. That which currently is called "truth" is expressed to rationalize the methods employed by the SBC ruling class to gain its objectives to control the nation's political elections.

- **_The Loss of Honor and Virtue—and Christian Values_**

Apparently, lying, cheating and slandering have become acceptable in the SBC. Instead of looking to Jesus as the model of life, numerous dishonesties are justified by claims that "all has been done for the glory of God." As a result, the level of integrity in Baptist life continues to drift toward accommodation with the lowest common denominator of personal and denominational conduct.

- **_The Loss of Trust._**

We are caught up in the most critical time in SBC history. Seemingly forsaking the gift of perception, some laypeople have been among the most gullible of Americans. In church settings lies have been accepted as absolute fact. We are skeptical about that which we should believe and we blindly embrace many things we should question. Even though we distrust men who have spoken blatant untruths about some of our pastors, ironically, many of us still consider those same men acceptable denominational leaders.

Widespread distrust abounds in the denomination though some Baptist writers and certain SBC leaders are afraid to discuss the loss of trust which is due to the loss of truth.

However, the dishonesties are taking their toll. The loss of confidence in the current SBC leadership seemingly is irreversible.

219

- ### The "Southern Baptist Advocate"—Intimidation and Fear

Among Fundamentalist publications that have risen and fallen in Baptist life since 1979, possibly the most scurrilous of these was the *Southern Baptist Advocate*. From its first issue (August 1980), it was used to undermine the hearts and poison the minds of gullible Southern Baptists. Its first editor was Russell Kaemmerling, Paige Patterson's brother-in-law. For eleven years the unscrupulous Fundamentalist journal ruthlessly unleashed hate and inflicted intentional harm against a significant number of Southern Baptist pastors and other denominational leaders. This *segregating* of good people for *"special treatment"* was extremely important to the Fundamentalists' successful takeover of all SBC institutions and organizations. Some Southern Baptists' tithes and offerings—gifts intended for investment in Christ-centered ministry and mission endeavors—were thus misused.

Following the Fundamentalist takeover of the *Baptist Press* in late 1990, the *Advocate* ceased publication in mid-1991. After eleven years of perfidy in print, the publication was no longer needed.

- ### Transformation of the Baptist Press.

From its inception, the *Baptist Press* served as a source of reliable information concerning all aspects of denominational life. Following the SBC Executive Committee's arbitrary termination of editors Al Shackleford and Dan Martin, credibility of the *Baptist Press* was compromised. From that day forward, SBC leaders, exercising absolute authority over the *Baptist Press,* have had opportunity to manage its news in ways to attempt justification of their worldly-powered control over the Convention. Thus, the *Baptist Press'* journalistic credibility has been seriously compromised.

- ### Introduction of the Associated Baptist Press.

Coincident with the change in control of the *Baptist Press*, numerous state convention paper editors formed the *Associated Baptist Press*. The ABP is viewed to have honored its commitment to maintain the highest level of fairness, honesty, balance and objectivity in its reporting of news. Accordingly, the *Associ-*

ated Baptist Press merits the encouragement and monetary support of *mainstream* Baptists.

- ### The Loss of Community.

The loss of truth and honor in the SBC has contributed to an ongoing erosion of civility and compassion in the denomination. The loss of respect between Baptists testifies to the ultimate cost of embracing biblically immoral control tactics, rather than the example of Jesus, as the model for personal conduct.

Pastors' Reflections

Pastors also talked about some of the external influences intended to interfere with the best use of their experience, time, energies, seminary training and gifts. Among those mentioned:

- **Threats.** Some have been bluntly threatened by Fundamentalists who have said, "You get right with our *cause* or you will have no future in the Southern Baptist Convention."
- **Get In Line!** Those who do not "get in line" with the spirit of Fundamentalism have become the subject of "whispering campaigns" against them individually as well as against the churches of which they are pastors. Derogatory whispering thrives in "behind-the-scenes politicking" at associational and state convention meetings as well as in the SBC.
- **"Is It Divisive To Discuss Morality"** Within their own churches, some laypeople who should know better are inclined to ask the pastor, "Please do not discuss the SBC controversy in our church for the matter could become divisive." The laypeople who make these suggestions should be led to understand that neither does evil correct its own ways nor are intentional ignorance and willful indifference honorable responses to evil. Perhaps those who are loathe to oppose wrongdoing will consider the Scriptures that admonish Christians to eschew evil and to separate themselves from it.

Absence of Personal Concerns

None of the pastors expressed undue personal concerns even as incidents of threats, vicious political labeling and insulting behavior continue unabated. Nevertheless, if your pastor is not a Fundamentalist, it is probable that he has been exposed to that rancorous spirit by having been called a theological "liberal." Yet, in SBC life it is the non-Fundamentalist pastors who seek to do that which is right in the sight of God.

- As an illustration, in the 1850s your pastor would have supported the abolishment of slavery in the United States and that would have been a "liberal" position for him to have taken.
- Your pastor also would have favored in the 19th Century the idea that American women should have a right to vote in every election.

He would have been against:

- One who would state, "My women will do as I tell them."
- One who would grab a younger pastor by the coat lapels and threaten him, saying, "You get right with our Fundamentalist 'cause' or you will have no future in the Southern Baptist Convention."
- One who would insult the Woman's Missionary Union or on every conceivable occasion attempt to persecute the WMU ladies in other ways.
- One who would tell our foreign missionaries that they are mere employees of the SBC and thus limit their freedom of expression.
- One who would suggest that foreign missionaries cancel their subscriptions to their state convention papers in order that they may be precluded from receiving truthful information.

Disturbing Matters

However, it was evident that there were matters over which they were disturbed. Typical of some that were mentioned:

- "The members of my congregation are wonderful people. They deeply desire to do those things that can glorify God. Regrettably, inasmuch as we don't know who to trust in Baptist life, our ministry and missions endeavors are mostly limited to the areas within only a few miles around the campus of our church."
- "I have been a pastor only since 1981. All that my contemporaries and I have known has been the incredibly harsh infighting that has gone on between Baptists."

- "Trust between Baptists has been broken because truthfulness no longer is a coin of the Baptist realm. Politicking is the order of the day."
- "My deepest concern is to lead as many men, women and children as possible to discover the saving grace of Jesus during the remaining thirty years or so of my active ministry. Yet Fundamentalist meanness seriously undermines Christian credibility."
- "No longer can I be a part of the SBC whose Fundamentalist leaders deny by their whispering campaigns that other *mainstream* Baptists and I have a place in Christendom."
- "I am only thirty-four years of age, but I am deeply concerned about what the next generation of ministry students who are being influenced by Fundamentalist rulers of the SBC will be taught in the seminaries concerning honesty, ethical conduct and morality."

Foundational Baptist Distinctives

Our pastors are fully aware of the price our forebears paid so that we might have the freedom to practice our religious beliefs. Our pastors also know that current Fundamentalist leaders of the SBC have ridiculed, opposed and, when possible, discarded most of our Baptist principles. While these latter-day "Baptists" may cling to some basic Christian beliefs, they neither cherish nor uphold the principles enacted during the life of Christ, and they are not committed to the Bible-based and time-honored Baptist distinctives.

On the other hand, the pastors to whom I listened stressed the importance of honoring and preserving distinctive Baptist beliefs. Among those long-held distinctives that are so important to all authentic Baptists:

- *Holy Scriptures.* The Holy Scriptures are the final authority and the foundation of our beliefs. No creeds, no confessions, no bishops, no cardinals and no popes can dictate to the Baptist conscience.
- *Baptism of Believers.* "Believers" means those who freely

accept Jesus as Savior and Master and believe the Gospel of Christ to be the guide of life.

• *Priesthood of the Believer.* The saving grace of Christ and the personal interpretation of God's Holy Word are available to every individual, without the mediation of any person or system.

• *Autonomy of the Local Church.* The local church is the sovereign, independent, all-powerful ecclesiastical unit—ordaining, calling, and conducting the affairs of the church as led by its head, Jesus Christ.

• *Separation of Church and State.* The most distinctive characteristic which the world has recognized as being Baptist in origin is religious liberty. However, some of the most prominent Fundamentalist leaders have called the separation of church and state, "the figment of some infidel's imagination." Fundamentalists want government money for their schools. They allow partisan politics to be paraded in their churches and some have become involved with the radical Reconstructionist movement.

• *Security of the Believer.* Salvation is a one-time experience that establishes a permanent relationship with God. Yet, some of the most prominent Fundamentalist leaders of the SBC are inclined to say, "Not to believe in Inerrancy is not to believe in God." *Mainstream* Baptist pastors and people are burdened by the evil of those who would say that we who were once accepted as fellow believers have fallen from grace. We are deemed unacceptable if we do not endorse their politicized "Inerrancy," that which, no doubt, is a sincere belief of some, but which has been transformed into a political vehicle of hate-induced harm to others.

Some of Our Pastors' Deepest Longings

While in the "listening sessions," pastors shared their heartfelt concerns and feelings with one another. Among them were:

• *Desire To Honor Christ.* Concerns were expressed regarding their work in God's Kingdom. Principally, how could the work and witness of the people of the church more greatly honor and serve the cause of Christ? Would the church seek to be all that the Lord would have it to be? Would its ministry make a measurable difference in the community, the state, the nation and the world?

• ***Desire to Help Laypeople.*** One pastor inquired, "If the church is to become all that Jesus would have it be, how can the pastor more effectively counsel, encourage and inspire more individual members of the congregation to be all that they can become? How can Christ's expectations be met in our 'everyday living' and thus, in our witness and work as believers?"

• ***Desire to Create New Beginnings.*** How can members of the church be encouraged to embrace—enthusiastically and eagerly—the development of a comprehensive plan for the church in regard to:

1) Having a new focus on growth.

2) Reaching more lost people and the unchurched.

3) Involving new members in that which is in the pastor's heart—ministries and missions.

4) Leading all members of the church to discover their spiritual gifts and then serve God accordingly.

5) Encouraging an ever greater number in the congregation to volunteer in Kingdom ministry.

6) Reaching out to people who are "not like us." Increasingly, we are in a multi-cultural, multi-ethnic, multi-social community and congregation.

7) Becoming more involved in the community, not necessarily so that all with whom we come in contact will come into our church building, but rather, how we may go to them more effectively.

8) Encouraging laypeople to become ever more involved in world witnessing and in world evangelism?

My perception regarding the pastors' comments was that they are greatly concerned for the lost. They have a deep desire to effect a more satisfying and exciting sense of teamwork between the pastor and people. The overarching objective of each is that all people in the churches of which Christ is the head become more Christlike in their outreach and serving of others.

Laypeople Respond
to Challenges

In the discussion sessions with laypeople, both individually and in groups, I learned of some things that I needed to do to enrich even the good relationship that I enjoy with my pastor and to "do my job" better in the congregation of which I am blessed to be a member.

I also detected a unique outlook among the men and women of the pews who articulated some encouraging expressions, i.e.,

• "Even though the SBC controversy is an embarrassingly unpalatable experience, some personal positives have come into my life. I realize that if public perceptions of Baptist life are to be improved, I must be involved in the effort. . . ."

• "The controversy has driven me to examine my relationship with Jesus. I have been led to a closer walk with him."

• "My church means more to me than ever before, possibly because I am more involved in ministries and missions than ever before. This has led me to understand the great value that every person in the world is to God. It has led me to understand that the dignity of every individual on earth is as precious to him or to her as is my own dignity to me. I have learned to understand that unless I recognize the value of every person and respect the dignity of every person, my saying, 'I love you,' to others is nothing but a hollow sound."

• "I have learned that both my pastor and we laypeople can be greatly blessed when we listen to our pastor as he shares his ideas about ministry and missions and when we as a congregation join him to reach conclusions regarding the prioritizing of ministry and mission programs for our church."

• "Instead of continuing to take for granted my personal life as a Christian and my membership in the congregation, I have learned that I am responsible to commit myself to the authority of the divinely inspired God-breathed Holy Scriptures. Therefore, I am certain the Bible is the authoritative rule and guide of my faith, practice and walk with the Living Christ. I have learned that I must stand by my faith. I have learned that it is a travesty against God to allow prideful, politically ambitious and otherwise self-serving men to strip me of my rights as a follower of Christ and as a Baptist.

I have learned the futility of attempting to persuade Fundamentalists to be Christlike; of dissuading them from lusting after the power to control minds, to seize institutions and to transform them to satisfy political avarice. Therefore, I have learned that I must separate myself from the spirit of Fundamentalism and get on with that which I know God expects of me."

Laypeoples' Communication with Pastors

Our pastors need the men and women of the pews to say, "Pastor, we want to listen to your visions to serve Christ through our church.

We want to work with you to develop a comprehensive plan that is right for our church.

We want to pray for you and ourselves that we may work more closely to focus on reaching the lost, ministering to the needy and being involved in local, national and worldwide missions—far more than we have ever done in the past."

Our Pastors Could Begin Bringing the "Baptist Mess" to an End

Throughout my lifetime, I have been privileged to meet hundreds of honorable Baptist pastors—men called of God to preach the gospel and minister to others in every way possible. On the other hand, I also have met many Fundamentalist preachers. I regret that some of those whom I have known have allowed the spirit of Fundamentalism to take over their lives. I pray that they will be able to break away from that addictive spirit as they would attempt to do were it the demon of cocaine, alcohol or another drug.

The many thousands of honorable *mainstream* Baptist pastors could devise a simple and Christ-honoring solution for the "Baptist mess" should they have opportunity to discuss the matter among themselves and with fellow members of their congregations.

I often wonder why we laypeople defer talking with our pastors about the controversy. The good men who provide spiritual leadership for our congregations do not know for certain if Judge

Pressler's plan to *put a man in every church* has been made manifest in their churches. But our pastors need to know where each of us stands regarding the spread of Fundamentalism, religious liberty, the right to follow the Holy Spirit's guidance regarding the use of our tithes and offerings, and our commitments, whether to Jesus or to Fundamentalism.

Our pastors need to know also that there are men and women who will not allow a Fundamentalist-supporting layman to abuse the pastor and/or rule the church.

The "Baptist Mess" controversy can be brought to an end; not in one fell swoop, but one step at a time.

The first step, I believe, is for responsible members of the congregation to discuss respectfully with their pastor the exercise of two cherished principles—religious freedom and the right of individuals to designate a portion of their tithes and offerings to undergird missions enterprises of their preference.

Enriching the Lives of Our Pastors

It is apparent that many of us laypeople have not invested enough of our time or capabilities to contribute fully to the enrichment of our pastors' calling. I share one pastor's comments:

> "The will of God for me is not a decision, it is a call. To do something simply because it is logical, appropriate or even good is not for me the right way. All of these human factors are to be considered, but the call of God is spiritually discerned and received.
>
> It is a gift of God to be answered and *obeyed*. My joy is in Sunday worship, pastoral preaching, personal involvement in conversions, baptisms, counseling, funerals and even weddings. I also have a consuming desire for spirituality and community among a group of people that I believe can best be fulfilled in the local church."

Disturbances in Congregations

The maintenance of excellent personal relationships with others obviously is far more vital than is the practice of preventive maintenance on automobiles or complex machinery.

From time to time when ministers and congregations have rediscovered love and harmony in their reconciliation through a new focus on their churches' goals, one realizes more than ever before that jeweled relationships reflect kindness, patience, courtesy, compassion and a genuine desire to love others.

Occasionally, we laypeople fail to show our pastors how much we love them. Usually, this is because we have not taken the time to evidence a heartfelt personal interest in them or to develop a good understanding of the difficulties with which they are confronted. Therefore, we have not sought to establish the level of comradeship that, surely, is the fertile soil in which friendships are grown.

The extent to which we Baptist men and women carry our troubles to pastors causes me to wonder how they can bear such heavy burdens. After we have told the pastor about some of our problems, do very many of us ever inquire, "Is there anything that I might do to be of some assistance to you?" Do we pause for a few moments in the pursuit of our own interests to mail a note of encouragement to our pastor? Do we inquire about him and his family members or express appreciation for his contributions to our own spiritual walk?

The Possibilities of Mutual Love

The most basic of all freedoms—religious freedom—is the foundation upon which rests all human rights. In the hustle and bustle of life, we frequently fail to respect the right of dignity that is precious to every person. We sometimes overlook the great worth of persons with whom we come in contact. Recognition of the dignity and worth of each person is the foundation upon which mutual love and effective work and witness in the cause of Christ can be developed.

When a pastor accepts the call of a congregation, a remarkable opportunity presents itself, both to the people and to the pastor, as together they embark upon a wonderful adventure. As in a garden a favorable combination of seeds, nutrients, water and sunshine can produce beautiful flowers, the work of pastors and laypeople can flourish as mutual respect, trust and appreciation develop into an abiding love for one another.

Special Opportunities Exist

We laypeople have many opportunities to engage in satisfying experiences. Throughout our lifetimes, we have enjoyed the growth and development of our children, grandchildren and other young people. We have applauded them for their educational and career achievements.

I know of a number of churches in small communities on the outskirts of cities in which universities and seminaries are located. Many members of these churches have gained a special joy while nurturing, encouraging and fostering the careers of student pastors whom they have called to preach His Word.

Over the years, as these young men have devoted their intellect, time, energies and skills to further His Kingdom in other sectors of the nation, some have kept in close contact with their first congregation. This has been a source of special satisfaction to the former pastors as well as members of these churches. I have known of some pastors who, upon reaching retirement years, have returned to live near one of the churches served in earlier days in order to join in the work and ministries of that congregation.

Adopt-A-Young-Minister

Some gracious *mainstream* Baptist pastors have chosen to give something special of themselves. They are establishing relationships with ministerial and seminary students, who, in due course, will spend time in their churches. Such mentoring processes will greatly bless the students' lives. Bravo!

A Straight Word to Fellow Laypeople

As previously indicated, many of our *mainstream* Baptist pastors have been subjected to Fundamentalists' public ridicule, insulting behavior and other abuse. Largely, we laypeople have not been fully aware of the mistreatment which they have endured for a very basic reason: To avoid any distractions in their ministry, *our pastors don't whimper.*

The more we laypeople understand some of the personal problems that are experienced by our pastors and the more quickly we extend appropriate responses to them, the more we will discover how our special support of the pastor in private will greatly undergird his preaching of God's Word from the pulpit.

230

14

Clear-Cut Choices
Remedies for the "Baptist Mess"

✾✾✾✾✾✾✾

In all things, be of good report—

". . . some leaders of the mass movement will live long enough to observe the downfall of the movement. A mass movement with a concrete objective, e.g., to take over and control an organization, is likely to have a shorter life than a movement with a nebulous, indefinite objective nurtured by chronic extremism.

"Oliver Cromwell was quoted by J. A. Cramb in his *Origins and Destiny of Imperial Britain* as having said, 'A man never goes as far as when he does not know whither he is going.' "

Clear-Cut Choices
Remedies for the "Baptist Mess"

Thank you for your interest and patience in considering the content of this book. It was prepared to provide straightforward answers to inquiries from many of my fellow Baptists—the people of the pews—regarding the loss of Christian integrity in some sectors of Baptist life.

Some of the laypeople's questions are shown below. I have added certain conclusions that have been made manifest to me:

- **What Caused the "Baptist Mess?"**
  The premeditated attack against the fifteen million unsuspecting Southern Baptist people.

- **Who Made the "Mess"?**
  The controlling oligarchy which is now comprised of approximately eighty radical Fundamentalists.

- **How Did They Do It?**
  By going into the Baptist hinterlands to foment hate sufficient to induce sizable numbers of other men and women to join in the Fundamentalist ideological movement.

- **Why Did They Do It?**
  In order to fulfill their ambitions to achieve more extensive worldly power in the United States.

- **What Has the "Baptist Mess" Left Behind It?**
  A disgraced and weakened denomination and a more vulnerable nation.

- **What Can Be Done About It?**
  That depends on the "people of the pews"—the Baptist men and women who perform much of the denomination's work and pay its bills. It is they who possess the abilities to do everything that is required to restore Christian integrity in Baptist life.

Please provide prayerful consideration to the content of these closing pages as, together, we identify ways to rid our denomination of the "Baptist Mess."

232

Certain Decisions Must Be Made

Decisions regarding these three questions will affect the desire and capability to bring the "Baptist Mess" to an end:

1) Do you believe it is vital to God's Kingdom, to your church and to your family members that integrity be reestablished in Baptist life?

2) If so, who is to restore honesty, truthfulness, fairness and other evidences of Christian conduct in Baptist affairs? Should I be unwilling to foster, practice and insist upon truthfulness among fellow Baptists, *or* should you and other laypeople choose not to do so, then *who* will take the first and succeeding steps to restore Christian integrity in our denomination?

3) Asked in another way, are you and I willing to be further manipulated by those who practice duplicity and other forms of dishonesty? If not, we would realize that moral soundness must be restored in the denomination.

How will you decide the answers to these questions? How will the other members of your congregation respond to them? Therein lie the answers to "What Can Be Done About the 'Baptist Mess.' "

First, A Review of Our Authentic Baptist Principles That Have Blessed Us in the Past

As mentioned in Chapter Two, Dr. Carl E. Bates, a trusted and revered Baptist leader who served as president of the SBC for two years in the 1970s, asked these questions: What makes one a Christian; What makes one a Baptist; and What makes one a Southern Baptist?

He answered the first question by simply stating that only God can make a Christian. He then enumerated the seven precious principles of authentic Baptist people.

1) The absolute authority and Lordship of Jesus Christ—we must do what Jesus commands, no matter what men may say.

2) The Bible is the only and all-sufficient rule of faith and practice—our doctrines and precepts are found in God's Word and are not in man-made creeds.

3) The competency of the soul in religion—no person, ordinance, or institution shall come between a soul and Christ.

233

4) An experience of Grace—a person must be converted to Christianity before becoming a member of a Baptist church.

5) The independence and autonomy of the local church—each church must govern itself, and all churches have equal, as well as separate, authority.

6) The separation of church and state—a free church in a free state.

7) The symbolism of the ordinances—baptism of believers by immersion and the Lord's Supper.

Southern Baptists, he explained, are identified by their "love for a lost world and a willingness to get on with the work for the glory of God—whatever it costs." In essence, these principles and total acceptance of God's Word as the inviolate standard of Christian conduct are the virtues of which authentic Southern Baptists are made.

Unquestionably, you and I stand on holy ground when we commit our hearts, minds and souls to the saving faith in Jesus, and when we accept the absolute authority of His commands—as evidenced in our love for a lost world and in our determination to pay whatever it costs to reach the world for the His glory.

Please Let Us Look Forward

There are many differences, of course, in the ways that our forebears lived and how we conduct our lives today. Our modes of travel, medical care and how we communicate with people throughout the world are but a few of the differences wrought by the changes that have taken place over the years.

Nevertheless, other matters that affect our lives and our usefulness to Christ remain unchanged. We, like the early-day Baptists, are identified by our "love for a lost world and a willingness to 'get on' with His work for the glory of God—whatever it costs."

Are we less reliant on our working with other Baptists—like-minded Baptists—than were our ancestors of a century ago?

I believe that our cooperative enterprises are more vital than ever before. We *mainstream* Baptists need to devote the best of our abilities, the use of our tithes and offerings and of our spiritual gifts to working with like-minded believers in ministries, evangelism, missions and other God-honoring endeavors.

234

The success of our cooperative endeavors, of course, is dependent upon our unanimity of purpose and mutual commitments to restore, and then to maintain, Christian integrity in the conduct of Baptist affairs. Truth, love and trust hang in the balance—as do our unflinching vows to increase our missions work and other testimonies to the cause of Christ.

Our Personal Decisions
Can Impact the Souls of Millions

One is unable to erase from memory the awesome implications of a statement made by Mahatma Gandhi. When asked, "Mr. Gandhi, what would be required to christianize India?" Gandhi responded, "For Christians to act as Christians."

What would be required to christianize America? Possibly this applies: "For Fundamentalists to act as Christians—as do *all* who genuinely follow Christ."

How extensively have Baptist leaders' deviation from Christ-mandated conduct over the last seventeen years injured our Christian witness? Is it too late to show the world that Baptists' commitments to Christ are sincere and to begin anew to *practice* what we *preach*? The answer largely lies in the hearts and minds of the pastor and people of every *mainstream* Baptist church.

Mainstream Baptists, who desire to remain spiritually sound, cannot allow themselves to remain besmirched by the stench of the Southern Baptist Convention's dirty politics. We must be credibly clean, as sincere Christians, to be effective in the telling of the Good News.

Choices Must be Made—By Christ-Honoring Decisions or By Default

Heard in early days was a saying about matters of conscience and heart: "If one is straddling the fence, already he is on the wrong side."

Laypeople today are being confronted—in both subtle and direct ways—to avoid fence-straddling by choosing:

235

1) to remain faithful to the cause of Christ, or

2) to embrace, either actively or passively, the spiritual schizophrenia evident in the spirit of Fundamentalism.

Baptist men and women of the pews cannot have it both ways. In due course, each of us will decide. Most will choose and honor their ongoing fidelity to the teachings of Christ, but some might chose to follow the elitist power of the Oligarchy of Eighty.

Failure to choose Christ will cast one adrift from God and will activate the gravitational pull of Fundamentalism upon that person's life and soul.

The choice that Baptist men and women make inevitably will have a lasting impact on families and congregations. The choice also will affect the U. S. Constitution-guaranteed religious freedom and individual liberties we now enjoy!

Therefore, I trust that each *mainstream* Baptist congregation will delay no further in deciding

1) to remain faithful to the cause of Christ, and in so doing,

2) to reject the spirit of Fundamentalism that, by its ungodly attitude and unchristian actions, has defined itself in the preceding chapters.

With that decision made, other vital matters await determination.

A Most Important Clear-Cut Choice
Alternatives to Fighting Fundamentalism

The *official* Southern Baptist Convention continues to undergo alterations that are unlikely to benefit Christendom or mankind in general. The changes currently underway and others likely to be initiated largely will undergird the worldly ambitions of the Fundamentalist Oligarchy of Eighty.

I believe a decision to *fight* Fundamentalism in the SBC would tend to intensify the existing negative impact on the denomination's Christian witness. Therefore, these comments are intended to encourage *mainstream* Baptists *not to fight* with Fundamentalists—whom I believe have no interest in changing their errant ways.

Remember SBC Annual Meetings of the Past

- It is 6:00 a.m. on the first day of the convention's meeting. Two thousand or more raucous Fundamentalist foot soldiers already are seated in the front rows of the huge meeting hall.
- They are there with beverage coolers and food—prepared to sit there the entire day. Their primary purpose is to look with disdain upon and shout derisive remarks and otherwise attempt to intimidate any and all who would not yield to their radical Fundamentalist leaders.
- Remember, please, the triumphalism of the SBC leaders of Fundamentalism as evidenced by their platform conduct.
- Remember how the Fundamentalists heaped scorn and abuse upon those who had been segregated as "opponents" when Fundamentalists encountered them in the corridors, elevators and hotel lobbies.
- Remember, please, the women who were called "whores of Satan."

Instead of Fighting Fundamentalists, Let Us Pay the Price—Whatever It Costs—and "Get On" with Mainstream Baptist Work

"Control" of the SBC has nothing to do with the advancement of Christ's Kingdom. Our concern is to "get on" with being Christians—Baptist Christians. This can be accomplished without fighting Fundamentalists—*but never yielding to their demands or wrongdoing*. We must resist Fundamentalism but not in its own mean-spirited ways for this would be an immoral use of our spiritual gifts.

Another Significant Clear-Cut Choice
What Will Your Church Become?

What will you choose for your church to be:
1) an authentic *mainstream* Baptist church;
2) a church controlled by the spirit of Fundamentalism; or,
3) one comprised of a congregation that has not yet decided that Fundamentalism is an affront to Christ, the head of His church?

Possibly the following comments regarding fence-straddling of some members of Baptist congregations are unduly direct. Nevertheless, those who are inclined to say, "I have friends on both sides . . .", "I don't want to be involved. . .", "Discussing the controversy could be divisive . . .", "I think both sides are wrong . . ." or "Our pastor ought to wait and see who is going to win . . . ." are likely to see their churches remain frail in their allegiance to Christ.

Such "fence-straddling" tends to weaken the Kingdom work of sincere Christians and authentic Baptists.

Nevertheless, some of our Baptist friends seemingly are unaware that when one straddles the fence regarding a moral issue, that indecision actually becomes a deterrent to those who seek to do that which is right in the sight of God.

What kind of a Baptist church is yours to be?

If you and fellow members of your congregation decide that your church is to remain a *mainstream* Baptist church, then you and they affirm that you will:

- Encourage one another to live in ways so that the world will recognize the word "Christian" as a noun which proclaims the lordship of Christ and not simply an adjective that describes a group of politicians or petty potentates.
- Respect the worth and dignity of fellow Christians and each potential believer in Christ.
- Attempt to restore trust among like-minded believers.
- Espouse love, rather than hate.
- Dare to stand and speak truthfully regarding all matters.
- Defend the liberty of individual conscience and the right of each believer to designate the use of his/her ministry and mission offerings.
- Dare to champion democracy in the church, as well as in the nation, for freedom is a treasured gift from God.

In these things, you and members of your church will have begun to restore Christian integrity in your congregation—and in the denomination.

The Decision That Will Impact All Other Choices:
Designating Our Tithes and Offerings

Surely, each *mainstream* Baptist will prayerfully determine if it is right in the sight of God to forward one's tithes and offerings to Nashville—where they will be controlled by the SBC Executive Committee—and where portions may be used to expand Fundamentalism's worldly powers, the use of which could be contrary to Christ-mandated conduct.

Special Message to Every Southern Baptist Church About Fairness, Equity, Honor and Justice

The Southern Baptist Convention's history is replete with accounts of members of "modest-sized" churches whose contributions as SBC officers led to the growth and success of the denomination.

- Owen Cooper, a layman member of the "modest-sized" First Baptist Church of Yazoo City, Mississippi, made exceptional contributions to the ministries, educational, evangelism, missions and other SBC enterprises throughout the world during his two years of service as president of the SBC. The account of his remarkably outstanding service was described in Chapter Eleven.
- I believe Dr. James Yates, who served as pastor of that "modest-sized" church, could have served with equal distinction as the president of the Southern Baptist Convention.
- However, as has been evidenced for many years, and especially in 1996, the Oligarchy of Eighty selects its nominee for president of the SBC and, therefore, the election of other persons is politically precluded.

Should the members of your congregation recognize that it would be impossible for one of their own—man or woman— to be elected as president of the SBC due to the Oligarchy of Eighty's total domination over the Convention, why would members of that congregation continue to send their tithes and offerings to Nashville?

The Ultimate Result of Fundamentalism's Greed

I believe Fundamentalism's greed for ever greater worldly powers ultimately will cast a pall of shame and disgrace over Southern Baptists. *Mainstream* Baptists have observed the damage that the spirit of Fundamentalism has done to their denomination's reputation for sincerity in service to Christ. Are they willing to allow further use of their tithes and offerings to result in more devastating travesties?

Inasmuch as I have shared vital information regarding Baptist life with you and reflecting on other information that is of record, I believe it would be immoral as well as imprudent for me to continue forwarding my tithes and offerings to be controlled by Fundamentalist leaders.

Is it not time to make the clear-cut decision that your individual tithes and offerings will be invested by your church only with like-minded Baptists whose commitments to Christian integrity, cooperative ministries and missions throughout the world are compatible with yours?

Should you have any concern regarding the ongoing support of our foreign missionaries, please review the section of Chapter Six in which that important matter is extensively discussed.

The Clear-Cut Choice About
Voting Rights

When one reflects upon the incidents of intentional hate that have been unleashed in the SBC to induce harm against honorable followers of Christ, many of whom have been *segregated* for *special treatment*, it is clearly evident that the acts of Fundamentalist persecution have inflicted recurring and terribly disturbing nightmares on its victims. Would you have voted for your denomination to be involved in the persecution of individuals—a group—*any group*—or a Baptist institution?

Unacceptable practices can be voted out of your city government. Every citizen has the right to vote on issues that impact his/her state and nation. Yet, the restriction of your voting rights prohibits the application of these democratic principles to the governance of the Southern Baptist Convention.

Every Baptist should have the privilege to vote on all matters of importance to his/her denomination. Is your congregation willing for Fundamentalist leadership to deprive you of the right to vote on such matters?

Democratic Voting Made Impossible by the Oligarchy of Eighty

Those who compose the Oligarchy of Eighty—the powerful men who hand-picked Dr. Jim Henry's successor as president of the SBC—hold the entire Convention in their iron-fisted grip. It seems evident those men will never willingly allow democratic voting, for if they did, no longer would they be allowed to control the Southern Baptist Convention. It is factual that fewer than one-tenth of 1 percent of all Baptists voted on matters at the 1996 SBC Annual Meeting at New Orleans.

Inasmuch as we are surrounded by electronic marvels, the entire meetings of state and national denominational organizations can be shown on screens in selected churches. In addition, other arrangements could be made for every member of a Baptist church to vote in person or *in absentia* on each important matter. Thus, individual Baptists who desire to participate in the meetings and to vote on all matters that impact their churches could do so without having to travel more than an average of approximately fifty miles from their home churches.

These Final Questions

"Who bears responsibility for the ongoing damage to the denomination that we have loved for so long?" "Can it be lessened?" "Can it be ended?"

Undeniably, Fundamentalists—in their pursuit of ever-greater power—have been destructive. They have tarnished and dishonored traditional Baptist witness.

However, *mainstream* Baptists also bear some responsibility for the disruption of fellowship in Baptist life. For much too long, laypeople have failed to demand that Christian integrity be reestablished throughout the denomination. Fundamentalists will continue to control the Southern Baptist Convention as long as honorable laypeople knowingly and willingly permit them to do so.

To a lost world, *mainstream* Baptists represent Christ. We would not continue to do business with dishonest bankers, bakers or candlestick makers. Why would unsaved men and women "do business" with Baptists who violate Christian principles that were established forChrist's followers' personal conduct?

Please review all that you have done *personally* over the last several years to prevent Fundamentalism from interfering with the Southern Baptist witness to God's grace and glory. Each of us will evidence w*ho* we are and *whose* we are by the action, or lack of action, we take regarding Fundamentalist evil.

Mainstream Baptists Will Resolutely Honor Their Witness to the Gospel of Christ

Many *mainstream* Baptist laypeople are committed to stand tall as sincere Christians, remain erect as authentic Baptists and to say to fellow Christians everywhere that the following are our positions of faith—as specified by God's Word and as imparted to our hearts and consciences by the Holy Spirit.

- *It is impossible for Fundamentalists to prevent us from publicly practicing the certitudes of our faith.*
- *We are among the groups that have been segregated by Fundamentalists for special treatment. We shall vigorously oppose further persecution of any Baptist individual, group or institution.*
- *We shall take exception and respond to further abuse of women and the slander of our pastors.*
- *We will invest our tithes and offerings with like-minded honest Baptists as we cooperate with one another to minister to a lost world.*
- *We will resist further Fundamentalist violations of Christian integrity and all attempts to silence mainstream Baptists who insist upon moral soundness in the associations and state conventions in which we participate.*

Epilogue

Men and women who now understand the spirit of Fundamentalism and continue to support its evil practices, in effect, are certifying to their approval of untruth, hate, slander and persecution in the church of which Jesus Christ is the head.

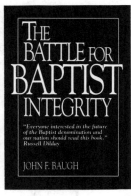

THE BATTLE FOR BAPTIST INTEGRITY

"Everyone interested in the future of the Baptist denomination and our nation should read this book."
Russell Dilday

JOHN F. BAUGH

ORDER FORM

_____

NAME

_____

STREET ADDRESS (NO P.O. BOXES)

_____

CITY   STATE   ZIP

_____

PHONE
     If delivery is to different address, please note.

Number of Books Ordered	
TOTAL PRICE (Price schedule on back of this form for Texas residents and non-residents)	$_____

Shipments will be sent on receipt of payment.

METHOD OF PAYMENT: ☐ check   ☐ VISA   ☐ MasterCard

Credit Card Number:

Expiration Date: ☐☐ — ☐☐

Signature: _____

Mail Orders To: Mr. John F. Baugh
                          1390 Enclave Parkway
                          Houston, Texas 77077

                          281-584-2721 FAX

TEXAS RESIDENTS

NUMBER OF BOOKS	BOOK PRICE	SHIPPING, HANDLING & STATE SALES TAX @ 8.25%	TOTAL PRICE
1	$12.95	$3.49	$16.44
2	$25.90	$5.08	$30.98
3	$38.85	$6.71	$45.56
4	$51.80	$8.86	$60.66
5	$64.75	$10.47	$75.22
6	$77.70	$12.08	$89.78
7	$90.65	$14.23	$104.88
8	$103.60	$15.64	$119.24
9	$116.55	$17.04	$133.59
10	$129.50	$18.45	$147.95
15	$194.25	$26.55	$220.80
20	$259.00	$34.65	$293.65
25	$323.75	$41.67	$365.42
50	$647.50	$83.34	$730.84
75	$971.25	$125.01	$1,096.26
100	$1,295.00	$166.68	$1,461.68

NON-TEXAS RESIDENTS

NUMBER OF BOOKS	BOOK PRICE	SHIPPING & HANDLING	TOTAL PRICE
1	$12.95	$2.24	$15.19
2	$25.90	$2.72	$28.62
3	$38.85	$3.24	$42.09
4	$51.80	$4.24	$56.04
5	$64.75	$4.74	$69.49
6	$77.70	$5.24	$82.94
7	$90.65	$6.24	$96.89
8	$103.60	$6.55	$110.15
9	$116.55	$6.86	$123.41
10	$129.50	$7.17	$136.67
15	$194.25	$9.72	$203.97
20	$259.00	$12.27	$271.27
25	$323.75	$13.82	$337.57
50	$647.50	$27.64	$675.14
75	$971.25	$41.46	$1,012.71
100	$1,295.00	$55.28	$1,350.28